Contested Christianity

Contested Christianity

The Political and Social Contexts
of Victorian Theology

Timothy Larsen

Baylor University Press
Waco, Texas USA

This volume is the forty-sixth published by the Markham Press Fund of Baylor University Press, established in memory of Dr. L. N. and Princess Finch Markham of Longview, Texas, by their daughters, Mrs. R. Matt Dawson of Waco, Texas, and Mrs. B. Reid Clanton of Longview, Texas.

Cover Design by Steven Day

Library of Congress Cataloging-in-Publication Data

Larsen, Timothy, 1967-
  Contested Christianity : the political and social context of Victorian theology / Timothy Larsen.
     p. cm.
Includes bibliographical references and index.
  ISBN 0-918954-93-2 (cloth : alk. paper)
  1. England—Church history—19th century. 2. Dissenters, Religious—England—History—19th century. 3. Christianity and politics—England—History—19th century. 4. Christian sociology—England—History—19th century. I. Title.

  BR759.L24 2004
  274.1'081—dc22

                                        2003025111

Printed in the United States of America on acid-free paper

For Mark A. Noll

Contents

Introduction

From a location in nineteenth-century England, this study seeks to shed fresh light on a range of subjects by introducing new conversation partners into a variety of discussions. The orientating discipline is religious history, more specifically the history of Christianity—and the other side of that coin in Victorian currency, the history of religious skepticism. Nevertheless, religious history is explored in this volume at its crossroads with other fields, both in religious studies (especially biblical studies and historical theology) and in historical studies, notably political, intellectual, social, cultural, and women's history. For example, how does a discussion regarding national politics change when theological voices are allowed to be heard? Or how is the direction of a conversation on the development of biblical criticism altered when plebeian radicals also make it onto the guest list?

The primary method used is the case study. By watching and listening closely to specific people, events, and controversies, many prevailing assumptions about what various groups in Victorian society were like, what they did, and why they did it, can be called into question and perhaps even overturned. The unifying category is contested Christianity. In other words, case studies have been chosen that expose an ideological fault line, either between Christians and unbelievers or between two different Christian communities, versions of Christianity, or lines of Christian thought. Christianity in nineteenth-century England, despite how it has often been portrayed, was not part of the air that the Victorians unquestioningly breathed; the Victorian era was not some imagined Christian golden age when religion was taken for granted as a matter of course. On the other hand, neither was Victorian Christianity, as it is alternatively presented by scholars (sometimes even the same scholars!), in crisis and retreat, being routed by doubt, crumbling on all sides against intellectual, social, cultural, and political forces for which it was no match; soundly conquered by principalities and powers ranging from

1

higher criticism to urbanization, from Darwinian thought to cycling clubs. In contrast to those two opposing pictures, it is more fitting and accurate to describe Christianity in the Victorian age as contested. More precisely, Christianity in nineteenth-century England was strong and pervasive, but it was also forcefully and vehemently attacked from without and given to rancorous disputes between different factions and versions of Christian thought within.

The central characters mark a fruitful shift of focus from that maintained in much current scholarship. Most notably, this study places Dissenters or Nonconformists—Protestants outside the Church of England such as Baptists, Congregationalists, and Methodists—in the leading roles. Although the Religious Census of 1851 revealed that close to half of the worshipping population of England was not Anglican, the Established Church nevertheless seems to exert a strong gravitational pull upon historians. There is a group of scholars that might be deemed the rising generation of established historians working on Christianity in nineteenth-century Britain—those who were awarded their doctorates in the 1980s and 1990s. It would seem that almost everyone in this group—one thinks of Arthur Burns, Grayson Carter, Frances Knight, Peter Nockles, Mark Smith, and Martin Wellings—has an Anglican focus to his research.[1] Nevertheless, many stereotypes about Victorian Christians generally, and Victorian evangelicals in particular, break down when Nonconformists are brought into the foreground. For example, chapter 1 offers a case study that reveals that evangelical Dissenting ministers in the early part of the nineteenth century were far ahead of English society as a whole in their commitment to gender equality. Their own theological resources enabled Congregationalists and Baptists to articulate a commitment to gender egalitarianism that was positively countercultural. Chapter 10 argues that what scholars have often seen as "secularization" ("the church" being "pushed out" of its place in society) appears from the perspective of Nonconformity as the hard-won triumph of an alternative theological vision, a Congregational ecclesiology of the gathered, voluntary, independent church. In addition to Dissenters, another set of alternative leading figures presented in this volume is plebeian social, political, and intellectual leaders. Although popular radicals have often been the focus of research in the fields of political and social history, this study endeavors to demonstrate the rewards that can be gained from allowing them to play central parts when pursuing the history of ideas.

As with a series of novels on Victorian life by Anthony Trollope—the "Palliser" political ones or the ecclesiastically inclined "Barchester Chronicles"—characters that take a leading role in one chapter are apt to make cameo appearances in others. For example, one meets the popular radical, Thomas Cooper, as a champion of D. F. Strauss's biblical criticism in chapter 4, only to have him reappear some years later in chapter 8 as a determined opponent of Strauss. The anti-Christian polemicists Joseph Barker and Charles Bradlaugh both appear briefly as Cooper's debating partners in chapter 8, but are leading characters in their own right in chapters 6 and 7 respectively. Harriet Knipe and Newman Hall, who are center stage in chapter 2, can be glimpsed again on holiday together in chapter 3. The eminent Baptist preacher C. H. Spurgeon is never allowed to play a major part in this study, but he has a habit of popping up occasionally in order to pronounce or withhold his blessing (the controversies of chapters 2 and 12 inspire him to bless, but he studiously refrains in chapter 11). One could go on like this. Indeed, in a sense, Jesus himself is a character in this drama, as several of the controversies covered in this volume came around at some point to questions of Christology (chapters 5, 6, and 8).

At the heart of this study, two dominant themes are addressed: firstly, the history of biblical criticism and intellectual currents perceived as challenges to the Christian faith; and, secondly, the political implications of Dissenting theology, experiences, and concerns. As to the first, an effort is made to show the actual, historical interrelatedness of two discussions that have been conducted separately in the existing scholarship: popular attacks upon Christianity by militant skeptics and the development of the (academic) discipline of biblical criticism and its dissemination among Christian leaders and thinkers. On the one hand, John Rogerson, a leading scholar of biblical studies in nineteenth-century Britain,[2] (and the entire vein of scholarship that he represents) is interested in explaining why biblical criticism was accepted so slowly in England, but this quest is hampered by his sticking to the high road, as it were, where only the scholarship of gentlemen, especially those associated with British and European universities, is brought into view. Edward Royle, on the other hand, is the foremost scholar of, to borrow a phrase from the title of one of his seminal works, "Victorian infidels."[3] Royle and the other scholars of popular unbelief have focused upon social and institutional history rather than intellectual history.

In this study, however, these two streams—the history of ideas and the world of popular unbelief—are allowed to mingle and influence one another, as they actually did in nineteenth-century England. For example, chapter 4 is a reception history that takes D. F. Strauss's *Leben Jesu* as its case study. Until now, the tremendous impact of Strauss's work in Britain has been accounted for by presenting it as more radical and destructive than anything that had gone before it. When the context of popular, infidel thought is brought into view, however, *Leben Jesu* is revealed to have been attractive to many Britons for the exact opposite reason: because it was more reverential, indeed more Christian, than the general run of radical literature then currently available. Likewise chapter 6 recovers the fact that many English Christians first encountered the lines of thought that were fundamental to the new discipline of biblical criticism (such as questioning traditional views regarding the authorship and dating of various books of the Bible) from militantly anti-Christian lecturers who presented these ideas in such a way that they were thoroughly jumbled together with bitter, sacrilegious attacks on the most fundamental beliefs of the Christian faith.

The controversy generated by the Old Testament criticism of John William Colenso, the missionary bishop of Natal, is analyzed in chapter 5. For the first time, the voices of Colenso's critics are allowed to be heard. In the past, scholars have caricatured the views of his detractors without actually having read them. This study of the Colenso controversy demonstrates how important the popular, pastoral context was for the reception—even by the elite—of biblical criticism in England. Many religious and intellectual leaders in Victorian society—even people as open to modifying or abandoning traditional theological views as F. D. Maurice and Matthew Arnold—believed that if ordinary people were receiving the impression that the Bible (and with it doctrine and morality) had been overthrown, then a stand needed to be taken against the source of such impressions. Tellingly, the adjective that was most often used to condemn the bishop's book was "dangerous." A recurring theme in this volume is the ironic fact that unbelievers often read the Bible in a more literalistic way than their Christian debating partners, and repeatedly grumbled that Christians ought to have a more conservative approach to Scripture than they actually did! (See chapters 6 and 7; chapter 5 offers a liberal Christian version of this same dynamic.)

Rather than, as it is so often presented, the "loss of faith" being the keynote explanatory narrative when it comes to the intersection between Victorian religion and modern thought, chapter 8 underlines the point that the nineteenth-century story is really one of contested Christianity rather than the ebbing of the sea of faith. Thomas Cooper, a popular, well-read, freethinking lecturer, found that the Christian faith ultimately won the contest in his own relentless quest for truth; and thereafter he traveled around the country giving addresses that engaged the latest scientific, philosophical, and skeptical thought from an evangelical point of view. Destabilizing other stereotypes about the Victorians, Joseph Barker is revealed in chapter 6 to be a scoffing infidel who was more absolutist about teetotalism, more prudish about human sexuality, and generally more committed to Victorian morality and respectability, than his evangelical opponents. Chapter 7, on Victorian Britain's most notorious atheist, Charles Bradlaugh, suggests that—at least at street level—Victorian skepticism was based more on a visceral antipathy to Christianity than on the cogency of any alternative body of thought. Victorian atheists were surprisingly open to alternative spiritualities or nonmaterialist views of reality such as Theosophy and Spiritualism. How large the Bible loomed over Victorian society—whether one loved it or hated it—is made apparent in many of these case studies (chapters 3, 4, 5, 6, 7, and 8). It is said that in Northern Ireland today atheists refer to themselves as "Protestant atheists" or "Catholic atheists." In a rather different sense, Victorian skeptics are shown in chapter 7 to have been "Protestant infidels" or "Protestant atheists." One could argue somewhat mischievously that their freethought seems to have been grounded in the Protestant principle of sola Scriptura as it was confined in large measure to attacking the Bible.

The second major theme of this study, how theology and church life informed national politics, is unfolded primarily in chapters 10, 11, and 12. Chapter 11 demonstrates how Nonconformity's own narrative of its spiritual lineage had direct political consequences. Dissenters had long honored as heroes of the faith the Puritan ministers such as Richard Baxter who were ejected from the Church of England in 1662. The commemoration in 1862 of the bicentennial of this event led to a significant deepening of the Nonconformist community's commitment to radical politics. The political divide between Anglicans and Dissenters is again underlined in chapter 12. In the bitter controversy explored there, English Baptists are shown to have sided with the black population of Jamaica against their own race and colonial representatives. The missionary impulse and solidarity with their co-religionists proved more powerful than patriotic and xenophobic passions.

Chapter 10, however, provides the wider, more far-reaching, revisionist argument on Nonconformity and politics. The ecclesiology of many Dissenters, particularly the theology of the church held by Congregationalists and Baptists, led these evangelical Christians into supporting a range of political objectives that defy current stereotypes. Evangelical Nonconformists were in the vanguard of pushing for religious equality before the law, including securing the civil rights of Roman Catholics, Jews, and atheists. In short, an evangelical, Dissenting theology led to the seemingly paradoxical result of a vision for a religiously pluralistic civic society. Also in contrast to the standard assumptions made in the existing scholarship, Nonconformists were often reticent to legislate for morality. Most of all, the theological vision of Nonconformists prompted them to want to remove entanglements between the church and the state, such as an established church and national days of prayer—changes that are often viewed as evidence for secularization in existing studies.[4]

Influence is not usually one-way, however. Chapter 9, a denominational study, recognizes that political commitments could also influence assumptions and preferences regarding church polity. The commitment to the principle of lay representation in the Methodist New Connexion was at least partially prompted by the value that its members placed on the liberal and democratic strains in modern political culture. The discourse of rights, liberty, freedom, emancipation, and representation was considered applicable in both ecclesiastical and civil politics.

These two dominant themes, one from intellectual history and the other from political history, are preceded at the beginning of this volume by a few, more intimate portraits of Victorian lives. In chapter 1, the line between public and private for Victorian women is shown to have been blurred in potentially liberating ways by Congregational ecclesiology. Notions of respectability, so important to Victorians, especially the aspiring middle classes, are explored in chapter 2 through a poignant account of the breakdown of a Congregational minister's marriage. In chapter 3, the volume offers an excursion abroad as Victorian Protestants, especially evangelicals and Dissenters, went on the first package tours of the Holy Land. Contested Christianity was not left behind even on holiday. These Britons were confronted by Roman Catholic and Orthodox versions of Christian spirituality at the sacred sites, were repelled by them, and felt compelled to denounce them. Nevertheless, these staunch Protestants could not resist longing to derive some spiritual benefits from encountering the "holy" land of the Bible, as they wistfully straddled the boundary between tourists and pilgrims. Moreover, even on holiday the fact that traditional Christian beliefs were contested by modern biblical critics could not be forgotten. Therefore, as members of Cook's tours of the Holy Land went sightseeing, they also kept one eye on the lookout for evidence that might prove the veracity of the Bible. It is only by drawing close enough in to see these very human struggles between different beliefs and practices that one can gain a truer understanding of the nature of Victorian Britain's contested Christianity.

This book is comprised of both original and previously published material. I am grateful for permission to use the previously published material, and wish to acknowledge those original contexts as follows: *Journal of Ecclesiastical History* 49, 2 (April 1998): 282–92 [ch. 1]; *Journal of the United Reformed Church History Society* 6, 8 (May 2001): 589–96 [ch. 2]; *Scottish*

Journal of Theology 50, 4 (1997): 433–58 [ch. 5]; *Journal of Victorian Culture* 5, 2 (Autumn 2000): 239–59 [ch. 5]; *Bulletin of the John Rylands University Library of Manchester* 82, 1 (Spring 2000): 115–34 [ch. 7]; Deryck W. Lovegrove, ed., *The Rise of the Laity in Evangelical Protestantism* (London: Routledge, 2002): 153–63 [ch. 9]; *Fides et Historia* XXXIII, 1 (Winter/Spring 2001): 109–19 [ch. 10]; R. N. Swanson, ed., *The Church Retrospective* (Studies in Church History 33; Woodbridge, Suffolk: The Boydell Press for the Ecclesiastical History Society, 1997): 459–73 [ch. 11]; D. W. Bebbington, ed., *The Gospel in the World: International Baptist Studies* (Studies in Baptist History and Thought 1; Carlisle: Paternoster Press, 2002): 165–86 [ch. 12]; R. N. Swanson, ed., *The Holy Land, Holy Lands, and Christian History* (Studies in Church History 36; Woodbridge, Suffolk: The Boydell Press for the Ecclesiastical History Society, 2000): 329–42 [ch. 3].

Mark A. Noll, McManis Professor of Christian Thought at Wheaton College in Wheaton, Illinois, as I have quipped elsewhere, is the original patron saint of my scholarly endeavors. This relationship began when I was still a Wheaton undergraduate student. Since I took several classes with him, he graciously agreed to supervise my BA thesis. After that, at the MA level, came a couple of independent studies and a research project on the Brethren that was subsequently published in a scholarly journal. Mark then hand-picked for me my other patron saint, David Bebbington, and sent me off to do doctoral work under his outstanding supervision. Mark has repeatedly ensured that I was invited to participate in scholarly projects (several careers could be made just out of the crumbs that fall from his table!) When it was time for me to come back to America, he commended me to my alma mater as someone who would be a worthy addition to the Wheaton faculty, and since that time he has been a most supportive and nurturing colleague. It is with deep gratitude, respect, and affection that I dedicate this book to him.

PART ONE

The Social Contexts of a Private Faith

Chapter 1

Gender Egalitarianism
The Baptist Women of the Mill Yard Church

The Mill Yard Seventh Day Baptist Church, founded in the seventeenth century, had by the 1820s dwindled to a group of just seven women without a minister. One of their seventeenth-century forebears, Joseph Davis, a wealthy linen draper, had established a charitable trust for the purpose of perpetually supporting the cause of Seventh Day Baptists. He had entrusted to it the Mill Yard property in London, which gave the congregation its name, and the task of paying the minister's salary, as well as listing some other suitable beneficiaries.[1] In 1830, however, the trustees at that time resolved to give the property to another congregation on the grounds that the historic Mill Yard church had ceased to exist. The members (all women) protested that they were a true church, and all parties agreed to take the case for arbitration to the General Body of Protestant Dissenting Ministers—a ministerial society comprised of the bulk of the Independent, Baptist, and Presbyterian ministers in London and its vicinity. Thus, for several days in 1831, many of the most prominent Nonconformist ministers of that era gave themselves to passing judgment on the theological legitimacy or otherwise of the unusual situation arrived at by a remnant of this obscure religious group, providing us with a unique opportunity to discover Dissenting attitudes during that period toward the relationship between gender and the very nature of the church itself.[2]

Curiously, those who have written the history of the Mill Yard church have uniformly failed to mention that there was a period in its history when it continued to function in the absence of male members and the case that this provoked. Indeed, the account given by the noted Baptist historian, W. T. Whitley, shows signs that he consciously chose to obscure the stand these women took.[3] F. H. A. Micklewright, who explored the church's history in considerable detail, also gives the impression that the congregation did not gather for worship during the period when there were no male members, as does the sketch of the congregation's history recently made by Bryan Ball, although it seems certain he is simply unaware of these events.[4]

It is particularly surprising that historians of the congregation would fail to record the case of these seven women because accounts of it have been included in other published sources, beginning with the biography of Josiah Conder. Conder, the editor of the *Eclectic Review*, represented the trustees before the General Body. His lifetime of work as a writer and editor provided a great literary service to Nonconformity, which offered ample material for a sketch of his life; and his advocacy on behalf of the Joseph Davis trustees was in no sense a significant event in Conder's career. It would appear that his biographer (who was also his son) took five pages to recount the case merely to bring some light diversion into his tale. His son tells us that when Conder was preparing the case, he happened to meet a Baptist minister whom he probed on his opinions of the issues at stake by using as his opening gambit the question: "How many sisters make a brotherhood?"[5] The *Wesleyan Methodist Magazine* took the uncharacteristic step of reprinting several pages of this biography, the account of the Mill Yard case.[6] One imagines that the magazine, which made few concessions to the human need for light diversion, was making a subtle point on the defects of Congregational polity as a small contribution to the ongoing debate on theories of church government.[7] Nevertheless, others seemed to agree with the apparent view of Conder's son that the Old Dissent was large and powerful and secure enough by the mid-Victorian era to be able to afford to laugh at an anomaly of its own making. The Independent John Stoughton also recounted the case in his history of Dissent during these decades (citing Conder's biography), although it is doubtful that he would have mentioned the Seventh Day Baptists at all, were he not tempted to amuse his readers with this curious episode.[8] So it is possible for us to be pointed toward the primary sources that provide a fresh view of attitudes toward gender and Nonconformity during this period because the Mill Yard women have been allowed to remain visible in the published historical record after all—albeit as jesters at the Dissenting feast.

Seventh Day Baptists officially distinguish themselves from other Baptists only by their belief that it is God's will that Saturday rather than Sunday be set apart for worship.[9] The willingness to break from the mainstream of Nonconformist thought that this necessarily implied, however, seems to have freed them throughout their history to adopt other minority positions as well: some Seventh Day Baptists of the Civil War generation had links with the Fifth Monarchists. During part of the Victorian era, the Mill Yard church adopted Unitarian beliefs, and an early twentieth-century minister of that congregation combined his Seventh Day convictions with being a zealous antismoker, vegetarian, Freemason, and Orangeman.[10] While a certain temperament undoubtedly revels in this kind of defiant witness, after the heady days surrounding the Cromwellian era, fewer and fewer people were willing to do so for the cause of the Seventh Day Sabbath. By the 1810s the Mill Yard minister, William Slater, was the sole male member of the church; his three nephews, including Joseph Slater, Jr., who was the leader of the trustees, had all "apostatized" and gone to the Church of England.[11] William Slater died in 1819. Joseph Slater, Jr., was now the sole surviving trustee, and he gained permission from the Court of Chancery to appoint some new trustees of his own choosing, none of whom were Seventh Day Baptists. Reading between the lines, one senses that perhaps public decisions might have been colored by a personal squabble within the Slater family. Nevertheless, the new trustees ensured that the Mill Yard building, which had fallen into disuse, was repaired and reopened; and they undertook to find a suitable minister for the little flock. Thomas Russell, an Independent minister, agreed to spend his Saturdays supplying the Mill Yard pulpit in the interim, beginning in March 1826.

The church belonged to the atrophied General wing of the Baptist family, and the task of finding an Arminian Baptist who believed that the Christian Sabbath was Saturday proved a daunting one for the trustees.[12] There was only one other Seventh Day congregation in all of London and it was small and Calvinist. When its minister died in 1826, this congregation called John Shenston to replace him and thereby deprived the trustees of their one reasonably promising applicant. Another candidate, Dr. Whitehead, applied in the summer of 1827, but it emerged through further communication that he was a Calvinist. Nevertheless, the trustees agreed to allow him a trial series of five sermons.

> The result was that the existing members intimated to the trustees an entire disapprobation of the matter and manner of Dr. W——'s addresses from the pulpit, and a determination not to attend on any repetition of them.[13]

There followed another couple of years of Russell's ministry. Two of the seven members from the time of William Slater had now died, and another had withdrawn from the congregation; but the clear leader of the faithful remnant, Elizabeth Slater, the minister's widow, had shored up the ranks by having those remaining receive into membership three of her daughters, restoring their number to seven.

In short, the congregation was comprised largely of Slaters, as indeed it was even during the final years of William Slater's ministry. His great-grandfather, Thomas Slater, had been one of the original trustees, and his grandfather and father had each in turn inherited this responsibility, passing it on to him. In terms of social position, William Slater was a Dissenting minister in a small and peculiar sect who supplemented his income by working as a schoolmaster. The couple lived in a house that was part of the Mill Yard property, and Elizabeth Slater continued to live there, together with their three daughters, after her husband's death. She noted in a letter to the trustees that it had been agreed in 1823 that a future Mill Yard minister could be paid a salary of £70 *per annum*. This figure gives some indication of the amount of income her husband might have earned from his ministerial dutes.[14] One of the daughters, Harriot, eventually married an Assistant Keeper of the Public Records who was also a Seventh Day Baptist minister. His income from his secular occupation was £260 *per annum* in 1844.[15] No other occupations or incomes related to the Slaters have been discovered. Nevertheless, these details do paint a likely picture of the family's social position: it seems probable that men from lower middle-class occupations such as schoolmasters, shopkeepers, or small masters would have been considered suitable matches for the other daughters.

In the fight that was to come, Elizabeth Slater proved to be a formidable opponent. Her actions are a telling case study of the way in which some women from this period might have been able to use the very roles allotted to them by contemporary notions of femininity as a base from which to extend their influence into spheres usually reserved for the male gender. In her case, the duty of a mother to see that her children are established in the faith was harnessed to affect chapel politics and a legal dispute. The supposed greater religious sensitivity of the female sex was arguably expanded into a public championing of these women's spiritual fidelity against the dulled spirituality (from the perspective of Dissent) of the leader of the trustees, and the derived status of a minister's wife was transmuted into an independent authority once she became a minister's widow.[16]

Thus the matter stood when in June 1830 the trustees resolved to hand the property over to Shenston and his congregation of Calvinist Seventh Day Baptists. This decision was explained to the General Body in this way:

> These Resolutions were adopted under an opinion [. . .] entertained
> by the trustees, that in the absence of any indications of revival, after a

trial of five years, it was impossible to consider the remaining members of the Mill Yard as constituting a church, or even the <u>nucleus</u> of a church [. . .].[17]

Elizabeth Slater responded defiantly, writing to the trustees:

> How very painful it will be to me and my family to be compelled to become hearers of Mr. Shenston, whose preaching would, we feel, be unprofitable to us all. It is, I submit to you, clearly contrary to all Dissenting principles to force any minister upon a congregation; for, although small in numbers, a congregation and church we still form.[18]

There followed a series of letters between the two parties and the establishment of Shenston's congregation in the property, before the persistent complaints of Elizabeth Slater and Thomas Russell led to an agreement to submit the matter for a binding judgment to the General Body. The ministers agreed to determine the answer to the question: "Whether the existing members of Mill-Yard Sabbatarian meeting are or are not a church, with the power of choosing a pastor?"[19]

The General Body called a special series of meetings in order to hear the case, convening for a full day once a week for three consecutive weeks. Dr. John Pye Smith, Principal of Homerton College and one of the most respected Nonconformist theologians of his day, chaired the meetings.[20] There were about fifty ministers present at each of the sittings, including such notable figures as the scholarly Independents Robert Halley and Robert Vaughan, the philanthropist Andrew Reed, the popular preacher Thomas Binney, and Baptist worthies such as Dr. F. A. Cox and the former president of Stepney Academy (now Regent's Park College, Oxford), Dr. William Newman.[21] Several provincial ministers were also invited to add their weight and wisdom to the proceedings. Josiah Conder, who in the following year would become the editor of the *Patriot* newspaper, had consented to plead the case of the trustees. Thomas Russell, whose own literary efforts—already achieved by this time—would secure him an entry in the *Dictionary of National Biography*, represented the Mill Yard seven.[22] It is hard to imagine a gathering more qualified to articulate the mature theological convictions of English Dissenters during this period.

The case turned on the question of whether or not the male gender was essential to the nature of a true church. In order to explain in brief why the women could not be considered a church, Conder prepared twelve "Reasons in the Negative," six of which explicitly related to the exclusively female nature of the group, and two more were preparatory points for those six. The first point cited an established definition of a local church as a group consisting of "a competent number of visible saints." He then proceeded in subsequent points to argue that an entirely female group is inherently a collection of saints of the incompetent variety. The reason this conclusion was sound, according to Conder, was that it was the custom in Dissenting churches to reserve for males alone crucial functions and activities, such as the diaconate and judging disputes between members. The latter function was particularly significant in his argument. In effect, he defined a viable church as enough saints to have a proper fight and, when looked at in this light, it was quite clear why men were essential. From this train of thought he was led to the conclusion that "no particular society can be possessed of entire competency, that consists of fewer than from six to ten male members." He also used the small number of people in the congregation as a point against them, but this was only a side argument for, according to Conder, "no number of women could themselves form a quorum, or an ecclesiastical assembly."[23]

Russell, on the other hand, in his "Reasons in the Affirmative," argued that the congregation was simply functioning according to Congregational principles of church government as it always had done. (Baptists and Independents both adopted this form of polity. In this chapter the term "Congregationalism" and variations thereof are not used in their standard sense to designate the Independent denomination, but instead refer to this pattern of church government and all those who adhere to it.) Russell noted that although it might be true that church officers must be male: "officers are not necessary to the existence of a church. The church is before them; appoints them; and can dismiss them."[24] Moreover, it was spurious to claim that a congregation must have within its own ranks individuals eligible to be officeholders for it was far more typical for a congregation to call a minister who belonged to another church and: "This course can as readily be adopted by a church of females only, as by one of both sexes."[25] Conder's argument allowed for a congregation to be completely deprived of female members without losing anything essential to the nature of a church; in his theological vision only the male gender was indispensable to the existence of a local church. Russell, however, claimed that the nature of the church was not gender dependent: "the abstraction of any given number of males or females, or of the whole of the one or the other, cannot deprive the church of its being [. . .]."[26]

The Mill Yard case served to lay bare the radical gender implications of Congregational ecclesiology. Maintaining that the government of the church resides with its membership, it was natural enough that some

Congregational churches would allow women to vote along with the men when choosing a minister, as no one would deny that women may be members. There was, however, no consensus on this. The eighteenth-century Baptist theologian, Daniel Turner, in his *A Compendium of Social Religion* (1758), argued that female members should not be allowed to vote on the grounds that this power "seems to imply rule" and that this "appears to me inconsistent with their state of subjection."[27] The eminent Independent minister, John Angell James, however, in his *Christian Fellowship* (1822), listed the reasons why it could be considered appropriate for women to vote, answering Turner explicitly point by point.[28] Nevertheless, this was not the practice of the congregation that James served, the Carr's Lane Church in Birmingham. The next occasion for the members of this congregation to vote on a minister came in 1854, fifty years after they had voted to receive James. This vote, which led to R. W. Dale, being invited to a copastorate alongside their elderly minister, was one in which only men could participate, although 370 of the silenced and disenfranchised women found an ingenious way to express their opinion by signing a memorial approving of Dale's ministry.[29] The first issue of the *Baptist Magazine* (1809) included a letter asking whether or not it was proper for women members to vote. It provoked a reply explaining at length why it was indeed appropriate. It also chided those in the correspondent's state of confusion for being so ignorant of "proper principles of dissent" and the "nature [. . .] of a Christian Church" as not to know why it was proper for women to vote.[30]

Even the founding benefactor of the Mill Yard church, Joseph Davis himself, might have held this conviction. He had written a kind of personal creed in which he said in regard to the local church:

> It hath been my professed Faith, according to the Word, near this sixty Years; that when Persons, Men, or Women, or younger Persons, do give themselves up upon the Lord, and to each other [. . .] with the Sacraments of Baptism, with Water, and the Lord's Supper, purely administrated: They are the Lord Christ's Church, and it is their Duty to Choose, from among themselves, such, as according to the Word are most fitly Qualified for such Offices; which Offices, are not by the Patron, to be thrust upon them, without their free Choice; but the whole Church is solemnly to wait upon God [. . .] depending upon the Spirit's Help and Direction, in the Choice [. . .]. [31]

Russell claimed that female suffrage was "now generally, if not universally, admitted and recognized in congregational churches," and Conder only countered this with the entirely compatible parenthetical grumble that it was "by no means universally recognized."[32] The fact that such comments could be made before the General Body, a group that would have had a fairly good understanding of the general habits of Dissenting congregations throughout the country, clearly reveals that the theory and practice of women voting already had a firm rooting in the Congregational world by this time.[33] In light of these realities, Conder did not even hint that women members should not have the right to vote; such an argument would have been in direct defiance of the practice of numerous churches and the teaching of some respected Dissenting ministers.

Nevertheless, Conder, who labored hard throughout his life to increase the respectability of Dissent, was clearly embarrassed that this bizarre case had so exposed the strands of gender egalitarianism woven into the fabric of Congregational ecclesiology. His final point seems to have brought to the surface his real fear, namely, that this case would bring Congregationalism itself into disrepute by so baldly asserting an attitude toward the rights of women that was at variance with the norms of English society as a whole:

> Because, the public sanction, for the first time, of the doctrine contended for, would tend to bring the rationale and constitution of Dissenting churches into contempt; [. . .] establishing a precedent hostile to the decencies of society, and furnishing occasion for scandalizing or ridiculing the pastoral relation, as supposed to exist, or to be capable of existing, between a small number of women, and a minister of their own creation or appointment.[34]

Less than a decade earlier, John Angell James had attempted to allay this fear by suggesting that his readers try not to think about it: "As to the supposition of females gaining a majority against the men, it is a case too improbable and extreme to sustain an argument."[35] The Mill Yard case was heard in the first year of William IV's reign; it would be a full generation before female suffrage was established for municipal elections and the whole of the Victorian and Edwardian ages would pass away before women secured the right to vote for parliamentary candidates. No wonder some Congregational ministers who longed to increase the respectability of Dissent were squeamish about highlighting the power given to women in this regard among their churches. Thomas Russell, on the other hand, seems to have felt that it was to their glory, not their shame:

> Every member has a right to vote in what concerns the whole body, sisters as well as brethren. It is a distinguishing feature of Congregational church-government, that in this respect no difference is made between the sexes [. . .]. [36]

Indeed, one can look at the case as a product of the tension between gender equality in regard to the rights of church membership taught by some Congregationalists and the marked inequality between men and women before the law. Many Congregational theorists were well aware that even though their principles of church government awarded no authority to trustees, the law invested them with a power that might be used to undermine this ecclesiastical model in practice. James wrote:

> Amongst some irregular and anomalous bodies of dissenters, the right of appointment is with trustees; but as this rarely occurs amidst the regular Nonconformists, and is so flagrantly an invasion of the people's right where it does occur, it will not be necessary for me to combat the practice, and expose its impropriety.[37]

Once again, he appears unduly sanguine. Of course, what to many minds today would seem to be the obvious way to have avoided the Mill Yard conflict—to have appointed some of the women as trustees to administer the property of their own church and denomination—is an anachronistic solution. In some circumstances before the Married Women's Property Act of 1907, and in all cases before the Married Women's Property Act of 1882, a wife was an unsuitable trustee because of her husband's power to interfere. In practice, this effectively barred all women. In Brook v. Brook (1839), the Master of the Rolls, Lord Langdale, denied a single woman the right to be a trustee on the grounds that "it was not the usual practice, and it might lead to inconvenience in case of her marriage."[38] Even in 1893, Mr. Justice North was reluctant to allow two unmarried women to become trustees.[39] Indeed, as late as 1901 a legal textbook, citing North's hesitancy in justification, commented:

> As regards married women, they used to be equally unsuitable for office of trustee—and this not only because of the inconvenience resulting from the legal unity of husband and wife, but also because of the reputed variability of the feminine temperament; and although the former of these two objections has, to some extent, ceased to exist, the latter of them still remains in its integrity.[40]

Congregational notions of equality of membership did not sit easily and were not easy to implement in a world such as this.

But neither were they abandoned under pressure. The Mill Yard women won their case. Eleven of the ministers voted that they were not a church, but nineteen voted that they were. The feelings of the majority having thereby been expressed, the ministers agreed unanimously that the seven women were a true church.[41] Unfortunately, there is no division list, so it is not possible to discover the opinion of individual ministers. Nevertheless, we may say that the majority of the Dissenting ministers who voted believed that masculinity was not essential to the nature of a church and were prepared to act on this conviction, despite Conder's warning that this would lead to Nonconformity's being mocked.

A compilation of biographical sketches of Seventh Day Baptists not only predictably has an entry on William Slater but has none on Elizabeth who—in her own time and way—was surely also a leader of the congregation. It even manages to credit him with having seven children without acknowledging his wife's assistance—or even her existence.[42] The Baptist historian, Karen Smith, has called for researchers to explore the way in which women "were able to cross over the boundaries from private to public spheres."[43] Elizabeth Slater, the woman who saved the church from extinction, is worthy of study by those who wish to understand the way in which some women were able to achieve a measure of success in realms usually considered unsuitable to the female gender, and a measure of honor by those who wish to celebrate the lives of Seventh Day Baptists. For, as her entry in the church minute book says, she was: "A *Mother* to this Church, during the long period of its troubles, and the vacancy of the Pastoral office, after her husband's death."[44]

Leonore Davidoff and Catherine Hall have noted that religious ideology in this period combined a doctrine of spiritual equality with a belief in social subordination.[45] The Mill Yard case demonstrates how the former had the potential to challenge and curtail successfully the division of functions by gender contained in the latter. The trustees were wrong to assume that the fortunes of the congregation were beyond hope of revival. The whole future history of the Mill Yard church is a tribute to the women who kept its light burning during those years. To them also belongs the credit for eliciting from many of the most prominent leaders of English Dissent a refutation of the notion that masculinity was part of the definition of a true church. To Conder's riddle, "How many sisters make a brotherhood?," they answered upon reflection: exactly the same number as it would take of brothers, because the nature of the church is not dependent on the gender of its members.

Chapter 2

Religious Respectability
The Reverend Newman Hall's Divorce Case

Christopher Newman Hall (1816–1902) was one of the most celebrated Nonconformist divines of the Victorian age, admired across the denominations. He was perhaps best known in his own lifetime as the author of the gospel tract, *Come to Jesus*. He published it in 1848, and by 1898 he could report that four million copies had been printed and it had been translated into perhaps as many as forty languages.[1] Also, Hall, using his own home, arranged for influential Nonconformists to meet the leader of the Liberal party; and, in our post-Christendom age, when he is still remembered by scholars, it is usually for his invitation to come to Gladstone rather than to Christ.

Moreover, in his own day, Hall would have been well known—once again, in circles well beyond the boundaries of Congregationalism—from the gossip and publicity surrounding the breakdown and dissolution of his first marriage. These events also have largely slipped out of the official historical record. Hall himself managed to write an entire autobiography of about four hundred pages without ever mentioning his first wife or marriage, let alone his divorce. Of course, when his autobiography was published, those events were in living memory and were therefore well known, but this reticent retrospective has also served as the principal source for Hall's life for subsequent generations. Indeed, one wonders if he wrote it precisely in order to make a biography unnecessary, since any biographer—however sympathetic and discreet—could hardly have ignored a marriage lasting over twenty years altogether. The *Dictionary of National Biography* tersely gives the bare facts in a few sentences, giving scarcely more than the dates of the marriage, the separation, and the series of legal events culminating in the decree nisi being made absolute.[2] Nevertheless, the trial is well worth revisiting, as it provides a rare glimpse into the intimate lives of respectable, middle-class, Victorian Nonconformists. Also, Newman Hall, whose fascination with the law occasioned the extraordinary fact that he pursued and obtained a LLB from London University while engaging in a prominent full-time ministry, gained the dubious honor of being immortalized in legal history for having established the precedent that someone who had withdrawn a petition for divorce was still at liberty to file again on the basis of the same evidence.[3]

Newman Hall married Charlotte, the daughter of William Gordon, MD, of Hull, on 14 April 1846, when he himself was a Congregational minister in Hull. She was eighteen years old at the time of her marriage, and he was thirty. Various statements were made at the trial regarding her having been spoiled as an only child, and her having been a demanding person whose emotional and physical well-being was easily disturbed; but it nevertheless appears that the couple had a reasonably successful marriage for the first fifteen years. As far as outward actions are concerned, the beginning of the end came in 1863, when Charlotte Hall informed her husband that she could no longer bring herself to have sexual intercourse with him. Mrs. Hall's personal habits also began to change in other ways: she was less inclined to attend public worship and she took up hunting and smoking. The divorce suit that Newman Hall filed in 1873 and then dropped only to file again in 1879 with success was based on the charge that Charlotte Hall had committed adultery with Frank Waters Richardson, a livery-stable keeper. Richardson was in his early twenties when this affair was said to have begun; she was forty. Richardson's parents ran a hotel in Tring where Mrs. Hall stayed when she went hunting, and when he moved to London in 1868, she began to go riding with him. This relationship became increasingly intense. She had her horse moved from stables near her home to Richardson's stables two miles away and would change into her riding clothes in his bedroom there. She had Richardson join her on holiday and even arranged for him to live in her and her husband's home for several weeks. She would stay up smoking with him in a back kitchen until two or three o'clock in the morning with—according to the servants—the door locked. When Newman Hall insisted that she break off this relationship, she left her husband and went to Brighton, arranging for Richardson to meet her there where he stayed in the same hotel as she. From her formal separation from her husband in 1870 until the time of the trial in 1879, Mrs. Hall lived with Richardson's sister while Richardson lived with Mrs. Hall's cousin, and they saw each other on a daily basis. Mrs. Hall did not dispute any of the facts presented so far at the trial, save that the door was locked when she was alone with Richardson, and that she was a smoker.

In other words, the crucial testimony was considerably more salacious. A parlor maid—an obligatory character in all such stories—claimed that while Richardson was living in the Halls' home, she had seen "Mrs. Hall, when only partially dressed, go into Mr. Richardson's bedroom before break-fast."[4] Mrs. Anne Francis had Mrs. Hall and Richardson as lodgers in sepa-rate rooms in her house in Brighton in October 1869. Her testimony was summarized as follows:

> They retired to their rooms at a late hour, and one night [the] witness and her husband were awoke several times by noises in the dining room, as if people were tumbling about. The witness went up to the room, and find-ing the door fastened, knocked loudly. Richardson answered the knock, and when the door was opened the witness observed that Mrs. Hall was lounging in the easy chair before the fire.[5]

The judge at the trial seemed to find the evidence of the staff at a hotel in The Strand particularly conclusive. Mrs. Jane Crispin Firth, the proprietress, made the most of her fifteen minutes of fame. She particularly excelled at describing the man who told her he was Mrs. Hall's husband:

> He had a pepper-and-salt suit. I thought at first it looked rather seedy. I thought he had a High Church curate's face. (Laughter.) I am sure he was clean shaven. He was not a stout man; more inclined to be slight than stout. I should think he was under 30—about 27 years of age. [. . .] As he went up to the second floor I could see he was not a clergyman from the manner in which his clothes were made. I was struck with his shaven and rather pleasing face. He looked like a man who had seen better days. His trousers were so tight about the knees that I was struck with it and saw directly he was not a clergyman. (Laughter.)[6]

Much more testimony was given in support of Newman Hall's suit, but these few examples should suffice.

Before the crisis in their relationship regarding Richardson, Mrs. Hall had written in a letter to her husband of her "revulsion" at the thought of having sexual intercourse with him. The defense, with a fair amount of inge-nuity, presented this as evidence that she was a desexualized creature:

> He knew his wife's nature, he knew that in her case there was the absence of normal natural inclination, and that what might be temptation and

opportunity for others was not temptation and opportunity to her. This
was the true explanation of her conduct [. . .].[7]

The judge, however, in his summing up, rejected this line of argument:

> She has to be judged by those whose experience tells them that a man and
> woman cannot remain alone together until a late hour at night with
> locked doors and indulgence in caresses without leading to sexual desire.
> She has to be judged by ordinary men and not judged by some mystic
> world of which we have no consciousness and where passion does not
> exist.[8]

And what of Newman Hall's sexual desires? He was certainly taxed by his
wife's cessation of intimacy. Mrs. Hall repeatedly complained during the trial
that he used to taunt her continually about this. A letter he wrote in 1867
was read in court in which he confessed that he found regular, morally sanc-
tioned sexual intercourse "a great help in making a pure mind and a healthy
body." He went on bitterly, "You cannot be justified in refusing this, and
doing what has driven many husbands into wickedness."[9] Indeed, Mrs. Hall,
more or less claiming that he was so driven, brought a countercharge of adultery against him. A Miss Mary Wyatt from Shropshire was named as the
other party. Interestingly, Newman Hall reported that he had met her in
1863, the same year that his wife's refusal had begun. Mrs. Hall asserted that
her husband wrote to Wyatt in a shorthand that others could not read, that
he was in the habit of kissing her good morning and good night, that she
wore "his portrait next [to] her skin," that they went for walks together, and
that he cut short a continental tour in order to come to her when he received
word that she was ill. Charlotte Hall's legal representatives then dropped this
countercharge, however, so Newman Hall was not afforded an opportunity
to recast this relationship in another light. For his part, the judge volun-
teered in his summing up that satisfying the sexual needs of her husband was
the "first duty of a wife."[10]

As soon as he had separated from his wife in 1870, Newman Hall sought
to escape his troubles through a Cook's tour of the Holy Land. On this trip
he spent a great deal of time with Miss Harriet Knipe, the woman who
would become his second wife.[11] Mrs. Hall claimed that in 1870, at the
same time that a certain advertisement about her appeared in a newspaper,
Newman Hall "was enjoying himself with Harriet Knype [sic], the woman
he was engaged to."[12] Mr. Willis, Q.C., forced Newman Hall to confess that
he wished to remarry and that he and Miss Knipe had more or less come to
an understanding:

Have you a person in your eye whom you would desire to marry if you
were free?
—I have.
Have you not communicated to her the feelings you entertain towards
her?
—Yes.
And do not your friends know of your object and purpose?
—Very few.[13]

According to the defense, Charlotte Hall was desexualized; and conversely,
Newman Hall was depicted as motivated by his sexual appetite: "at the date
of the letter Mr. Hall had an eye only on a Heavenly inheritance; now it was
on another and different inheritance. (Laughter)." And still more bluntly:

Two lines which he (Mr. Willis) remembered from boyhood, and which
he never expected to quote in a case like the present, occurred to him,—
"Old folks say there are no pains
Like itch of love in aged veins."
(Laughter.) But the heyday of life was not yet past with the Rev. Newman
Hall.[14]

The stereotype that the Victorians were prudes when it came to sexual matters undoubtedly has been overplayed, but it would seem to be a genuine difference between their age and our own that this line of attack was considered
so damaging as to necessitate a counteroffensive by his own legal representatives in which Newman Hall was now desexualized. The final sentences of
the final speech made in support of his suit were as follows:

She who ought to have brought sunshine to the petitioner's house had
brought upon it the cloud and shadow of a great sorrow, and had left him
to sit alone by the hearth whose ashes were cold and scattered; and now
at the close of life, unmoved and uninstigated by passion, he asked for the
companionship which she denied him. In his name and that of justice the
learned counsel claimed for him that verdict which would deliver him
from a grievous and unreasonable bond.[15]

Apparently a sixty-three year old man was expected to have a content mind
and body without the aid of passionate love.

The case of Newman Hall's divorce also presents interesting sidelights on
the issues of religion and respectability. Hall's reputation as a popular minister was unavoidably part of the subtext of the case. Hall himself admitted
that one of his reasons for withdrawing his earlier suit was that he was in the

middle of the fundraising campaign for that £60,000 Dissenting cathedral, Christ Church, Westminster Bridge Road, and he judged that "under the circumstances, my wiser course was not to expose my affairs."[16] Mrs. Hall seemed to resent his exalted position or find it difficult to bear; at the very least it was a source of tension. Undoubtedly it placed tremendous pressures on her such as most wives never experienced. She claimed that her husband had confided to Richardson, "Mrs. Hall is a dangerous woman. I should have been the most popular man in England but for her."[17] A letter from Mrs. Hall to her husband was read during the trial in which she declared, "Your punishment will yet come, and when poverty, illness, and unpopularity comes I shall be your best friend."[18] His unpopularity would have been easier for her to bear than the demands that his popularity placed upon her. The constraints of her husband's profession were felt as such. Mrs. Hall explained that she knew Richardson much better than her husband knew him because she and Richardson would stay home together on Sundays whereas "Mr. Hall was away so much preaching the Gospel at his chapel."[19] She reported that her husband had said to her, "I forbid smoking in my house, as it is inconsistent with the position of a minister of the Gospel."[20] Mr. Willis, Q.C., speaking on behalf of his client, Mrs. Hall, said of her:

> From an early period of her married life Mrs. Hall was subject to the most dreadful thoughts and fancies. She was never a pastor's wife, and did not, as was the custom in all the Dissenting communities, share with her husband in church labours. A more terrible situation for a man in Mr. Hall's position—a leading minister, a popular preacher, and prominent figure in the religious world—could scarcely be conceived. It would have been better for them if they had parted long before they did, and buried the secret of their relations in their own hearts. Mrs. Hall rode and hunted—a thing unusual with a minister's wife.[21]

Mrs. Hall was very alive to issues of respectability. She boasted that after her formal separation from her husband, friends from Surrey Chapel still continued to call on her.[22] Indeed, this might have been her Achilles' heel: the fact that she could not bring herself to admit publicly that she was a smoker helped to seal her fate. The judge noted, in his summing up:

> Now, with regard to the truthfulness of the lady. Mrs. Hall has said that she has not smoked. It is not of much importance. There are countries where ladies smoke. It is unusual in this country, and I hope it will remain so; but while it is unusual it is a matter in which a husband should be obeyed, because it must be remembered that with man and wife the rep-

utation of the one is the reputation of the other. She says that she has never smoked; but is it possible to accept her explanation after passages in her letters of this kind [. . .] "I have been accustomed to smoke with friends for 14 years" [. . .]?[23]

Richardson, on the other hand, the product of a humbler social background, seemed oblivious of middle-class niceties. He cheerfully admitted all kinds of things that Mrs. Hall had denied in her own testimony: that he would drink spirits at her house (she claimed she did not allow drink on the premises), that he was in the habit of putting his arms around her waist and kissing her (she would only admit to a kiss on her birthday), that he was alone with her a great deal (she claimed that she almost always had a lady companion). He seems to have been concerned only about avoiding the admission of something actually criminal rather than merely below the standards of polite society. Thus, the difference in class and social position between Mrs. Hall and Richardson was another subtext that had a habit of reemerging during the trial. It was pointed out that he was not a gentleman, that he had only a rudimentary education, that he had been brought up "in no school of strict devotion," and that he was much younger than Mrs. Hall. Sir Henry James, Q.C., speaking on behalf of Newman Hall's case, noted dryly that, given their differences, all Mrs. Hall and Richardson appeared to have in common was "the love of horses."[24] Assuming, as one must, that they really were lovers, one does feel for Charlotte Hall as she carried this burden of notions of respectability—doomed to persevere doggedly year after year with the nuisances of the farce she had constructed; a lover who could only be a day visitor, a live-in chaperone who always had to be near to hand, but not too near. Perhaps the divorce gave her the courage to choose in which world she really wanted to live: afternoon tea with earnest chapel friends or late nights with the smoking set.

Knowing the history of Newman Hall's first marriage sheds a fair amount of light even on his autobiography. Although Charlotte was never mentioned, Newman Hall spent no less than six pages paying tribute to her father, the capstone of which is a sonnet, *In memoriam*, which he wrote himself.[25] Most of all, there is the heightened emotional tone of the chapter on his marriage with Harriet Knipe, including the frequent references to (unspecified) past trials and sufferings. He reprinted a long and tactfully worded letter of congratulation from the trustees and elders of his congregation, Christ Church, on the occasion of his second marriage, which referred to "the heavy trouble which had long pressed upon you," and which was unequivocal in its effusive praise for his past and present conduct. Newman

Hall was known as "a Dissenters' Bishop," so it was not easy for him to appeal to a higher human authority, but he nevertheless managed to let it be known that his second marriage had the blessing of a Dissenting archbishop: "To Metropolitan Tabernacle [. . .] After a grand sermon from C. H. Spurgeon, I introduced her to him. Several times he warmly grasped her hand with benedictions."[26]

Chapter 3

Spiritual Exploration
Thomas Cook, Victorian Tourists, and the Holy Land

During a visit to Palestine in 1853, A. P. Stanley, then canon of Canterbury, sent missives to friends as he went along, describing his reactions to the Holy Land. Goldwin Smith, a fellow at University College Oxford, enthused, "You have nothing to do but to piece together your letters, cut off their heads and tails, and the book is done."[1] *Sinai and Palestine* (1856) became his most popular work. When the Prince of Wales decided to visit Palestine in 1862, he asked the canon to accompany him: Stanley had been Regius Professor of Ecclesiastical History at the University of Oxford in the later 1850s, and he was the nephew of a peer. Although his position in the social order excelled that of many other Eastern travelers at midcentury, Stanley serves well to evoke the kind of encounters between religiously minded Britons and the Holy Land that were experienced in the era before modern tourism.

Thomas Cook (1808–92), a man from humble, provincial, Dissent-ing roots, represented a very different segment of society from men such as Stanley (let alone the Prince of Wales).[2] Cook made Palestine accessible to his own kind of people: not, of course, to the bulk of the working classes, but to various segments of the middle classes and notably, for the subject in hand, to a steady stream of Dissenting ministers. The first Cook's tour to Palestine occurred in 1869, and one of its members was Jabez Burns, a Baptist minister. The opening paragraph of Burns's account of his journey reads like a manifesto for the newly liberated middle classes:

> Such a tour as I have to describe was undertaken in former ages only by crowned heads, wealthy grandees, or by influential pilgrims. Many months, and often years, were spent in its accomplishment. [. . .] Now,

29

by railroads and first-class steamers, we safely effect the round of Eastern travel in ten or twelve weeks, and by the principle of co-operation it can be done by persons of moderate means at a comparatively small expense.[3]

Hitherto, the Holy Land had lacked both the necessary amenities and policing to make travel there an inviting prospect for any but the more adventurous, resourceful, or powerful of Westerners. Cook had long dreamed of "organized" trips to the biblical lands, and he judged that the time was right to make a start in the late 1860s. He negotiated arrangements for safe passage and accumulated a vast amount of useful kit in order to make life in Palestine less primitive for his clients. These provisions, together with improved methods of transportation and the more reasonable prices that economies of scale could deliver, opened the door to the Holy Land for a much broader spectrum of British society.

The purpose of this chapter is to explore the religious reactions to the Holy Land of early members of Cook's tours and some other travelers to the region in the 1860s and 1870s—especially the spiritually minded among them—as they straddled transitions such as those from elite to mass travel, from narrow- to broad-minded views, and from pilgrims to tourists.

There are two relevant precursors. Firstly, a party of six Dissenters led by the Congregational divine, John Stoughton, organized their own Palestinian tour in 1865. This group neatly illustrates the change that was taking place: their social position looked forward to the mass tourism that was coming, but their letters of introduction from Stanley spoke of the exclusive world that had not yet passed away.[4] Secondly, a ruthless preemptive strike on any potential wide-eyed pilgrims was made by the celebrated author Mark Twain, who in 1867 went on the first American package tour to Palestine. Twain's incredulous approach to the question of the historical veracity of sacred sites and his the-Sea-of-Galilee-has-nothing-on-Lake-Tahoe approach to the biblical landscape emboldened some of the new tourists to cast a jaded eye on their surrounds.[5]

Cook's clients usually crossed continental Europe by rail, then went by steamer from Italy to Alexandria. Accounts by the early tourists often begin with an initial reaction to encountering non-Western cultures. Many of these refer to life in Egypt, where scenes common throughout the East were often first viewed. Muslim practices were particularly fascinating. Few could resist the urge to comment on the sight of veiled women, especially as this made more difficult the right that traveling Englishmen presumed they possessed to judge the local female beauty. One senses a note of spite when William Leighton, an Anglican layman on the 1874 Cook's tour, comments on the use of veils: "It is rarely worth the trouble however, for nearly all the pretty faces belong to Christians or Jewesses."[6] Even the Baptist minister Samuel Manning, who was on the 1873 Cook's tour, did not find it inappropriate to reflect in a devotional work that the women of Bethlehem were his favorites.[7] Polygamy likewise was exotic enough to warrant inclusion in most narratives. Thomas Cook himself, writing while on a preparatory trip in 1868, managed to combine all these spectacles: "One passage [. . .] was occupied by a harem, consisting of a Turk and four wives, one of the latter most gaudily attired, her beautiful face generally hidden in folds of white muslin."[8]

From the very beginning, tourists tried to bridge the cultural gap by importing the trappings of life at home. Burns described Palestinian tent life on the first Cook's tour: "we had English ham and bacon from Yorkshire; pickles, potted salmon and sardines, from Liverpool; well preserved fruits, marmalade, &c., from London; and prime Gloucester and Cheshire cheese."[9] A common strategy for negotiating the spiritual gap between the travelers and the sites of other religions which they visited was—depending on one's point of view—to consecrate or desecrate them by engaging in Christian worship. In a typical instance, George Jager, a layman on the 1874 Cook's tour, recorded in his diary: "we had Service in the Temple of Jupiter: and there, where heathen rites had been celebrated thousands of years ago, we tried to praise our Father. [. . .] I think that all felt the salutariness of the Service."[10] The eminent Congregational preacher Newman Hall, who went on the 1870 Cook's tour, tells this anecdote:

> We climbed the Great Pyramid, and on the summit held a short service, which was disturbed by the disputing of our guides respecting "baksheesh," when I suddenly in my prayer changed the name of Deity, saying, "O Allah! O Allah!" At once and to the end there was reverential silence.[11]

Stanley did his bit to make alien things seem more Christian and familiar by observing that a sculpture of Cleopatra looked remarkably like the Bishop of Oxford.[12] The indigenous people sighted by tourists traveling through Palestine were often deemed "savages." By 1873, however, Cook had already repackaged this as an attraction, promising his American customers, "We are sure to be visited at night by natives [. . .] who get up a sort of Indian warcry and dance, in the style of savages."[13] There is scant evidence of any desire by early tourists to engage in a serious intercultural or interreligious dialogue.

Nor were their impressions of the historic Christian traditions that they encountered a triumph for ecumenism. Burns's censorious comments on the kind of spirituality that could be found at the Holy Sepulchre are representative:

> It is taught by the clergy, and believed by the fanatics, that the "holy fire" descends on Easter-eve upon the sacred Tomb. This monkish superstition is the grand attraction to most of the pilgrims. [. . .] Nothing can possibly be more opposed to the simplicity of Christ than the gorgeous decorations, costly shrines, and superstitious ceremonies of the "Church of the Holy Sepulchre."[14]

Henry Allon, a Congregational minister who accompanied Stoughton, attended worship at the Orthodox convent near Mount Sinai. He claimed that despite "the catholic feeling that recognizes every form of devotion which travel produces [. . .] we found worship utterly impossible." His judgment is unsparing: "Anything farther removed from spiritual feeling and devotional significance it is impossible to conceive."[15] Edwin Hodder, an Evangelical layman remembered as Lord Shaftesbury's biographer, went on a Cook's tour in the early 1870s. He attended Greek Orthodox worship in Jaffa and his main impression was that the faithful could kiss the Bible, but not open it.[16] A common fascination with the geography of salvation history did not lead Dissenting or Anglican travelers into a sympathetic appraisal of the non-Protestant forms of Christianity with which they came into contact.

The alien nature of these Christian traditions for low Protestants induced a dissatisfaction with the main sacred sites, which were, of course, usually in the care of either Orthodox or Catholic communities. This was often coupled with incredulity regarding their historical accuracy. Mark Twain set the standard for this approach, recording, for example, his joy at discovering that the Church of the Holy Sepulchre also contained the tomb of Adam: "How touching it was, here in a land of strangers, far away from home, and friends, and all who care for me, thus to discover the grave of a blood relation."[17] Leighton had read Twain's book and often adopted his tone in his letters. On Lazarus's final resting place he writes: "As to the genuineness of the tomb why there were no less than 3 candles burning over it."[18] What is interesting about this reaction is that it is not so much an irreverent or cynical one as it is Protestant. The instincts of the ministers on these tours were the same, albeit they did not usually express them through sarcasm. The most sacred sites were the worst. The tourists invariably felt that the keepers of these places had overplayed their hand by claiming that too many events had happened in one place, that specific events could be too precisely localized, or that buildings or artifacts were originals when they were obviously from a later period. The pejorative phrase "monkish legends" abounds in the narratives. The alien spirituality which they encountered sometimes almost made them want the sites to be false. Manning writes tellingly on the Chapel of the Nativity:

> Whilst feeling that the balance of probability is in favour of the authenticity of the site, there was one consideration which made me wish to come to a different conclusion. The degrading superstition and the disgraceful discord which prevail here are a scandal to the birth-place of Christianity.[19]

Such feelings became most heightened at the Holy Sepulchre. Hall wrote:

> I cared little for the numerous relics, which are so highly prized and for most of the "Holy Places," so called. [. . .] The Church of the Holy Sepulchre has little interest for me. I cannot regard it as occupying the site of the sepulcher, while the imposition practised is gross and revolting.[20]

It is not surprising, therefore, that when he returned to Palestine in 1886 he quickly convinced himself that the alternative site for Christ's tomb that General Gordon had identified in the intervening period was the correct one.[21] Likewise the popular Methodist minister Hugh Price Hughes, "did not accept the traditional site, but took General Gordon's view."[22] Allon's biographer summed up well this aspect of British Protestant reactions, "With all travelers, too, he felt the tremendous distance between the real associations of Jerusalem and the lying legends which abound in it."[23]

Nevertheless, the Holy Land could still inspire strong feelings of devotion in the hearts of these tourists. The prompt for such emotions, however, was transferred from sites to scenery. The River Jordan, the Dead Sea, fields near Bethlehem where shepherds watched their flocks—these were the kind of places that roused their hearts to reverent awe, delight, and worship. Leighton followed Twain's lead, pronouncing the Sea of Galilee "the tamest and most uninteresting lake I have ever seen, not excepting Bala in North Wales."[24] This attitude however was atypical: most were seduced. Burns described the Sea as "this most interesting of all sacred scenes."[25] Allon enthused about Mount Sinai. He contrasted it with the disappointing sites in Jerusalem—even a place of nature such as Gethsemane "has been desecrated into a trim and graveled garden, with gaudy flowers in partitioned beds." As for Sinai, however, "its sacred associations have been preserved so inviolate." When his party first beheld the mountain, there was "an intensity of feeling that imposed silence upon us all, and that deepened into awe."26

Cities, towns, and villages could evoke the same reactions when contemplated as a whole. Hall treated Lazarus's tomb at Bethany with disdain, but reminisced that "it was delightful to think of our Savior coming to visit Martha and Mary and their brother in this village."27 Manning described the moment when his Cook's party first glimpsed Jerusalem: "There is nothing imposing or impressive in the sight, and yet every traveler halts; even the most frivolous are awed into silence. Not a few gaze with tears upon the scene."28 Stoughton confessed: "as I caught sight of the walls and the gate, I am not ashamed to say, my eyes were full of tears."29

Such emotions arguably aligned them closer with the Orthodox and Catholic religious devotion that they saw around them than they realized. It is not an accident that so many of the ministers on Cook's tours were Dissenters—especially Baptists and their ecclesiological twins, Congregationalists—as Cook himself was a staunch evangelical General Baptist. Letting his religious sensibilities override his business instincts, he wrote in his promotional newspaper that when parties visited the Jordan River sometimes "the superstitious and ritualistic fill phials of 'Jordan water' for the christening of English and American babies."30 Nevertheless, was it any less an act of superstition (or alternatively appropriate piety) when members of Cook's tours who held Baptist convictions chose to wait to be baptized until they had arrived at these sacred waters? Leighton writes of the 1874 tour: "We first made for the Jordan where to our great astonishment two baptisms took place: one of Dodge by Mr. Gale the Baptist minister and one of Mrs. Blake by her husband, who is not acknowledged to be a clergyman by anyone of the party, but—himself."31

Hughes, even though he endorsed Gordon's alternative site for Christ's tomb, responded to this shrineless spot in a way that was not particularly Protestant. In the words of his daughter, "he lay full length as gently and reverently as the knight of the legend who has visited the spot of his desires. 'My Master lay here,' he murmured; 'see, I stretch myself where He lay.'"32 Tourists invariably employed the language of "holy" places, especially referring to Jerusalem as "the Holy City," although arguably a strict low Protestantism would disallow this.

Nevertheless, these were true Protestants whose imaginations were steeped from childhood in the stories of the Bible. Cook himself captured these feelings well in an article recounting his first visit to Palestine: "These Bible histories engaged the attention of my earliest reading exercises, and it was then pleasing to believe without sight. But the sights of places once regarded exclusively as matters of faith, awakened emotions of new and intensified interest."[33] Hodder, Manning, and Burns often reduced their narratives to a mere recounting of all the biblical passages in which a given town is mentioned. Many of Cook's tourists had come to place the biblical drama, which they knew and loved so well, upon its original stage.

Such people were continually on the lookout for scenes that reminded them of a portion of Scripture or, better still that illuminated a difficult passage. Jager was not the only traveler to come away with a story about a gate called "needle's eye" as a more palatable explanation of Christ's apparently overly pessimistic calculation regarding the probable fate of the rich.[34] Even something as mundane as seeing a walled garden could send Manning off chasing through both Testaments for allusions. A sudden storm, which arose when he sailed across the Sea of Galilee, caused him to appreciate the unpredictability of such events and to empathize with the disciples' fears, but, alas, he did not attempt to rebuke it. He found new allegorical meaning in a familiar passage upon investigating when Palestinian shepherds separate the sheep from the goats, and hit upon an involved solution to the apparent unreasonableness of Christ's cursing the fig tree.[35] Few travelers could resist the temptation to use modern Palestine as a living biblical commentary.

Furthermore, it was frequently argued that the veracity of the Bible was proven by an examination of Palestinian geography. Few things thrilled the hearts of these travelers more than to find a proper wasteland upon a spot that had been cursed in the Bible. Cook wrote with relish: "It is a great event of a life to come and see the 'desolations done in the land,' [. . .] in the desolation of which our belief in the Divine Word is most powerfully strengthened."[36] Burns claimed that Tyre's condition exhibited "the most complete verification of prophecy that the world can furnish."[37] Manning revealed that apparently an entire Cook's party took part in an experiment to determine whether or not the Law could have been heard by the Israelites if read from the mountains of Ebal and Gerizim. Their efforts were rewarded: "Infidels have made merry over the assumed incredibility of the narrative. But no real difficulty exists."[38] The triumphal nature of these accounts belied the fact that the most they could prove was that the biblical author had an accurate knowledge of the physical setting of the drama. Manning remarked optimistically, "It was the VALLEY OF AJALON, where Joshua commanded the sun to stand still. Again the topography [. . .] confirmed the narrative."[39] Stoughton was not the only one to observe gleefully that even the skeptic Ernest Renan had admitted that he was struck by the geographical fidelity of the Scriptures, but this very concession should have warned him that such evidence did not offer proof of the supernatural claims made in or for the Bible.[40]

Drawn to their Bibles afresh, and repulsed by the Christian traditions
that monopolized the sacred sites, these travelers zealously homed in on the
few beacons of Protestantism that could be found. In Beirut, Burns attended
an American Presbyterian and then an English Episcopal church, and
although he had just left the Holy Land, he was prompted to say, "Here we
felt ourselves to be in a center of Christian light, with institutions for the
education of Syrian girls, the training of the blind, and an asylum for crip-
ples."[41] In fact, the industrious ladies who ran missions such as these had
their names praised throughout the literature, and a tour of their facilities
became a standard attraction on Cook's itineraries. Miss Arnott, a
Glaswegian who ran a school for girls in Jaffa, was a particular favorite.
Hodder not only lauded her in his narrative, but also included an appendix
describing her work, directing those who wished to know more about
Eastern missions to *The Female Missionary Intelligence*.[42] It was perfectly
natural for Cook to note in a tour prospectus, amid more traditional points
of pilgrimage: "The schools of the late Mrs. Thompson, now under the man-
agement of Mrs. Motte, and the educational arrangements of the American
Mission, are all intensely interesting."[43]

Although the Holy Land did not inspire a sense of Christian solidarity
with Orthodox and Catholic believers, it did facilitate pan-Protestant fellowship. The task of officiating at worship services during the tent-life portion of a Cook's tour was rotated among the ministers in the party,
irrespective of denominational affiliation. Stoughton, pleased with his own
liberal-mindedness, recorded regarding his Sundays at Mount Zion Church,
"I received the Lord's Supper at the hands of Episcopalian brethren."[44]
Harriet Knipe, an Anglican, was on the same Cook's tour as Newman Hall.
Some years earlier a friend had suggested that they attend a lecture of his,
but she rejoined, "No; I do not care to go and hear a Dissenter, and in a
chapel, too."[45] The latter of these objections was removed by the Bishop of
Jerusalem, Samuel Gobat, who asked Hall to preach in Mount Zion Church,
thereby scandalizing a "Ritualistic newspaper" in Britain. Knipe's prejudices
were so greatly eroded on this tour that she eventually married Hall.[46] Such
rapprochements notwithstanding, the real yearning was to find, amid foreign surroundings, which were so intensely religious, a group who spoke
one's own native spiritual language. Having just spied out the land in preparation for his first tour, Cook wrote a letter titled "An Invitation to
Jerusalem" to the *General Baptist Magazine*, announcing this new service that
his company was launching. While a skeptical mind might surmise that he
was simply trying to drum up business, this was a very small pool in which
to fish. He could have just as convincingly written to a panevangelical organ

and reached a far wider audience. Perhaps his motives were just what he said they were—a longing to have in such a place a companion with precisely the same religious sentiments. He contrasted his affection for their little denomination with the unsatisfactory alternatives he had to encounter in his travels.[47] Visiting a Protestant mission or traveling with a coreligionist was perhaps the spiritual equivalent to importing Cheshire cheese.

Travel to Palestine was being transformed in these years, not least by the laborers of Thomas Cook and Son: a place once difficult to visit was being made accessible. Cook wrote as the first tour was about to enter its Palestinian phase: "I am now trying a great experiment and hope to show that it is possible for large and happy parties thus to move about with considerable comfort and without much personal inconvenience."[48] By 1873, only the fifth year of his Eastern tours, around 450 people had already toured the Holy Land in the care of his firm.[49] By 1891, the figure was 12,000, and most Westerners visiting Palestine were doing so with the aid of Thomas Cook and Son.[50] William Howard Russell, the famous journalist, was very pleased to be a member of the Prince of Wales's party in 1869— and not at all amused to discover that the East had to be shared with the first group of Cook's tourists. He complained that it was "a nuisance to the ordinary traveler [. . .] to see his pet mountain peak crested with bonnets and wideawakes, to behold his favourite valley filled up with a flood of 'mere English, whom no one knows.'"[51] In other words, he did not wish to see common people encroaching on places that he viewed as special preserves. Nevertheless, on this first Cook's Eastern tour, the masses almost literally did overtake the elite as Cook allegedly began to stalk the Prince.[52] A three-day gap was almost closed but, the entrepreneur noted forlornly, "our hopes of giving the heir-apparent of the English throne and his amiable Princess a really English cheer on the Nile were frustrated by the march of the party being a very little faster than our own."[53] Russell claimed that the royal party was thrown into a great agitation by an alarm that mercifully proved false, "The tourists are coming!"[54] But the race is not to the swift, and ultimately Cook triumphed. By 1882, when the Prince of Wales wished his sons Prince Albert Victor and Prince George (the future King George V) to visit the Holy Land, he entrusted them to the care of Thomas Cook and Son.[55] The role of keeper of the secrets of Palestine had passed from men like Stanley to the organizers of travel for the masses.

But what was the role of religion in what Cook was doing? He had no qualms about transacting business with people whose religious sentiments he disliked: his firm escorted Catholic pilgrims to Rome and helped Indian Muslims on their way to Mecca.[56] Nevertheless, although his personal convictions did not lead him to forego these kinds of business ventures, they did inspire others. From his first effort as a tourist agent when he organized a temperance outing, Cook hoped that his business could do some social and religious good. He viewed Holy Land tours in this light, describing the first one as "the greatest event of my tourist life."[57] He even saw it as a return to the more explicit connection that he had had with religious work when he was a village missionary as a young man, writing to the *General Baptist Magazine* while on his first Eastern trip: "The two ends—the first and the last—of my traveling life seem to come into closer proximity the nearer I approach to the culminating point of this long and interesting journey."[58] In his company newspaper, he made explicit his hope that these tours would prove spiritually fruitful:

> It is a joyous event to see the "mountains round about Jerusalem"; but its culminating glory would be to look beyond those mountain ranges to the "Jerusalem above"; and if a tour to famed attractions of Palestine should inspire all who accompany us to see the "better land," a rich reward crown our labours.[59]

Thomas Cook was able to go to the Holy Land in 1868 because John Mason Cook could run the business while he was away, and one senses that the son viewed his father's plans as an indulgence in private preoccupations. Tensions grew. In 1873, Thomas Cook wrote to his wife while he was in the East about their son:

> I have received a painful letter from him in reply to the one I wrote on the Red Sea. [. . .] He does not like my mixing Missions and business: but he cannot deprive me of the pleasure I have had in the combination; it has sweetened my journey and I hope improved my heart without prejudice to the mercenary object of the tour.[60]

The Eastern tours did eventually prove profitable for the company and perhaps even because of, rather than in despite of, their pious overtones. Cook always carefully arranged the itineraries so that there was no Sunday traveling. In 1877, the company announced that it was offering "Biblical Education and General Tours to Egypt and Palestine [. . .] Designed especially for Ministers, Sunday-School Teachers, and others engaged in promoting Scriptural Education."[61] In 1879, they offered a tour "In the track of the Israelites" for which the Congregational minister Arthur Hall would "act as Chaplain to the party."[62] The firm was not afraid to allow its Holy Land tours to have a religious hue.

The company also made arrangements for traditional pilgrimages, notably a party of a thousand French Catholics in 1882; but how did the members of his standard tours view themselves—as pilgrims or tourists?[63] The language of "pilgrimage" is ubiquitous in their writings. Newman Hall, for example, wrote: "I went to Italy to join a party of pilgrims to Jerusalem, under the care of Mr. Cook."[64] But was such language primarily a literary flourish or was it a reflection of a sincere desire to derive spiritual benefits from visiting a sacred place? There was certainly an earnestness about the Holy Land tours that it is hard to imagine tourists to other parts of the world adopting. It was standard practice during the month-long period when they lived in tents for the whole party to gather for worship every evening.[65] Often they responded to specific sites by singing a hymn, or praying. Moreover, one senses that they longed for a deep religious experience. Low Protestantism did not make room for traditional notions of pilgrimage, so perhaps being a tourist might actually have been a new, acceptable way for evangelicals to express a widespread religious impulse. Chaucer has planted in the popular mind the notion that people who were officially pilgrims might also have hoped to gain some pleasure from the journey. These tourists, conversely, were people who were officially pleasure seekers, but who longed to derive some spiritual benefits from their travels.

In conclusion, however, it is necessary to remember once again that those coveted benefits were ones that fitted a Protestant milieu. Cook summarized them this way:

> A new incentive to scriptural investigation has been created and fostered; "The Land and the Book" have been brought into familiar juxtaposition, and their analogies have been better comprehended; and under the genial influence of sacred scenes [. . .] enquiring and believing spirits have held sweet counsel with each other. Devoted ministers have [. . .] returned richly laden with new additional and corroborative facts to enrich their ministrations. [. . .] It is not in time that the full benefits of Travels in Bible Lands can be fully realized.[66]

There were middle-class, Victorian Protestants who believed that a trip to the Holy Land would enrich their faith, and Thomas Cook made Palestine accessible to them, creating a hybrid situation in which the comfort, security, and ease of access required by tourists were combined with the spiritual yearnings of pilgrims.

PART TWO

The Social Contexts of a Contested Faith

Chapter 4

Biblical Criticism
and the Crisis of Belief
D. F. Strauss's *Leben Jesu* in Britain

Perhaps no other book written in the nineteenth century induced more crises of faith in Victorian Britain than David Friedrich Strauss's *Leben Jesu*, the first volume of which appeared in 1835.[1] The most serious rival for such a claim would be Darwin's *On the Origin of Species* (1859). The English Congregational theologian A. M. Fairbairn, observed in 1876, "This century has been rich in books that create epochs, but no one was more directly destructive, more indirectly creative, than the *Leben Jesu*. The only one that can be compared with it in importance and revolutionary force is the 'Origin of Species'."[2] Yet, although a whole harvest of scholarship has been produced on the influence of Darwin's work, no study has ever been made of Strauss's impact in Britain.[3] The fact that *Leben Jesu* undermined the faith of a significant number of Britons has long been known. Edward Royle noted in 1974 that the book "became one of the works to precipitate the mid-Victorian 'crisis of faith'."[4] To take a random, lesser-known example, when the Congregational minister J. Guinness Rogers took up his first pastorate at Newcastle in 1846, he discovered that the situation was so bad there that even one of his own deacons had lost his faith "by the study of Strauss's 'Leben Jesu'."[5] John Henry Newman and E. B. Pusey swapped letters in 1839, anxiously wondering what to do about the fact that "Strauss's book is said to be doing harm at Cambridge."[6] Moreover, listening carefully to responses to Strauss will also illuminate revealing fault lines within the religious landscape of Victorian Britain.

The natural orientating point for any discussion of Strauss's *Leben Jesu* in Britain is the publication in 1846 of George Eliot's English translation.

This work, however, came eleven years after the first German volume, and thus the start of the controversy over the book and what happened during those interim years is crucial for understanding aspects of the British debate. Eliot's was not actually the first English translation. Strauss's work had been circulating in plebeian, infidel circles in a translation that had been made, not from the German original, but rather from a French translation. (It is worth recalling that very few Britons indeed at that time—not exempting Oxford and Cambridge dons—had even a basic knowledge of German.) It would appear that this edition was published in parts in Birmingham by Henry Hetherington (1792–1849), a radical who endured several prison sentences in the struggle for a free press, including one on the charge of blasphemy. In other words, Strauss's work was quickly captured by a defiantly skeptical camp and set within the context of popular anti-Christian thought. This populist milieu was alight for several years with the report that Strauss had decisively and irrefutably overthrown the Bible before anyone in Britain attempted to write a critique of *Leben Jesu*.

The first British reply to Strauss came only one year before the Eliot translation: J. R. Beard, ed., *Voices of the Church, in Reply to Dr. D. F. Strauss, Author of "Das Leben Jesu," Comprising Essays in Defence of Christianity, by Divines of Various Communions* (1845). This volume was a collection of English translations of replies to Strauss that had been penned in German and French. Beard himself contributed two original essays, and these were therefore the first indigenous responses. British reviewers and critics of *Leben Jesu* leaned heavily upon *Voices of the Church* in the years to come. Beard, himself an English Unitarian minister, credited three other English Unitarian ministers with having helped him with the translations and index.[7] Strauss had presented his work as a contribution from within the church rather than an attack from without, but it is indicative of how unconvincing that position appeared to many in Britain that a group of Unitarians—the most liberal Christians in the land—led the attack on Strauss. Tellingly, Beard had long been preoccupied with defending Christianity against the attacks of popular radicals. As far back as 1826, he had published replies to the English infidel leaders, Robert Taylor and Richard Carlile.[8] Beard's anti-Straussian volume was intended as a continuation of this struggle against popular unbelief:

> This reply was undertaken in consequence of the wide diffusion in this country—not least among the labouring classes—of opinions and impressions adverse to Christianity, derived more or less immediately from the efforts and publications of DR. STRAUSS. Even where the

Leben Jesu was not known, and could not be read, a conviction has pre-vailed, that some great work had been put forth in Germany, which, as being destructive of the Christian religion, its ministers in England wished to keep from the knowledge of the people, and were afraid even to study themselves.[9]

From this perspective, whether one was apt to celebrate it or decry it, Strauss's work was viewed as the most radical and effective attack on Christianity then currently on the market.[10]

The "respectable" English translation has its own background. George Eliot, who was then still a young woman named MaryAnn Evans and not the celebrated novelist that would emerge in the years ahead, had been a devout evangelical Christian during her late teens. Her letters from that period are filled with pious, earnest sentiments informed by this faith. Her evangelical sensibilities were so exacting as to cause her to disapprove of ora-torios even if their lyrics were merely texts of scripture. Her second occasion to pronounce this stricture ended in the reflection that "it would not cost me any regrets if the only music heard in our land were that of strict worship."[11] In 1841, she moved in with her widower father near Coventry. There she became friends with Charles and Caroline Bray and their Unitarian circle of friends and relations.

Caroline's brother, Charles Hennell, had written *An Inquiry Concerning the Origin of Christianity* (1838), a volume that Strauss himself had judged similar in methods and conclusions to his own, prompting him to ensure that it was translated into German. Hennell's volume played a crucial part in Eliot's own move away from orthodox Christianity. In his *Inquiry*, Hennell rejected the miraculous altogether. This stance, however, was hardly new in a British context as it had been a staple of deistic and infidel criticism for quite some time. What was new was to combine such a conclusion with a genuinely reverent tone. Hennell heaped unstinting praise upon Christ and Christianity, and expressed the hope that his position could be construed as within the faith rather than without:

> Although the belief in the miraculous origin of Christianity forms at pre-sent a prominent feature in the creeds of all sects of professing Christians, it would be an unnecessary and perhaps injudicious limitation to hold that the relinquishment of this belief is equivalent to an entire renuncia-tion of the Christian religion. [. . .] The author of this volume would therefore willingly have it considered as employed in the real service of Christianity, rather than as an attack upon it.[12]

Hennell even worked his way toward an eloquent reassertion of Christian doctrines within the bounds of natural religion: "Enough is understood to enable us to see, in the Universe itself, a Son who tells us of a Father, and in all the natural beauty and moral excellence which meets us in the world an ever-present Logos, which reveals the grace and truth of its invisible source."[13] The appeal of Strauss's *Leben Jesu* for Eliot and this new circle of hers was that it was in this same spirit. It was the kind of work that could lead one outside the orthodox realm or allow one to roam there in a dignified, respectful way. Like Hennell, Strauss was not rabidly denouncing the faith; he, too, was trying to maintain an identity that might still be labeled "Christian."

Even Strauss's strongest claim to originality, the application of a mythical interpretation to the gospels, was not entirely new in a British context. The most influential work of biblical criticism in British, popular, radical circles was Thomas Paine's *The Age of Reason* (1793/1795).[14] Paine's treatment of the virgin birth is as follows:

> It is the fable of Jesus Christ, as is told in the New Testament, and the wild and visionary doctrine raised thereon, against which I contend. The story, taking it as it is told, is blasphemously obscene. It gives an account of a young woman engaged to be married, and while under this engagement to be married she is, to speak plain language, debauched by a ghost, under the impious pretence (Luke c. 1, v. 35) that "the Holy Ghost shall come upon thee, and the power of the Highest shall overshadow thee." Joseph afterwards married her as his wife, and in his turn rivals the ghost. [. . .] This story is, upon the face of it, the same kind of story as that of Jupiter and Leda, or Jupiter and Europa, or any of the amorous adventures of Jupiter; and shows, as is already stated in the former part of *The Age of Reason*, that the Christian faith is built upon the heathen mythology.[15]

Strauss, although, of course, he had quite a different conception of myth, offered no advance on this in terms of the radical nature of his criticism; what he offered was a volume conducive to someone who, on the one hand, could no longer believe in the virgin birth but, on the other, had no inclination to revel in scoffing at the idea. When George Eliot wrote a letter to her father in February 1842 in which she attempted to justify her move away from orthodoxy, she acknowledged that she regarded the Bible as "histories consisting of mingled truth and fiction," but also hastened to add in the very same sentence that "I admire and cherish much of what I believe to have been the moral teaching of Jesus himself."[16] Indeed, for Eliot, even Strauss's clinical approach was hard to stomach at times. Caroline Bray wrote of Eliot as she approached the end of the translation in 1846: "We have seen more of M. A. [George Eliot] than usual this week. She said she was Strauss-sick— it made her ill dissecting the beautiful story of the crucifixion, and only the sight of her Christ-image and picture [religious art in her study] made her endure it."[17] Charles Hennell was the person in their circle behind the project to translate Strauss. Elizabeth Rebecca Brabant had initially taken on the task, but upon her marriage to Hennell in 1843, Eliot was persuaded to step into her place. It is highly suggestive that both the English translation of *Leben Jesu* and the first British reply to Strauss arose out of Unitarian circles. This reveals a fault line within English Unitarianism between a supernaturalist, more biblicist camp and a naturalist, more freethinking one. It also illuminates a more general cleavage in the controversy between those who viewed Strauss's work as a new height in anti-Christian polemics and those who viewed it as reassuringly respectful in tone.

But, the translation having been published, who would actually read it? Daniel L. Pals assumes that popular radicals were not up to the task: "If Strauss was read by workingmen, it is difficult to believe they were really convinced by his arguments, or even understood them. [. . .] if Strauss did appeal, therefore, it was likely to be in an indirect fashion, as a symbol of defiance to be held before the churches."[18] Eliot herself was doubtful: "Glad am I that some one can enjoy Strauss! The million certainly will not."[19] And even more pessimistically: "I do really like reading our Strauss—he is so klar und ideenvoll but I do not know *one* person who is likely to read the book through, do you?"[20] While these assessments do not prove to be true as general statements, they are painfully apt for some of the book's reviewers. A widely disseminated essay was the one by Henry Rogers titled "Reason and Faith; their Claims and Conflicts" in the October 1849 issue of the *Edinburgh Review*. In fairness to Rogers, *Leben Jesu* was not actually named as one of the volumes under review. On the other hand, the first of the three items so named was, rather pathetically, a thirty-year-old spoof by his friend, Richard Whately, *Historic Doubts Relative to Napoleon Buonaparte*, which had fresh resonance as the wag's oblique response to Strauss (and it even came to be "known in Germany, having been translated with special reference to the work of Strauss").[21] Nevertheless, Strauss was discussed at greater length than any of the three volumes ostensibly under review, and it was primarily as an answer to *Leben Jesu* that Rogers's essay secured its popularity. It went through eight impressions as a separately published item, and it was even translated into German and published in Berlin.[22] It was so successful that Rogers eventually published a volume of his essays with it as the lead one that gave the collection its title.[23] Nevertheless, it is all-too-obvious that

Rogers had not read Strauss when he had attempted to answer him. Although other books (including those under review) were carefully cited with pagination, *Leben Jesu* was never directly cited at all. When Strauss was quoted (which was not very often) the passage is invariably lifted from Beard's *Voices of the Church*. Reading between the lines, one can sense Rogers's reticence actually to plow through Strauss in his dismissing of *Leben Jesu* as "some mystico-metaphysical philosophy, expressed in language as unintelligible as the veriest gibberish of the Alexandrian Platonists," and in his daunted description of it as "two bulky volumes of minute criticism."[24] No doubt quietly repenting of this cavalier approach, for the book version Rogers dropped the list of ostensible items under review altogether (these items being "no longer likely to interest the reader"), and included an article-length "appendix" that did tackle the actual contents of *Leben Jesu* from a firsthand reading.[25] The review in the *British Quarterly Review* rather suspiciously avoided the main body of Strauss's work and its conclusion, covering this deficiency with the words, "We shall best gain these ends by examining, as freely as space permits, the Introduction which he has placed in the front of his work."[26] Most embarrassingly of all, the Unitarian journal, the *Inquirer*, noticed the publication of Eliot's translation in June 1846 and declared its intention to review it.[27] It then went silent on the subject for three and a half months, apologizing in October that "[w]e have delayed the fulfillment of this promise longer than we wished," and then offered a review that confined itself, quite literally, to discussing only the first sentence of Strauss's work![28] The *Eclectic Review* opted to review Beard's *Voices of the Church*, rather than *Leben Jesu* itself.[29]

The indolence of these "respectable" reviewers merely serves to underline how wrong Pals was about who actually imbibed Strauss's work: the evidence is clear that some plebeian radicals did give the book a careful reading and reflect rigorously on the ideas it contained. The best-documented example of this is that of Thomas Cooper (1805–1892), a former shoemaker from Gainsborough who had become a Chartist leader and had spent two years in prison in the first half of the 1840s for seditious conspiracy. Cooper recorded in his autobiography how religious skepticism had become compelling for him during his imprisonment, before recounting:

> I never proclaimed blank atheism in my public teaching. And I feel certain that I should have broken away from unbelief altogether, had I not fastened on Strauss, and become his entire convert. I read and re-read, and analysed, the translation in three volumes, published by the Brothers Chapman: the translation begun by Charles Hennell, and finished by the

authoress of "Adam Bede." I became fast bound in the net of Strauss; and at one time would have eagerly helped to bind all in his net [. . .].[30]

Cooper expounded Straussian biblical criticism to the masses in a series of detailed lectures under the general title of "Critical Exegesis of Gospel History, on the basis of Strauss's 'Leben Jesu'" at two freethinking halls in London—the Literary Institution, John Street, Tottenham Court Road, and the Hall of Science, City Road—during the years 1848–1850. He then published these lectures throughout 1850 in his popular, radical *Cooper's Journal*. The clergyman and author Charles Kingsley was duly impressed and alarmed:

> But there is something which weighs awfully on my mind,—the first number of *Cooper's Journal*, which he sent me the other day. Here is a man of immense influence, openly preaching Straussism to the workmen, and in a fair, honest, manly way, which must tell. Who will answer him? Who will answer Strauss?[31]

There is no doubt that Cooper had made a careful reading of the book, digested it, and made it his own. Indeed, it is highly likely that if a young, aspiring biblical scholar of liberal inclinations would have been able to stomach the rough atmosphere, he would have gained a better introduction to the latest currents in gospel criticism from Cooper's lectures than from any to be had at that time at the universities of Cambridge, Oxford, or Edinburgh. It is important to underline the high degree to which Cooper was faithful to Strauss, but, nevertheless, what is most illuminating for present purposes is the way that he reflected distinctives of the British debate. Firstly, as with Eliot and the Hennell circle, Cooper was attracted to Strauss not, as the stereotype would have it—because he offered the most virulent attack on the Bible and Christianity to hand—but rather because of his reverent tone. In contrast to the bitter anti-Christian abuse that one could often hear at the Hall of Science and the Literary Institution, Cooper was sincerely of a different temperament:

> All who are afraid of thinking, and who dread that the People should think, on the most important of all subjects, will censure me for the publication of these discourses. Let none of these, however, misrepresent my motives. I yield to none in fervent admiration and love for the character of Christ. [. . .] I seek to multiply, not to lessen, the number of his true disciples. [. . .] I know no higher teaching than Christ's: I acknowledge none. But his religion no longer commends itself to me by mysterious or

miraculous sanctions. I hold it to be the most perfect version of the
Religion of Humanity; and for that reason, desire to see it divested of all
legendary incrustations that may prevent its reception with sincere and
earnest thinkers. The great work of Strauss assisted me much in coming
to a clear and determined conclusion respecting the source of the corruptions in the real history of Christ [. . .].[32]

Secondly, and this is a general theme in the British debate as well,
Cooper was not interested in Strauss's attack on the rationalists. Strauss had
structured his work by, biblical passage after biblical passage, first ruling out
supernaturalist and rationalist interpretations, and then proposing the mythical as the true one. Therefore, Strauss had spent much of his work opposing, if not ridiculing, rationalists. The subtlety of this approach was either
unabsorbable or deemed unserviceable in a British context, and therefore
Strauss's work was generally presented both by his friends and his foes as a
continuation of the rationalist tradition rather than an attack upon it. When
forced to follow Strauss's argument in this direction, in order to avoid using
the word "rationalist" in a pejorative way, Cooper first used the cumbersome
circumlocution "a class of commentators who are inclined to find *natural*
interpretations of the Miracles," then gestured back to it with the phrase,
"[t]he class of commentators just alluded to."[33] He soon decided, however,
not to waste any time on that line of argument on the grounds that all that
mattered (one might add, in a British context) was whether or not supernaturalist interpretations were valid.[34]

Finally, Cooper continually introduced issues which revealed that while
Strauss might have been able to take for granted joining a discussion that
had reached a certain point, in Britain no such prior work could be assumed.
One of Cooper's main mantras was that what was uncovered in Strauss's
work was incompatible with the notion of the "plenary inspiration" of the
Scriptures. It almost seems at various points that it would have been enough
of a victory for Cooper just to persuade his audience to abandon that doctrine as untenable. He also wielded the assertion that we do not know who
wrote the Gospels in a way that assumed it to be a new and deeply disturb-
ing discovery worthy of repetition. The subject of eternal punishment and
the perceived orthodox view of the connection between salvation and assent
to dogma was another running theme.[35] In Britain, issues such as the persistence of a high doctrine of Scripture and the soteriological implications of
adopting certain scholarly views could not be bracketed out of the debate.

While those themes, to greater and lesser extents, were indicative of the
wider British debate, Cooper also betrayed his distinctively plebeian context
at points. His lectures were sprinkled with folksy adaptations to a British

context such as when he declared of certain gospel narratives that "they were plainly and palpably legendary, and deserving of no more credit as facts, than the fables of King Arthur and Merlin the Prophet"; or that, if the account of the wedding at Cana were literally true, then Christ made for a drunken crowd a quantity of wine equivalent to "from 800 to 1,200 English pints!"[36]Cooper could also engage in more forthright polemics, typical of that world of popular radicals, when roused by certain traditional doctrines he found particularly offensive. Here, for example, is his treatment of substitutionary atonement:

> Why, is it the pouring out of a red fluid, which has been formed by the digestion of bread and meat and vegetables, that can alone satisfy an Infinite Existence for transgression, not of the being who suffers, but of the other unnumbered millions of the world? If thy brother had offended thee would not thy nature feel it to be more noble to forgive freely, without a human slaughter? And do you really form to yourself a God for worship with a less exalted nature than your own?[37]

Finally, at points, the lectures offer an unintentional autobiographical glimpse as the autodidact, former shoemaker, who felt himself endowed and destined to lead great movements that would help the people of the land, reflected upon Jesus of Nazareth:

> Nothing is more natural than the supposition that Jesus early practiced the trade of his father. But his intellectual development must have been of the grandest order. He was one of those lowly born, but gloriously endowed children of Nature, which she brings forth at seasons, few and far between, to exercise a commanding influence upon mankind. His enemies assert (John, vii ch., 15 v.) that he had never learned letters; and he does not contradict them. His townsmen being astonished to find so much wisdom in him, we are compelled to infer that he had not, to their knowledge, been a student. [. . .] With the Essenes, consisting chiefly of the toiling classes, Jesus must have felt a strong sympathy [. . .] His burning love for mankind, his zeal for purity, his ardent attachment to justice, his pity for the oppressed—filled his expansive heart, and stimulated his intellect. It was impossible for such a character to remain all his life a carpenter at Nazareth.[38]

One of the most astute British readings of Strauss was an article in the *Westminster Review* by James Martineau, the leading English Unitarian theologian of the Victorian era.[39] Martineau's reaction to *Leben Jesu* was respectful—and far from emotive—but nevertheless his overall judgment was that he was not persuaded. He even contrasted Strauss with "the competent critics of Christendom."[40] Typical of the British debate was the fact that Strauss's work was discussed primarily as a negative achievement, a tearing down of traditional beliefs. Martineau observed that it would be so, "Indeed, by far the greater part of it, and, to the English reader, we venture to believe, the most impressive part, is but a clearance of the ground to make room for his own hypothesis."[41] As Cooper would, Martineau saw this achievement as helping to dislodge traditional notions of biblical inspiration: "We cannot believe that henceforth any instructed theologian will waste his strength in attempting to *harmonise* the gospels; or that laymen will be expected to make nothing of their discrepancies."[42] Not holding a high doctrine of Scripture himself, Martineau was unusually free to make a particularly incisive attack on Strauss's theory. Strauss built many of his mythical interpretations of biblical passages on the supposition that, rather than being historical, these narratives had arisen in order to give concrete form to Jewish expectations derived from their reading of the Hebrew Scriptures regarding what the Messiah must be like. The English Unitarian theologian, however, was not convinced:

> How often has it been noticed, that the prophecies quoted out of the Old Testament in the New, fit very indifferently to the incidents on which they are put! But would this have been, if the incidents had been manufactured to the pattern of the prophecies? What then was to prevent the neatest correspondency? The outrages upon David and Isaiah, prove that the writers were reduced to their last shifts for a quotation by the inflexible nature of their facts. [. . .] No; they reported all this, because it was *forced* upon them by its historical reality.[43]

Martineau also laid his finger on a certain lack of psychological imagination in Strauss's thought. Once again, as a Unitarian, he could grasp Christ's humanness without any nervousness:

> The agony in the garden is so unintelligible to Strauss, that he must hunt through the Old Testament to find "materials for the formation of this scene." [. . .] To our author, however, fresh from the cold bath of his philosophy, these things appear otherwise. What was all this sorrow about? Death had often been endured by philosophers, and even by common mortals, without fear; and could not a prophet bear the calamity with quietness? And what was the use of such a "vain repetition" as saying the same prayer, and having the same sorrow, three times over? If once did not suffice, why not four times? *Three* is a suspicious number [. . .].[44]

Martineau ended his analysis of the contents of *Leben Jesu* with a delicious deflation of Strauss's achievement: "He has found a fulcrum for moving the globe: but he does it under the human condition: he swings across half the universe; and he stirs the world—an inch."[45]

Strauss's thoroughgoing British opponents can be dealt with more collectively on the basis of their common themes. A ubiquitous reaction was to observe that Strauss was not the objective scholar he might have appeared to be, but was rather ensnared by questionable presuppositions, and was campaigning on behalf of those positions. What these critics found particularly annoying was what Strauss's admirers found most reassuring: the German scholar's refusal to align himself with the enemies of the Christian faith. Henry Rogers, already amply mystified by Hegelian dialectics, was at his wit's end with the religious identity of this new breed of German critics exemplified by Strauss: "They are so greedy of paradox, that they, in fact, aspire to be Christians and infidels at the same time."[46] William Gillespie was an Edinburgh lawyer and Christian apologist famed for his restatement of the a priori argument for the existence of God and known to debate atheists when the opportunity arose.[47] Gillespie also published a volume in response to Strauss, *The Truth of the Evangelical History of our Lord Jesus Christ: Proved, in Opposition to Dr. D. F. Strauss, the Chief of Modern Disbelievers in Revelation* (1856). It was a tangled, prolix, mess of a book in sore need of a good editor; and more to the point at hand, it proceeded on the assumption that "*Strauss* must be pronounced to be an Infidel."[48] Even J. R. Beard was not ashamed to take on the tone of an exposé on occasion: "a system which, under the mask of friendship, and with a Judas-kiss on its lips, has attempted, in the person of Strauss, to destroy the faith of the Christian church in its very foundations."[49] Many critics observed that Strauss had declared his inability to believe in any miracle on philosophical grounds, but that such a position could by no means be taken for granted, especially in Britain.[50] The *Inquirer*, which tellingly must be classed with Beard as one of the Unitarian opponents of Strauss, averred: "But the important point at present, is, that Strauss's rejection of revelation in any proper sense—of the whole supernatural element—is not to be regarded as the result of which he arrives from his examination [. . .] but follows, of course, from certain philosophical principles received by him."[51] It was important to Strauss's critics to strip away from him the cloak of an impartial judge, exposing him as a partisan in the dispute.

The old deists and the then current anti-Christian popular radicals had not hesitated to denounce key elements of the gospel story as fraud, lies, a sham. One of the great appeals of *Leben Jesu* for its admirers was that it avoided such harsh judgments. In fact, Strauss went out of his way repeatedly to assert that the myths could well have formed without any conscious intention to deceive.[52] His critics, however, preferred the tidiness of the old polarities and were apt to try to align Strauss with the less charitable theory. Beard was particularly effective at this. He directed an unflinching gaze upon the dead body of Jesus of Nazareth.[53] It was gone, ergo, either he had risen indeed or there was indeed some deliberate deception being perpetrated. It is absurd to imagine that the body was not gone:

> All the time these delusions were going forward, there was at hand an infallible test. Jesus (according to the theory) was in his tomb. [. . .] Even supposing that, for any case whatever, not one of the disciples had either the sense or the honesty to apply this test by a visit to the grave, surely the enemies of the cross would not have failed to try its power [. . .].[54]

In such an argument, Beard was taking advantage of one of Strauss's more vulnerable points: the German critic's lack of interest in the significance of the indisputable residue of historicity that even his own work admitted was there. One senses that Strauss's imagination was captured by pure ideas, and he was impatient with mundane facts. Even Martineau was frustrated by this: "He thus distinctly admits an historical element; though he endeavours to disguise the admission by including these traditional memories under the name of historical *mythi*. [. . .] [Jesus] who is mentioned only to retire into the mist; who gives our author some trouble by his death, but very little with his life."[55] Likewise the *British Quarterly Review* pressed home the view that a better explanation was required as to how Jesus had become the focus of these myths:

> He assumes that the belief in a miracle-working Messiah was so strong among the Jews that it gave birth to this whole cycle of myths concerning Jesus; and he builds upon this the position that a man of humble descent, in poor circumstances, who did no miracles, and in no way answered to the universal expectation of the Messiah, nevertheless conceived the idea that he was the Messiah, succeeded in persuading others to the same belief, and gathered around him a multitude of followers who perseveringly ascribed to him all that he was not, but what they believed the Messiah was to be![56]

It was sometimes pointed out that myths, by definition, are not about historical figures (legends are about real people) and therefore Strauss's interpretative frame was misapplied. It was argued over and over again that myths take more time to develop than even Strauss's own chronology would allow: "The myths of India are the slow growth of many centuries; so were those of Egypt; so were those of Scandinavia; and so have all popular mythologies been. [. . .] The popular mind is not a hot-bed in which growth can be forced. Mythology, like its own phoenix, has a birth only once in a lapse of centuries."[57] A related, favorite cluster of arguments was that the mythical view did not provide an adequate cause for the willingness of early Christians to suffer martyrdom, for Gentiles to have embraced the nascent faith (given the weight that Strauss had put on projections of Jewish expectations) and, in general, for the rise and growth of Christianity in a hostile environment.

Critics also routinely offered more specific cavils concerning Strauss's way of handling material in the Gospels. It was widely claimed that he was too quick to assume that a discrepancy existed, that there was no possible explanation that could preserve the veracity of the statements under question, and that this alleged flaw fatally undermined the historicity of the entire account. The British temperament seems to have had a particular affection, if not weakness, for historical spoofs. Again and again Strauss's methodology was applied to well-known figures with the ostensible result that they were revealed to be mythical. Beard tried his hand at Milton: "These discrepancies look very suspicious. Was Milton any thing more than a poetical impersonation of the republican spirit which produced the Commonwealth?"[58] Rogers opted for Jonathan Swift for his own original effort.[59] And so it went on. Strauss had argued that the process of myth formation tended to add names and other specific details to stories, but he also used the lack of specifics as an indicator that a narrative was not historical. This lose-lose methodological bind was pounced upon by his British critics. As Gillespie put it: "*How*, according to *Strauss's* estimation, *could an Evangelist have written*, WITHOUT *writing in a legendary way?*"[60] Henry Rogers, in his appendix on *Leben Jesu* in the book version of his essay, catalogued and illustrated with examples the methodological flaws he had observed in Strauss's project.[61] In short, the German scholar, according to his critics, had rigged the rules of the game.

It is worthwhile to return to some themes alluded to already in the context of Strauss's admirers from the perspective of his critics. In a British context, the issues of biblical inspiration and authorship were central, and Strauss could not be discussed without that ground being traversed. The *British Quarterly Review* was still ready to defend the validity of the traditional answers to the question of the Gospels' authors. It had no time for obfuscating theories that perhaps some other "John" wrote the gospel that comes to us under that name:

> No doubt there were many Pauls and many Johns among the Christians
> in the days of the apostles; just as in England there were doubtless many
> Bacons, and many Newtons and many Miltons living at the same time
> with the great authors of the "Novum Organum," the "Principia," and
> the "Paradise Lost." [. . .] When, therefore, any Christian writer attests
> that John did so and so, or wrote such and such books, it is as certain that
> he means the apostle John, as with us the expression "Milton wrote such
> and such a work" [. . .].[62]

The doctrine of Scripture also loomed large. Gillespie began his anti-
Straussian monograph with the words, "The question of questions of the day
regards the inspiration of the Scriptures."[63] The *British Quarterly Review*
complained regarding Strauss's treatment of the Johannine discourses: "The
question to which this test can alone apply is, Assuming that John was
assisted by the Spirit of God, is it credible that he could report exactly such
long discourses?"[64] The British debate was at a different point from the particular discussion (which, of course, did not reflect the whole range of views
among German scholars) that Strauss was joining on the continent: Britain
was at a place where an antisupernaturalist *had* to be a rationalist and where
it could not be assumed that traditional views on miracles and biblical
authorship and inspiration had been discredited.

In conclusion, to return to an earlier theme, the "respectable" reviewers
were often nervous about the interest in Strauss's work that was being shown
by popular radicals. Too often they also patronized them. The earlier translation from the French was soundly abused. Beard, to take a typical example, pontificated that *Leben Jesu* had been "'done into English' in a
disgraceful manner, and sold in low-priced numbers, to satisfy the truly infidel cravings of a portion of our towns populations," and that this translation
"has not the slightest literary value whatever, being obviously brought out to
supply food to the unhappily depraved appetite for sceptical productions, so
prevalent in these times among our manufacturing populations."[65] Likewise
the *Eclectic Review* anxiously reflected:

> We do not ourselves apprehend much danger to our educated youth,
> from the diffusion in this country of the views and principles of interpre-
> tation of which the name of Strauss affords the most convenient designa-
> tion. The danger is to our manufacturing population in large towns,
> where we find a good deal of rude, uncultivated talent, and a smattering
> of knowledge, which unhappily, the possessors are but too prone to
> think it most clever and most original to display in carping at established
> truths. To such minds, and to the publications which feed them, a bad

translation of Strauss, sold cheaply, affords rare materials, greedily received, and unsparingly applied.[66]

From today's perspective, however, what is more worthy of comment is that this earlier translation was evidence that these overworked, underpaid Britons with scant formal education really did want to read the book rather than just refer to it.

Even Strauss himself gave these popular radicals no encouragement, writing in the original preface to his *Leben Jesu*:

> For the laity the subject is certainly not adequately prepared; and for this reason the present work is so framed, that at least the unlearned among them will quickly and often perceive that the book is not destined for them. If from curiosity or excessive zeal against heresy they persist in their perusal, they will then have, as Schleiermacher says on a similar occasion, to bear the punishment in their conscience, since their feelings directly urge on them the conviction that they understand not that of which they are ambitious to speak.[67]

But Thomas Cooper did understand whereof he spoke when he lectured on *Leben Jesu*; and he understood it significantly better than some of Strauss's "respectable" reviewers. Moreover, Cooper was sincere when he paid homage to Christ. Ultimately, this enduring love affair with Jesus of Nazareth helped to lead him back to Christian orthodoxy. By way of contrast, those anti-Christian lecturers and authors who truly were permanently immune to the allure of the realm of faith, were not particularly interested in Strauss's work. George Jacob Holyoake, a leading Secularist and the editor of the *Reasoner*, for one was not enamored with *Leben Jesu*, and he grumbled at the time: "*Cooper's Journal* abounds in eulogies upon the character of Christ so extravagant and fulsome that they must be particularly distasteful to Christ if he is conscious of it."[68] It was the same with Charles Bradlaugh, the foremost spokesperson for atheism in Victorian Britain. Although he devoted much of his energy to debunking the Bible, and he did own a copy of the Eliot translation, it seems to have made no significant impression on him.[69] On the other hand, Henry Rogers was aware of a new kind of British skeptic who was likely to be tempted by the tone of *Leben Jesu*:

> Sometimes the spirit of unbelief even assumes an air of sentimental regret at its own inconvenient profundity. Many a worthy youth tells us he almost wishes he could believe. He admires, of all things, the "moral grandeur"—the "ethical beauty" of many parts of Christianity; he condescends to patronize Jesus Christ [. . .].[70]

In summary then, in a strange way, the wild rumors notwithstanding, Strauss's real appeal in a British context was that he was *less* radical than alternative skeptical voices; his approach was *more* palatable for those with lingering pious convictions or sensibilities. As A. M. Fairbairn, reflecting on the controversy thirty years after the appearance of the Eliot translation, aptly observed:

> Strauss was no revived eighteenth-century infidel, or vulgar official controversialist against an accepted faith. He was a critic by nature and discipline, scientific in spirit, veracious in purpose. His attitude to Christianity was not Voltaire's. He approached it from within, not from without, his primary aim being to reform and refine rather than abolish it.[71]

Chapter 5

Biblical Criticism
and the Desire for Reform
Bishop Colenso on the Pentateuch

In October 1862 John William Colenso (1814–83), bishop of Natal, published a book titled *The Pentateuch and Book of Joshua Critically Examined.* Although this volume proved to be only the first of seven parts, and the bishop's life was eventful in other ways, the controversy surrounding this volume did more than any other single factor to determine Colenso's enduring reputation. To his critics, the publication of such a book was an outrageous and heretical act. When the book was discussed in the Lower House of Convocation, C. E. Kennaway was convinced that it should be labeled "Poison!" and Archdeacon Denison declared that "No book can ever be brought under our consideration of a worse character than this" and that "if a man asserts such things as are in this book—*anathema esto*—let him be put away."[1] In the end, both houses of Convocation resolved that "the main propositions" of the book "involve errors of the gravest and most dangerous character."[2]

Colenso himself, on the other hand, presented his work as a labor on behalf of the cause of "Truth," as revealed by scientific investigation.[3] He wrote to a friend, "the 'scandal' they complain of is not caused by me, but by those who maintain a state of things in the Church opposed to the plainest results of modern science."[4] He boasted that the "men of science and literature are almost in a body with me," and there was at least some evidence to support this claim: the eminent geologist Sir Charles Lyell became friends with him, and he was received into the Athenaeum Club. Colenso even talked of forming a scientific society, like one might have for geology or astronomy, for the study of the history of religions.[5] Therefore, while his critics compared him with heretics such as Arius, the defenders of his memory evoke the names of scientists like Galileo—people who discovered great truths that the world ultimately would not be able to suppress.[6]

The term "biblical criticism," in this context, refers to the modern discipline as it has evolved and not older attempts, whether negative or orthodox. On the Continent, most notably in Germany, the modern discipline of biblical criticism had already been well established for decades before Colenso's work. In Britain there was, of course, a portion of educated people who were reading the European literature and agreeing with some of its methods and conclusions. A few of them had even published writings that reflected this influence. Benjamin Jowett, tutor at Balliol, was one such person, and his *Epistles of St Paul*, published in 1855, was one such work; however, it was not a significant contribution to the field of biblical criticism, and the controversy that it generated did not focus on this aspect of the work.[7] Samuel Davidson's *The Text of the Old Testament Considered*, published in 1859, deserves special recognition. Although it was far more conservative and less sensational than Colenso's work, Davidson was enough of a student of the new discipline to provoke a conservative backlash, which caused him to be driven out of his professorship at Lancashire Independent College.[8] The controversial *Essays and Reviews*, published in 1861, sought deliberately to force upon British society some of the findings of Continental biblical critics; therefore, this work should be viewed more as containing an appeal on behalf of the discipline rather than an actual embarking upon its work. Moreover, the notion that biblical criticism was a powerful tool that could no longer be ignored was not central to the heated public discussion that the book provoked.[9] From his vantage point at the end of the century, T. K. Cheyne, in his *Founders of Old Testament Criticism*, unequivocally reserved for Colenso the place of founder in Victorian Britain. When he came to discuss Colenso's book, Cheyne dramatically exclaimed, "At length, in 1862, the hour came, and the man; and strange to say, the champion was a bishop."[10] Even though Cheyne might have overstated the case, we may nevertheless safely admit that Colenso's book was the first thoroughgoing, indigenous attempt at modern biblical criticism that brought the young discipline to the general attention of British society.

But what a strange book it is upon which to place so much passion and weight! Irrespective of whether one is looking for shocking heresy or seminal science, the actual book can hardly live up to the excitement that it generated. The substance of it is based almost entirely upon mathematical calculations derived from the numbers recorded in the Pentateuch. Before he had been ordained, Colenso had been a mathematician. At Cambridge, he had been second wrangler in the mathematical tripos and then went on to teach mathematics at his college, St. John's. During this early period of his adult life, he wrote several highly successful mathematical textbooks. The numbers given in the Pentateuch were examined by the mathematical bishop and were found to prove that the narrative contains internal inconsistencies and implies physical impossibilities. Most of these calculations begin with the statement made in Numbers 2:32 and other passages that Israel had around 600,000 warriors. From this number it was estimated that the whole people must have numbered around two million, and this, in turn, was found to be an unwieldy number of people to force into various other passages. For example, such a number would imply that the Israelites' camp in the wilderness would have needed to have been approximately twelve miles square, which would have made the command in Deuteronomy 23:12-14 to go outside the camp in order to attend to a call of nature a burden to the point of absurdity.[11]

Patiently, similar problems were unfolded: how could two million people have been told in one day about the need to keep the Passover? How could enough sheep to serve the needs of two million people have been found for the Passover? How could Joshua have read the Law in the hearing of two million people? And so it goes, on and on. Each problem is usually given an entire chapter in its own right, which is filled with an exhausting trail of assumptions, estimations, and calculations. For example, on the question of the number of lambs that would have been needed for the Passover: (1) explanations are given as to different theories concerning the probable number of people sharing a lamb; (2) calculations are made as to the total population of a flock compared to the number of firstborn males that it produces; and (3) sheep-tending authorities from New Zealand and Australia are cited on the amount of land needed for grazing per sheep— all in order to come to the conclusion that, according to the Pentateuch, the Israelites must have had "an extent of country considerably larger than the whole county of Hertfordshire"; the probability of this actually having been the case and the other difficulties that this fact would necessarily entail are then explored.[12] Although Colenso had read German biblical criticism and had imbibed many of its methods and ideas, for this first and crucial volume he confined his work almost exclusively to these kinds of numerical critiques.

A fair number of the problems which Colenso explored were well known "difficult passages" that had already been addressed explicitly—however inadequately—in existing works. Colenso, however, found the standard answers unconvincing. Instead, he said that the honest course was to admit frankly that these difficulties were insurmountable. Therefore, upon the evidence of his calculations, despite their relentlessly narrow focus, he was led to a breathtakingly sweeping conclusion: "very considerable portions of the Mosaic narrative" are "unhistorical" and the account of the Exodus "*is not historically true.*"[13] Indeed, in its initial form, which was printed privately in Natal, he had declared that his sums led him to conclude that "the whole story of the Pentateuch is fictitious from beginning to end"; but those whom he consulted, such as F. D. Maurice and A. P. Stanley, persuaded him to avoid the word "fiction" in the version to be published in London for general circulation.[14]

One cannot help but be curious as to the experiences and the process of thought that led him to undertake this study and to follow it through to such a conclusion. Colenso gave his own account of this intellectual journey in the book's preface. He admitted that he had begun to study the matter only in the early part of the previous year. Doubts about the Pentateuch had been thrust upon him when an "intelligent native," who was helping him translate the story of the deluge into Zulu, had innocently asked him, "Is all that true?"[15] This story won him the sympathy of many people who had come face to face with honest doubt. For example, the freethinking journal, the *Westminster Review,* said of the book, "The account given of its origin is the simplest possible, and one which must win for it a candid perusal from all but the bigoted and narrow-minded."[16] On the other hand, this story also won for Colenso the disdain of his critics, who taunted him as the missionary who was converted by the natives. Therefore the story has been retold endlessly, and uncritically, as the origin of his thinking—whether by his critics, such as the Evangelical Anglican newspaper, the *Record,* or his defenders like Cheyne, or sources which particularly strive for neutrality like the *Encyclopaedia Britannia.*[17] Nevertheless, it might prove instructive if the tale of the questioning Zulu were critically examined.

The most obvious point that needs to be made is that his translator was not troubled by biblical arithmetic. His question concerned the accuracy of the biblical account of the deluge. Colenso admitted that he himself was suspicious of this passage even when he had been ministering to the natives of Norfolk rather than Natal, and he had already decided it was impossible to believe in the literal, historical truth of the story *before* his encounter with his Zulu colleague. Moreover, he admitted that in holding these opinions he was no different from numerous other clergymen who also treated the early chapters of Genesis in a manner different from the subsequent history.[18] In short, Colenso did not need to go to Africa in order to encounter skeptical questions concerning the deluge.

Secondly, it is illuminating to realize that this story is similar in kind to other remarks by Colenso—that it fits into a pattern of persuasion of which he was fond. For example, elsewhere in the book, Colenso cited Exodus 21:20-21, a passage that ruled that a master who beat a slave was not to be punished unless his victim died immediately, on the grounds that a slave was the equivalent of money. Colenso then wrote:

> I shall never forget the revulsion of feeling, with which a very intelligent Christian native, with whose help I was translating these words into the Zulu tongue, first heard them as words said to be uttered by the same great and gracious Being, whom I was teaching him to trust in and adore.[19]

The heated subject of clerical subscription—the requirement that all clergymen had to swear at the time of their ordinations that they believed unfeignedly certain documents and doctrines—was tackled by Colenso in a similar way. He argued that his missionary experience highlighted the need for change. A Zulu ordinand could not possibly give his unfeigned assent because "the nice distinctions of the Athanasian Creed for instance, cannot possibly be translated into his language."[20] This argument, however, could only go so far in helping the numerous clergymen whose difficulty with the Athanasian Creed was that they understood what it said all too well.

In 1861 Colenso published a commentary on the letter to the Romans in which he attempted to overturn traditional doctrines such as substitutionary atonement and eternal punishment and to advocate a form of universalism. The subtitle of the work claimed that Romans would be "explained from a missionary point of view," and the preface claimed that it was "the results of seven years of Missionary experience."[21] Even an extremely hostile review of this work conceded that developing intimate relationships with so many damned heathens, over a prolonged period of time, must have been a great psychological pressure on the bishop.[22] This picture, however, is misleading. Before Colenso had even begun his missionary work, on his first voyage to Africa, he had taught his companions in a series of addresses the basis of his later book—his nontraditional interpretation of Romans.[23] Peter Hinchliff has shown that Colenso was airing some of these views such as universalism as early as the 1840s at gatherings of the Depwade Clerical Society.[24] In the case of his book on Romans, he was raising such issues as eternal punishment, and then it was as if he were encouraging his readers to imagine the whole heathen world asking the question: "Is all that true?" One final example of this rhetorical habit: his biographer tells this anecdote of Colenso: "Looking at one of his own children in the innocence of her infancy; he asked a friend how anyone looking on a babe could be a Calvinist."[25]

This habit is illuminating because Colenso's desire to personalize—his critics would say sentimentalize—an intellectual issue betrays a Romanticist way of thinking. This, of course, is more profoundly illustrated by his theological views; his growing revulsion with ideas such as substitutionary atonement and eternal punishment reveals a theological evolution that was being guided by the sensibilities of Romanticism. Jeff Guy has shown how Colenso's encounter in 1842–43 with the writings of S. T. Coleridge and F. D. Maurice filled him with an excitement almost akin to a conversion experience.[26] This influence was reinforced by his becoming friends with Maurice shortly thereafter. This exposure was the dominating influence upon Colenso's intellectual development, deprived as he was of any formal theological training. During his first year of work in Africa, when he was confronted with the ridiculous charge that he was a Tractarian, he confided in a letter how baffling it was that "I, a Maurician" could be so mislabeled.[27] Colenso drank deeply from wells dug by Romanticists, and he imbibed their moral and theological instincts in the process. In this light, one could see his commentary on Romans as a kind of last-ditch attempt to show that his Romanticist convictions were reconcilable with the teachings of Scripture.

In short, what was growing inside Colenso was a moral critique of certain passages in the Bible. Despite the narrow focus of his book, this factor emerges to the surface in the last biblical difficulty Colenso addressed: the story in Numbers 31 of the war with Midian. He also found in this passage internal inconsistencies and impossibilities chiefly based on the numbers that it contains. His calculations upon the number of Midianites, however, enticed him to make other points:

> We may fairly reckon that there were [. . .] altogether 80,000 females, of whom, according to the story, Moses ordered 48,000 to be killed, besides (say) 20,000 young boys. The tragedy of Cawnpore, where 300 were butchered, would sink into nothing, compared with such a massacre, if, indeed we were required to believe it. [. . .] How is it possible to quote the Bible as in any way condemning slavery, when we read here, v. 40, of "Jehovah's tribute" of slaves, thirty-two persons?[28]

In other words, the numbers reveal that the narrative is unreliable, which proves it is unhistorical. This frees us from having to embrace those passages that offend our sensibilities. Romanticist instincts caused Colenso to wish to be freed from the letter of the Law, and, paradoxically, the Enlightenment tool of science became a weapon that allowed him to liberate himself from these bonds in the name of truth.

Therefore, his new convictions regarding the Bible actually brought a great psychological release to the bishop. At times, he seemed intoxicated with the possibilities that he imagined his discovery heralded. He wrote to a friend: "The movement, however, is begun which will end, I cannot doubt, in a revolution of the English Church."[29] In his original, unguarded draft of the book, he announced that his conclusions necessitated "a very considerable modification of Church dogmas and formularies."[30] This ulterior reward enticed him to marshal whatever evidence he could find and place it in as damning a light as possible, sometimes with results that seemed comic to many. For example, because the Pentateuch claims that the Israelites lived in tents during their sojourn in the wilderness, Colenso took a chapter to inquire suspiciously where they obtained them and to attempt to prove that it would have been physically impossible for them to have carried the required tents out of Egypt. Leviticus 8:3-4 claims that Moses obeyed the Lord's command to gather "all the congregation together unto the door of the tabernacle"; however, after careful calculations and measurements, Colenso deduced that only nine grown men could actually fit in front of the door, as opposed to the two million that the text required.[31] In the minds of his critics, passages such as these betrayed a perverse desire to manufacture difficulties.

If Colenso came to the point where he wanted to disbelieve the Bible, many of his critics, of course, had the exact opposite disposition. The Bible for them was not a source of bondage to be shed, but a source of security and certainty to which to cling. They, therefore, did not concur with Colenso's assumption that once one had noticed numerical difficulties in the Pentateuch, there was an inevitable momentum of thought, leading to the abandonment of some of the most cherished doctrines of the Church. Moreover, Colenso was not short of critics. The high and low wings of the Established Church, together with the Evangelical Nonconformists, all made common cause against him—that is to say, the vast majority of the religious world.

So the religious world set out to attempt to answer him. It was easy enough to pick one of his weaker arguments and give it a good working over in a letter to a religious newspaper or in an article. For example, Colenso had made much of the duty of the priests, as commanded in Leviticus 4:11-12 to carry the carcass of a bull whose fat had been used for an offering outside the camp. He argued that, given the size of a camp for two million people, it would have been a long and difficult trek for the beleaguered priests to make, and therefore was an absurdity when compared with their small number and numerous other duties. His critics, however, were quick to claim that the Hebrew verb in this passage merely meant that the priests were to cause this action to be done rather than necessarily do it themselves. This critique had the added advantage of arousing the suspicion that Colenso was not a credible scholar. Joseph M'Caul, in a letter to the *Record*, claimed smugly, "His palpable ignorance of the Hebrew idiom is calculated to excite a titter amongst true critics." A letter to the High Church newspaper, the *Guardian*, from the clergyman, J. P. Gell, covered similar ground, only it confined itself to making a scholarly point.[32] It was true that Hebrew was not Colenso's strong point. After a worse linguistic blunder was made in the next part of his study, Colenso enlisted his erstwhile critic, Gell, to examine the third part in advance in order to save himself from further embarrassments.[33] Other passages in Colenso's book were also attacked quickly on other grounds. The requirement to relieve oneself outside the camp, for example, was declared, when read in context, to refer to encampments of soldiers during military campaigns rather than to the whole congregation. The Congregational magazine, the *Christian Witness*, never reviewed the book, humbly confining itself to attempting to resolve only one of Colenso's difficulties.[34]

Colenso's critics were also quick to ridicule his tendency toward "a perverse literalness," such as his legalistic handling of the passages that claim that the people gathered in front of the door and that the whole people heard the Law read.[35] A letter in the *Guardian* provided a spoof critical examination of Colenso's book *Ten Weeks in Natal* that did a fine job of sending up his literalism; likewise, the Anglican Evangelical journal, the *Christian Observer*, applied Colenso's methods to the standard history of King Edward I's attempt to assemble an army with which to fight William Wallace, showing that, if valid, these methods would prove that account to be unhistorical as well.[36] Perhaps, however, conservatives should have looked first to the mote in their own eye: in his book, Colenso patiently, and without ridicule, dealt with a conservative scholar's theory that the fact that every tribe's census produced a round figure—Judah, 74,600; Issachar, 54,400 and so on—was proof of a special providence of God in their birth rates.[37] Nevertheless, some of the bishop's points were shown to be particularly vulnerable to a counterattack. Undoubtedly, it was these passages, along with a bit of confidence-boosting bravado mixed with wishful thinking, that enticed some of his critics to dismiss the whole book as so obviously erroneous that one should hardly waste one's time answering it. The archbishop of Canterbury himself, Charles Longley, provided one of the foremost comments along these lines, pronouncing Colenso's objections: "so puerile, that an intelligent youth, who read his Bible with care, could draw the fitting answers from the Bible itself,—so trite, that they have been again and again refuted, two hundred years ago."[38]

Eventually, some of his critics took a stab at answering every one of his objections, one by one. The *Record* did not actually begin to review the book until over a month after it had begun to denounce it—apologetically claiming that it was delayed due to "accidental circumstance."[39] It then began to review the book in parts, the first two of which simply gave background, context, and denunciations; and then it took a week off—pleading insufficient space—before it actually began to answer the arguments that the book contained. Nevertheless, it did eventually attempt to answer every one of Colenso's difficulties. Others did the same; the controversy generated publications with such hopeful titles as *Solutions of Bishop Colenso's Bible Problems* and *The Nineteen Alleged Impossibilities of Part I of Colenso on the Pentateuch Shown to be Possible.*[40] This kind of response might have come close to a tacit admission that Colenso's slippery slope was a valid one—that if one unanswered difficulty remained, then the authority and inspiration of the entire Bible would be undone.

A slightly less absolutist response was the hypothesis of the transcriber's error; a ploy much loved by conservatives faced with a seemingly insurmountable difficulty. A letter to the *Record* suggested the possibility that somewhere along the way a mistake had been made that changed tens of thousands to hundreds of thousands. Thus it was actually 60,000 rather than 600,000 warriors.[41] The scholarly journal of the Evangelical Nonconformists, the *British Quarterly Review*, also cast doubt on the perfect transmission of all the numbers, adding: "an error of this kind once introduced being so liable, not only to be repeated, but to lead to further corruptions that other figures might be brought into harmony with it."[42] It was quick to affirm, however, that it was quite possible to assert that "these errors of copyists whether coming in as oversights or from design, have left, not only the moral and religious teaching, but the chain of historical facts contained in the record, undisturbed."[43] However probable or improbable this theory might be, it did expose the narrowness of the bishop's attack: if these concessions were granted, then the vast majority of his catalogue of difficulties would be swept away in one (false) stroke.

Even more broadly, some of his critics argued that even if Colenso's difficulties were real, they were not of sufficient import to justify overturning the historicity of the Bible. The High Church journal, the *Christian Remembrancer*, took this line:

Let it be repeated—we are not attempting to explain a difficulty, but place it in the strongest light we can to further Dr. Colenso's purposes. We are supposing—what is perhaps not to be supposed—that it is insurmountable; and we ask, what then? [. . .] It is a pregnant fact that such difficulties have been seen by everybody, have been commented upon, have exercised the ingenuity of expositors with more or less of success or failure, and that the Christian world has paid very little attention to the matter. If it is asked what is the reason of this, the obvious reply is, Because the authenticity of the books of Moses is abundantly proved from external sources of various kinds, and because they are unmistakably endorsed by the whole subsequent history of the Jewish nation, and by the writers of the New Testament. People have been content to leave difficulties unexplained, for which they could see no probable solution, and which, after all, did not affect their belief either way, whether explained or unexplained.[44]

Likewise, the *British Quarterly Review* conceded, "We do not mean to say that the matters set forth by Dr. Colenso as difficulties are in no case real difficulties." Nevertheless, the testimony of the New Testament—of so many righteous witnesses—to the truth of the Old, although it "would not warrant us in receiving statements as true which we see to be contradictory and false," "should dispose us to accept of any explanation of difficulties in the Hebrew Scriptures that may take with it probability, or even possibility, rather than discard those writings as untruthful." Indeed:

Every allowance of the kind indicated is due in sheer justice to writings which have come to us from so remote an age, with a purpose so limited, in a language so ancient, and through processes so perilous to their literal accuracy.

The bishop of Natal, however, like a man with no respect for due justice, had run a trial in which the rules were: "The presumptive evidence in favour of the defendant, however strong, shall be wholly ignored, and the circumstantial evidence tending the other way shall be retained, and urged to the letter."[45] The *Record* complained that many of Colenso's critics had conceded too much ground in the debate, grumbling that it would not do to have a "half infallible" Bible, but some others were content to allow some difficulties to rest unanswered.[46]

The fame of Colenso's book can be largely attributed to the near hysteria that it produced in the Christian camp, but to what can this panic reaction be attributed? Inside the Church of England there was already a great deal of unease. The Church was divided from within into various factions, assaulted from without by Nonconformists and—it had only recently begun to realize—rendered by the courts virtually powerless to thwart theological or liturgical mavericks. The uproar caused by *Essays and Reviews* was still raging; Colenso's book coming so soon on the back of it might well have made loyal churchmen wonder if the dam had now broken, releasing a torrent of heresies, of which this was but the beginning. Therefore, particularly for High Churchmen, Colenso's status as a bishop was especially alarming. One of the fathers of the Tractarian Movement, Edward Pusey, wrote to Bishop Tait: "Had he been *Mr.* Colenso still, his book would have been stillborn. Now it is read by tens of thousands because he is a Bishop. It is his office of Bishop which propagates infidelity."[47]

Concern over Colenso's position as a bishop was often fueled, as Pusey's comments implied, by a pastoral concern for the effect that the book might have had on the public. This concern was shared by the majority of the bishop's religious critics, irrespective of their denomination or the wing of the Church to which they belonged. If the masses were to hear a rumor that the Bible had been overthrown, would this have caused vast numbers of people to lose their faith and morals? One of the most popular adjectives for the bishop's book was "dangerous." Chancellor Massingberd, despite the fact that he had opposed the condemnation of *Essays and Reviews* by Convocation, wanted to see the gathered leadership of the Church take a stand against Colenso's work. Alluding to one of the Lord's strongest statements of condemnation, he felt that the book had gone a long way toward "offending Christ's little ones."[48] Colenso himself had helped to provoke this reaction; he had made an appeal to laymen in the preface of his book, and it was clear throughout that he was writing with one eye on influencing those without pretensions to scholarship.[49] His critics, likewise, pitched many of their comments with the gallery in mind. A letter to the *Guardian* from a vicar in Wiltshire recommended the book as "a short and easy answer for simple-minded and hard-working men to the doubts which are now being raised as to the truth of Bible history."[50] Many of Colenso's critics wrote books that they would have deemed highly successful if found worthy of such a recommendation.

The pastoral dimension of the controversy is well illustrated by an address given by Canon John Miller, a well-known Evangelical clergyman in Birmingham, which provoked such interest that the aisles were filled with those who could not find a seat and numerous others were not even able to enter the building. Miller sought to strengthen the faith of those who might have been shaken by reaffirming his faith in the Bible. With disarming frankness, he admitted that it might well be true to say that he was "unable to follow all Bishop Colenso's calculations, unable to correct his Hebrew, and unable, in other commentaries to find the difficulties he had raised solved." He went on to say:

> Understand, then, the existence of difficulties is not denied—difficulties in philology, in chronology, in ethnology, in geology. But, in a world full of difficulties—difficulties in God's works, in God's providence, in God's grace, where to yourself your very self is a mystery, will you, on this ground, reject God's Word, or any, even the least portion of that priceless book?

He then went on to advise that those who read Colenso's book also read "something else" and to recommend some titles, both more substantial works and ones that were more likely to be "within reach both of your purse and your ability."[51] Cheap volumes were wanted in order to secure the place of that priceless book in the hearts and minds of the people. Miller was neither the first nor the last of Colenso's critics to use the simplistic, but forceful, tactic of quoting Christ's words: "For had ye believed Moses, ye would have believed me: for he wrote of me. But if ye believe not his writings, how shall ye believe my words?" (John 5:46-47 AV). Moreover, some of the bishop of Natal's condemnations of the Pentateuch were so sweeping as to make this response more compelling than it might have been. Colenso and his critics were both grabbing crude weapons which they imagined would be effective on the masses; and both, therefore, could readily find reasons to charge the other with using unworthy arguments. A scholarly debate was deeply intertwined with the desire to influence the thinking of the general populace.

Although reciting the words of Christ was not an answer to Colenso's criticisms, Evangelical and High Church critics continually trumpeted the argument that the numerous references in the New Testament that attribute quotations from the Pentateuch to Moses and refer to the events recorded there as if they were historical, did indeed settle these issues for believers. Even the report produced by a special committee in the Lower House of Convocation, which had come from a sober process of carefully winnowing down the charges to those that could be best defended, made much of this point. Colenso had tried to preempt the retort that he was accusing the Lord of being mistaken by suggesting the answer that perhaps Christ's comments were merely reflecting the common assumptions of his day; but this concession had the reverse effect—causing many of his critics to suggest that his comments contained the seeds of Christological heresy.[52] Indeed, this was one of the points upon which he was found guilty at his ecclesiastical trial in Capetown:

> In imputing to our Blessed Lord ignorance and the possibility of error, the Bishop has committed himself to a most subtle heresy, destructive of the reality of the Incarnation, and he has departed from the Catholic faith [. . .].[53]

Such arguments were difficult to sustain theologically. It was demonstrated by his supporters that Colenso's remarks were consistent with those made by numerous well-respected divines.[54] These charges were undoubtedly highlighted because they had the polemical advantages of substantially increasing the seriousness of Colenso's crimes and of being far easier for people to understand than the complex trains of thought often involved in biblical criticism. Raising the stakes, however, meant that either party might lose more. The short-term gains, which such arguments might have made, were at the price of making pronouncements that could not be sustained if the legitimacy of the modern discipline of biblical criticism was to be recognized and an endless battle against its most fundamental assumptions and findings was to be avoided.

At a time when the church had just begun to struggle with the theories of Charles Darwin, a nerve seemed to have been touched when Colenso's critics had thrown at them the counteraccusation that they were opposing science. This appears to have been an area where hidden anxieties lurked; and perhaps ones that had to do with their own, internal, fears rather than just fears concerning public perceptions. Criticisms of the book were often coupled with strong denials that there was any desire to suppress valid pursuits of the discipline of biblical criticism. For example, the report condemning the book produced by the Lower House of Convocation denied that its authors had any such intention, claiming that: "On the contrary, they insist upon the duty and the advantage of bringing all the appliances of sound scholarship, and all the real results of learned and scientific investigation, to bear upon the Books of Holy Scripture."[55] The anxieties behind such statements are perhaps more apparent in some wistful comments made by Canon Stowell, when he made reference to the controversy over Colenso's book that was then just beginning:

> The use that is made of science at present in certain quarters is utterly unlike the use that was made of it by Newton, the prince of science [. . .] now-a-days the study of many scientific men seems to be to discover discord, and not harmony, and to find in science, not the handmaid of revelation, but the antagonist.[56]

Colenso might not have been a terribly frightening opponent, but his new weapon was perhaps an ominous sign of things to come.

Broad Churchmen and liberal-minded clergymen did not rally to the
defense of Colenso's book either. Indeed, what is perhaps most striking
about their reactions is how much common ground they share with those of
the Evangelicals and the High Churchmen. One might have imagined that
if anyone would have defended Colenso it would have been his friend F. D.
Maurice. When Maurice had been himself under intense attack for alleged
heterodoxy during the previous decade, Colenso had bravely dedicated a
book to him. Nevertheless, this new controversy ruined their friendship.
Maurice wrote to a friend:

> The pain which Colenso's book has caused me is more than I can tell you.
> I used nearly your words, "It is the most purely negative criticism I ever
> read," in writing to him. Our correspondence has been frequent but per-
> fectly unavailing. He seems to imagine himself a great critic and discov-
> erer [. . .] his idea of history is that it is a branch of arithmetic.[57]

Maurice felt so strongly on the matter that he decided to resign his living so
that no one would be able to claim he was not defending Colenso in order
to save his own position. In the end, his bishop did not accept his resigna-
tion, and his alarmed friends dissuaded him from pursuing that course of
action any further.[58] The relationship was so strained that Colenso's mother-
in-law felt a need to attempt to thwart the plan of the bishop and his wife to
take up lodgings in Russell Square, lest this would prove embarrassing for
Maurice, whose residence was also there, and it never recovered.[59]

In fact, it is very hard to find anyone, particularly anyone influential in
the religious world of Victorian Britain, who was willing to give a hearty
defense of Colenso's book. Liberal and Broad Churchmen usually distin-
guished themselves from the crowd in this controversy by their willingness
to defend the bishop himself against persecution. The religiously liberal or
secular press was sometimes willing to make strong statements in favor of
applying scientific techniques to the Bible and against the prejudices of conservatives, but it is not easy to find a wholehearted defense of the publication itself. For example, the *Edinburgh Review*, in an article that was officially
meant to be a review of the bishop's volume and related works, scarcely discussed the book at all, choosing instead to make general statements about
the need for the old view of the Bible to be overthrown. Moreover, it did
concede, in a rare allusion to Colenso, that he had "pressed a narrow line of
argument to extreme conclusions, which, in our opinion, it fails to support."[60] The British men of science who rallied to the bishop's side belong in
this same category. There is no apparent evidence that any of them defended
the volume's intrinsic worth, and the botanist Sir Joseph Hooker, the one of

their number whose letters contain a lengthy passage on the controversy, admitted at the outset of his remarks that he had not read it. Moreover, after his social interaction with Colenso increased, he confided to Charles Darwin, "I have seen a good deal of him, and consider him sanguine and unsafe."[61]

The Broad Church publication, the *Spectator*, repeatedly condemned the *Record* for the way in which it was attacking Colenso.[62] Nevertheless, this stance did not translate into a defense of the book itself. Its own review freely conceded that the Pentateuch's "numerical statements are magnified by the mists of time and the imaginative arithmetic of Orientals (who habitually use numbers much as we use a varnish of sentiment)." This might be a problem for some conservatives, but not for the *Spectator*. Nevertheless, it went on:

> This once admitted, what remains on which we differ from the Bishop of Natal? [. . .] that whole undercurrent of thought which seems to imply that when once we have detected bad arithmetic in the Pentateuch, we may entirely change our *attitude* of mind towards the narrative—cease to feel under any divine obligations to its history, and thenceforward, though we may pick and choose from its text little bits of spiritual sentiment that we like or fancy better than the rest, as oases in the desert, dismiss all idea of studying the developing purpose of God's revelation in the history as a superstition which only those can afford who are satisfied with every detail in the numeration.[63]

Dean Stanley, who was far more sympathetic than most, also made many familiar points. He, too, felt that Colenso had tried to draw far too many conclusions, when all he had really called into question was the accuracy of the numbers. He admitted to a friend, "I regret the book extremely" and in correspondence with Colenso in response to a copy of the original draft, which the bishop had sent to him, he told him, "I regard the whole plan of your book as a mistake." Moreover, he reaffirmed the essential historical accuracy of the narrative "from the time of Abraham downwards." As to the specific points that Colenso had raised, he answered in a way that would have resonated with many Broad Churchmen, "Whether any answer can be made I know not, nor do I much care"; and perhaps an even wider audience would have identified with a comment he made to another correspondent, "Of course the arithmetic is entirely beyond me."[64] Benjamin Jowett, who was one of the contributors to *Essays and Reviews* and himself an author of biblical criticism, does not seem to have praised the book. On the other hand, he apparently confined his criticism of it, given in a letter to Stanley,

to the comment: "I think the tone is a good deal mistaken." Neither agreeing nor disagreeing, praising or denouncing, he simply took the apathetic
view that he and Colenso worked in different ways.[65]

Bishop Tait, who championed Colenso's rights against his persecutors,
nevertheless spoke of the bishop of Natal's "rash and arrogant speculations"
and of his own duty to warn "the people committed to my care against his
errors, and what appears to me the very unbecoming spirit in which they are
urged."[66] Connop Thirlwall, bishop of St. David's, was the only member of
the Upper House of Convocation who voted against the resolution condemning Colenso's work, arguing that it failed to show how the bishop had
violated the doctrines of the Church.[67] Thirlwall himself was a student of the
new German scholarship; he had translated Schleiermacher's *A Critical Essay
on the Gospel of St. Luke* and published it in 1825 along with his own learned
introduction.[68] Nevertheless, he charged Colenso with possessing a "very
rash and wild" skepticism and his book with:

> confounding the accuracy of arithmetical calculations with that of the
> premises on which they are based. Difficulties are magnified into "plain
> impossibilities"; seeming discrepancies into direct contradictions.
> Whatever is narrated so as to raise such difficulties, is pronounced "unhis-
> torical."

Moreover, the bishop of St. David's strongly rebuked Colenso for his pastoral
irresponsibility and declared that his arrogant style was particularly distasteful.[69] Even the leading Broad Church clergymen and the most sympathetic
bishops did not approve of Colenso's book.

Matthew Arnold—who was not a clergyman, and therefore was not prey
to the Church's muzzle, and who belonged, at least intellectually, to the liberal and broad wing of the laity—nevertheless disapproved of the book so
much that he determined without solicitation to publish an article condemning it.[70] He purported to judge the book by the standards of literary
criticism, and finding in it nothing new to add to educated debate and nothing edifying to make it a useful popular work, he decided that "the Bishop
of Natal's book cannot justify itself for existing." Arnold ridiculed Colenso's
method, claiming that it would have been possible to write the book on "a
single page" because all one would have needed to do would have been to
offer one calculation that produced a faulty sum per book of the Pentateuch;
for, according to Colenso's way of thinking, one of these was sufficient to
dispose of an entire volume. He contrasted Colenso's work with that of
Spinoza, the latter, however unorthodox his opinions might have been, having had genius enough to stimulate the elite—and discretion enough to

write in Latin.[71] Arnold's not-in-front-of-the-children approach to biblical criticism naturally enough laid him open to the charge of snobbery. He hit back, however, claiming that he, too, had a pastoral concern for the masses; that he was not against the dissemination of ideas, but only their careless introduction without a sufficient attempt to help people integrate them into their existing spiritual lives.[72] Liberal and Broad Churchmen often agreed with many of the criticisms of Colenso that were made by Evangelicals and High Churchmen.

In a recent study of Colenso, Jeff Guy has made a quixotic effort to defend the bishop's first volume on the Pentateuch. In doing so he is, as he is well aware, defying the considered opinion of the vast majority of weighty figures (let alone the rest) who have taken the time to evaluate the book, from Colenso's contemporary, F. D. Maurice, down to Guy's own contemporary, Owen Chadwick.[73] In addition to several secondary lines of reasoning, he offers as his central explanation for this alleged critical injustice an argument bordering on a conspiracy theory in which the clergy, and particularly the hierarchy, of the Established Church successfully used their wealth and influence in order to place a lasting slur on the book's reputation: "They had access to the men who ruled the nation [. . .] the newspapers and journals in which they could make their views known, and funds to attract and support men in their cause."[74] This argument is unconvincing. The leadership of the Church did not have the ability to suppress unwanted religious opinions, as witnessed by the power of Nonconformists to disseminate effectively views that annoyed the Church; and the entire religious world—Dissenters and Churchmen together—was not capable of burying whatever awkward contributions might emerge, as Charles Darwin's *On the Origin of Species*, published just two years before Colenso's work, amply proved. In fact, the other Church controversies of the era clearly reveal that Church leaders were often unable to bring their influence to bear upon undesirable views which arose within their own ranks, let alone manipulate the opinions of society as a whole. Colenso's book was not the victim of a clerical conspiracy.

One of Guy's secondary lines of argument is that in the prudish Victorian age readers were offended by the bishop's willingness to address "the physical aspects of the biblical narrative." In order to substantiate this argument, he quotes Maurice's comment:

> To have a quantity of criticism about the dung in the Jewish camp . . . thrown in my face, when I was satisfied that the Jewish history had been the mightiest witness to the people for a living God against the dead dogmas of priests, was more shocking to me than I can describe.[75]

The part of the quotation that Guy deleted was the phrase "and the division of the hare's foot."[76] Maurice was not shocked by allusions to the necessities of nature, but rather by the fact that someone could imagine that queries regarding such trivial aspects of the story would cause anyone to jettison a narrative with such manifest liberating power. The attempts by both Guy and Rogerson to evaluate Colenso's critics are substantially weakened by their failure even to acknowledge that one of the most fundamental flaws of the bishop's first volume—a flaw that was central to its widespread rejection—was its unconvincing assumption that difficulties in the details of the narrative, the existence of which had long been known, must inevitably lead people to abandon vital parts of the story of salvation history and fundamental doctrines of the church.[77]

The emergence of biblical criticism in Britain was inevitably going to have been difficult. Nevertheless, it certainly was not inevitable that it would have been this strange and emotive. Conservatives could hardly be expected to react well to biblical criticism in the hands of a bishop who had already proven himself—to their satisfaction—to be a heretic. Colenso's work was polluted with some crass and dubious arguments, and he dramatically overplayed the conclusions that could be drawn from his evidence; therefore, it was an awkward gesture to embrace him as a champion of truth and the herald of a new science, even for the friends of biblical criticism, let alone for the defenders of orthodoxy he had already alienated by his commentary on Romans. None of these peculiar facts, however, could justly be used by Colenso's critics to disprove the validity of the entire discipline of biblical criticism or to suppress its emergence in Britain. Unfortunately for those who were wishing for a path of peaceful coexistence, the rhetoric of many of these critics, despite their protests to the contrary, did not position the religious world well for a reconciliation with the findings of this new discipline. The great biblical scholar J. B. Lightfoot lamented, when the bishop of Natal's book was first published, that "a more frank and liberal treatment of the difficulties of the Old Testament, if it had been general, would have drawn the sting of Colenso's criticism," but now he feared the effect of the book would be "to discredit reasonable inquiry" and "to divide men into two extreme parties, who will wage fierce war against each other and trample the truth under foot between them."[78] The way in which Colenso's critics handled this controversy did not lend itself to creating an environment in which a more liberal attitude toward biblical criticism could immunize the community against extremist positions; and, for that matter, neither did the actions of Colenso himself. In the end, if they wished to remain credible in the eyes of the wider world of thinking, spiritual men and women, both

Colenso and his critics needed to moderate their claims and rhetoric. Both the Bible and biblical criticism were there to stay—to imply that the stories of the former had no foundation in history, or that the theories of the latter had no foundation in science, was to fight a losing battle. Biblical criticism already existed, and British society was going to be exposed to it whether Colenso's critics wished it or not; but the Bible, despite its great antiquity, and excited rumors to the contrary, was not in danger of being killed off by the young discipline. Indeed, its very age pays tribute to its profound resilience.

Chapter 6

Biblical Criticism
and Anti-Christian Rhetoric
Joseph Barker and the Case against the Bible

Despite the fact that Joseph Barker (18075) was a prominent figure in his day and that his name regularly appears in new works of scholarship on the nineteenth century, he has never been the subject of a biography.[1] His talent for renouncing the ideas and communities he had once vigorously championed inevitably fostered a tendency to minimize or ignore his previous achievements in those fields. From a working-class background and largely self-taught, he became a Methodist New Connexion minister as a young man, gained a reputation as an anti-Owenite lecturer, and rose to become one of the denomination's most popular preachers. His emerging heterodoxy, however, and his arrogant, confrontational personality, led to his expulsion from the denomination in 1841. As his exodus provoked a major schism that was the greatest crisis in the history of the New Connexion, he is remembered only briefly in Methodist historiography, and almost entirely as a troublemaker. In the 1840s he continued his ministry as an independent religious leader, forging links with the Unitarians. In the latter half of the decade he became increasingly preoccupied with radical politics, eventually championing Chartism in his popular journal, *The People.*[2]

Perhaps none of Barker's efforts has more often gone uncredited than his prominent work in the world of Victorian popular freethought. He was once viewed as one of the most important, national leaders in that movement, taking his place alongside a handful of others whose names and reputations are still well known such as Charles Bradlaugh and G. J. Holyoake. His subsequent reconversion to orthodox Christianity, however, created an incentive for historians of freethought to endeavor to forget him.[3] For example, J. M.

79

Robertson did not mention Barker once in the over 600 text-crammed pages of his encyclopedic effort, *A History of Freethought in the Nineteenth Century* (1929), although he did have room to include sections on more tenuous contributions to freethought such as the absence of much religious teaching in the novels of Charlotte Brontë.[4] Likewise, J. M. Wheeler did not include Barker among the thousands of entries in his *Biographical Dictionary of Freethinkers of all Ages and Nations* even though he included lesser figures in the history of freethought from Barker's own generation and milieu such as Patrick Lloyd Jones and figures whose contributions to this cause were—to say the least—less overt, such as William Shakespeare.[5]

Should Barker have died around 1860 rather than live to reconvert, his name would have held an honored place in such literature. Indeed, this counterfactual scenario has rather better evidence than most speculations of its kind as his death was falsely announced in 1856. The militantly Secularist journal, the *London Investigator*, ran an obituary article in which it declared him to have been "the ablest man who has risen from the working classes since the time of Cobbett" and went on to opine: "He has fallen a signal martyr to liberty. Take him all in all we may never see his like again in our generation. Freethinking has sustained an irreparable loss. In exposition he was unrivalled, and in controversy invincible. His friends and admirers were legion."[6] Charles Bradlaugh, who would go on to become the most prominent atheist in England, helped to edit a series of *Half-Hours with the Freethinkers* in 1857. The lives and writings of twenty-five figures were included in this effort, ranging across the nations and centuries to include people such as Epicurus and Spinoza. To Joseph Barker, however, was reserved the honor of being the only living person to be included. Ironically, his entry begins with the words, "In any work, purporting to be a record of Freethinkers, the name of Joseph Barker cannot be omitted."[7] In 1895, Bradlaugh's daughter tried to explain (and excuse) what appeared then to be the surprising fact that Barker had been one of the original editors of the great freethinking newspaper, the *National Reformer*.

> His coming [back from America] was heralded by a flourish of trumpets—literary trumpets, that is—receptions were arranged to welcome him, and there was evidently a widespread notion that Joseph Barker was a very great man indeed. It is difficult for us to-day, having before us his whole public career, with its kaleidoscopic changes of front, to realise the enthusiasm which his name provoked in 1860. But be that as it may, it is quite evident that at that time his reputation stood high amongst English Freethinkers; and, in an evil hour, Mr. Bradlaugh, thinking that the cooperation of such a man would be a great advantage to the cause he had

at heart, suggested to the Sheffield committee that Mr Barker should be invited to become a co-editor with himself.[8]

In short, if one revisits the primary sources, it becomes readily apparent that Barker was once regarded by popular English freethinkers as one of their greatest champions and as a man of extraordinary talent and ability. Nevertheless, although Barker's name and some of his achievements are recorded in more recent scholarship on the history of freethought, notably Edward Royle's pioneering study, *Victorian Infidels*, his once celebrated work in this field has not yet been the focus of a scholarly work.[9]

Moreover, Barker's main freethinking efforts were as a popular critic of the Bible, and scholars of biblical criticism tend to neglect popularizers as thoroughly as freethinkers neglect reconverts. To start at the beginning, although J. Estlin Carpenter's *The Bible in the Nineteenth Century* is a hymn in praise of eradicating all confessional instincts from the study of the Scriptures, nevertheless its author seems to have thought—if his complete neglect of Secularist texts is anything to go by—that this achievement only "counted" when made within a Christian milieu.[10] This blinkered approach has persisted to the present. For example, after discussing a work by F. W. Newman published in 1847, John Rogerson, in his *Old Testament Criticism in the Nineteenth Century: England and Germany*, claimed, "Nothing as radical and far-reaching as this was to come from an English writer until the appearance of the later parts of Colenso's *The Pentateuch and Joshua* in 1871 and 1879."[11] While admittedly popular authors did not usually write volumes that dealt solely with the Hebrew Scriptures, this remark ignores the existence of infidel literature that explicitly challenged traditional notions of authorship, composition, and dating and generally dealt with the Old Testament in a way that was certainly equal to Newman's effort in terms of its radical nature. While it might be argued that it is reasonable that scholars such as Rogerson should examine only the more erudite works in the field, this approach militates against their preoccupation with explaining the reasons for the slow acceptance of these ideas in Britain. That theories akin to those of the scholarly biblical critics were being propagated by declared infidels in an avowed attempt to destroy the Christian faith is certainly germane to such an inquiry. In short, an important aspect of the social and religious context of the mid-Victorian debate regarding biblical criticism has been routinely ignored.

During the 1850s Barker was widely considered the preeminent English infidel biblical critic. During a debate on the Bible at Halifax in 1855, Barker's opponent, the Congregational minister Brewin Grant, feigned to be surprised at the ignorance he claimed Barker exhibited on the subject, noting that freethinkers had been confidently saying: "the others of our leaders are more in the philosophical way, but Mr. Barker is our Bible man."[12] Barker, as a reconvert, claimed that he undertook his anti-Christian work in the spirit of a calling and a mission: "I vowed,—I felt as if duty required me to vow,—eternal war against Churches, priesthoods, and religions."[13] Nevertheless, he almost invariably struck at these targets via an attack on the Scriptures. Barker published in 1858 a challenge to the celebrated Chartist and author Thomas Cooper, who had recently reconverted, to join him in a debate, but when Cooper chose the subject "the belief in a personal God and a future life," Barker was uneasy, despite having publicly repudiated these notions.[14] Barker had recently, and apparently somewhat rashly, declared himself to be an atheist rather than merely a freethinker, and his son, Joseph Barker, Jr., was afraid that his father would be maneuvered into trying to prove a negative:

> However, I think you can easily get over it. You really don't deny anything; you only deny a *present* belief from present data [. . .] [George (another son)] does devotedly hope you will not take what he calls the *insane* ground that there is no God and No Future State. [. . .] Cooper wants to force you into a very untenable position, so as to be able to escape what *he* knows will be a complete and dreadful defeat if he *is* obligated to prove that the Bible is of divine origin.[15]

He agreed to Cooper's terms nonetheless, but perhaps regretting it, grumbled at the end of the discussion, "I have now merely to state that I did not seek this debate. I sought a debate on the Bible. I wished to free the people from slavery to an old document. That was my object."[16]

The printed British Library catalogue lists nine items under Barker's name that were published during the 1850s. Two of these are accounts of his loss of faith, but the other seven all deal with the Bible question. He first began to publish statements against traditional views of the Bible around 1845 and did so for the last time in 1863. In 1851 he emigrated to America. His talents as an anti-Bible lecturer were sufficiently recognized there for him to be elected the president of two major freethinking gatherings on this theme: the Salem (Ohio) Bible Convention (1852) and the Hartford (Connecticut) Bible Convention (1854).[17] In January 1854 Barker took the negative side in a celebrated debate with the Reverend Dr. J. F. Berg on "the origin, authority and tendency of the Bible," which was held in Philadelphia. He returned to England for a long stay in 1854–55, during which he gave anti-Bible lectures and took part in several debates, the most notable of which was his ten nights' discussion with Brewin Grant in January–February 1855. Barker returned to Britain again in January 1860 and remained settled in England until some years after he abandoned his anti-Bible views in 1863. During the 1850s Barker recycled the same arguments against the Bible in lecture after lecture, debate after debate, and publication after publication. Moreover, his arguments were cheered, lauded, and parroted by rank-and-file popular freethinkers and even by other leaders in the movement. An examination of these arguments will provide a useful window into radical, popular thought at midcentury.

His first attack was usually an argument regarding textual transmission. The fact that there is no guarantee that errors or interpolations have not crept into the text over the centuries and the fact that translation is a process that may result in a loss of the original meaning proved (according to Barker) that the Bible currently in existence cannot justly be said to have divine authority. For Barker, this argument by itself was decisive: "Supposing it could be proved, therefore, that the originals were written by God, or were of Divine authority, it would not affect the question under discussion. [. . .] This, therefore, in reality settles the question as to the Divine origin and authority of all existing Bibles."[18] It would be difficult to overestimate the weight that this argument seemed to carry in Barker's own mind: one senses in his attitude the portent that might be given to certain facts not commonly understood when discovered by an inquisitive, self-confident, self-educated person who is accustomed to possessing greater intelligence and knowledge than most other people in his social world. Moreover, this line of reasoning seems to have gone down well in popular freethinking circles. For example, the English Secularist leader G. J. Holyoake was so pleased with Barker's speech at the Salem Bible Convention, which had this argument as its main theme that he printed it as a pamphlet, claiming in a postscript: "Both in America and in this country it is considered the ablest Mr. Barker has delivered."[19] Nevertheless, as it was based on facts that every educated person took for granted, this line of attack was hardly calculated to disconcert a debating opponent. Without fail, they answered that this was not an argument against divine authorship but against any authorship. John Bowes, for example, whom Barker debated at Stockport in 1855, retorted, "We have not the original of Shakespeare, does that prove that we are not in possession of Shakespeare's writings?"[20] Barker would obligingly fall into this trap and therefore make his point susceptible to being portrayed as a pedantic one. In this debate he claimed of Shakespeare's plays, "we cannot tell but that they are all wrong" and even conceded the same for his own, early publications.[21] Grant won a similar admission and capitalized on it to the full:

> He declares we have, by the press, a copy of Locke, but there is no author-
> ity for any quotation as really Locke's, except Locke should come back
> to endorse it. Very well, that is all I want you to see. I want you, as a plain,
> simple matter of reasoning, to understand this,—that the very argu-
> ment which he employs to overthrow the Bible, would destroy all litera-
> ture [. . .].[22]

His opponents invariably conceded that there were probably some errors and
interpolations that had crept into the text. Barker, however, thought such an
admission decided the matter: "if there has been only one single alteration
made in the whole Bible, and we were unable to tell what that alteration was,
that single fact would destroy the doctrine of the absolute Divine authority
of the book."[23]

In light of their flat denial that these facts carried the implications he
claimed, Barker sought to strengthen his argument. He did this by arguing
that the extent of the corruption of the biblical text had been very great. A
favorite fact he liked to air was that the German scholar J. J. Griesbach had
compared some manuscripts of the New Testament and found 150,000 variations.[24] The reply to this was sometimes an appeal to less pessimistic scholarship but, more crucially, an assertion that these were overwhelmingly
minor variations that did not call into question the meaning of any vital
statements of Scripture. Barker's inflammatory counterattack was a conspiracy theory. He had been deeply shocked by reading Mosheim's *Ecclesiastical
History* (a volume to which he refers in most of his writings and debates),
and one of the ideas he had taken away from it was that the early Christians
freely indulged in "pious frauds" because they did not believe lying and
deceit were sins if done with the aim of promoting Christianity. Moreover,
this claim was routinely extended into a vitriolic attack on his Christian contemporaries whom he claimed still covertly acted on the same principle. In
a typical remark, he offered one audience this exposé: "Christians distinguish
between lying, and using falsehood for the good of souls. They contend, that
to deceive people for their good, and the cause of God, is *not* lying."[25]
Whatever else could be said for or against this approach, it certainly removed
any sense that the debate had narrowed into a discussion of obscure scholarly points.

Barker also used the well-worn infidel technique of highlighting contradictions in the Bible.[26] To his critics, most of these were either trivial—how
important is it to know definitively whether Solomon had 40,000 or 4,000
stalls for his horses?—or dependent on a perverse reading of the text. As they
were not fighting for an infallible existing text, they could easily put the former down to copying errors, although it was undoubtedly still worth it just

for the entertainment value for Barker to highlight the point in a biblical list of kings at which the numbers given made one man two years older than his father.[27] More substantial points were probably only effective if Barker's hearers either had never habitually attended sermons or if they were ready to see familiar texts with entirely fresh eyes. It is hard to see how an earnest Christian would be likely suddenly to see a contradiction in one of the most famous verses of the Bible on one of the most central ideas of the gospel: "One passage calls God immortal, while another represents him as dying. John iii: 16."[28] Likewise one would need to be able to ignore a well-established narrative of the unfolding of salvation history to be troubled by the fact that "in one passage it says, circumcision *shall* profit, whereas Paul says, circumcision profiteth nothing."[29] Such objections were akin to another trait in Barker's biblical criticism—his insistence that various passages be interpreted literally. Some of his standard observations included: (1) contrary to the story of the post-Fall curses, dust is not the food of snakes; (2) contrary to the account of Noah's flood, there are no windows in heaven through which water may fall on the earth; (3) contrary to the prophecy against Ninevah, the stars have not fallen from the sky; and (4) contrary to the prophecy that said the Messiah would be called Immanuel, the New Testament claims that he was actually named Jesus. Moreover, if people's thoughts were only evil in the time of Noah, then mothers would not have cared for their children and this society would have destroyed itself; if everyone's hands had been against Ishmael, he would not have been able to go on living; if the descendants of Abraham did become as numerous as the dust of the earth, they would not all be able to fit on the earth, and so it goes on. His insistence on literal interpretations and on the necessity of an inerrant existing text both illustrate an ironic dynamic that repeatedly came into play in which Barker asserted that his opponents' beliefs ought to be more conservative or narrow than they actually were.

A train of thought related to the idea of scriptural contradictions that loomed large in Barker's mind was that the Bible itself contradicted orthodox views. Anthropomorphic language in reference to the divine being he took literally and thereby purported to demonstrate that the Bible taught that the deity had a physical body that performed functions such as breathing and smelling. Also, "God is represented as tired and exhausted with the six day's work of creation, and as resting on the seventh, Exodus xxxi: 17, and being refreshed."[30] Moreover, the biblical deity is not omnipotent: "Thus you see there is a wrestling match,—Jacob and God,—and Jacob beats God."[31] His opponents had two main responses to this line of attack. First, they noted that neither Jews nor Christians, despite—or, more

accurately, because of—their great devotion to the Bible, have ever enter-
tained any of the notions Barker imagines are taught there. In his debate
with Grant, Barker asserted that many Christians did believe that God had
a body. Grant repeatedly demanded that his opponent give some examples
until Barker was forced to answer by naming the Swedenborgians and the
Latter Day Saints. Grant then triumphantly responded that these were the
exceptions that proved the rule, as both of these communities had extra-
biblical sources of revelation that informed their theologies.[32] Secondly, his
opponents claimed that Barker seemed to lack even the most basic ability to
comprehend how language was commonly used—an argument that was
employed in response to all his literalist readings and some of his other
attacks as well. Grant did a fine parody of Barker's method by offering a literal reading of the statement from the Salem Bible Convention, which
Barker had signed. Barker, however, fell into this trap as well by grumbling
that he had not written it, thus opening the way for Grant to point out the
occasions at which Barker used nonliteral language in their unfolding debate,
such as his claim that he "saw the hand of a priest" in a certain passage of
Scripture.[33] Nevertheless, Barker's attacks on biblical portrayals of the deity
did bolster a wider claim of his that probably was rhetorically effective. Until
1858 (by which time his major anti-Bible writings and debates were already
completed), Barker was not an atheist, but rather a Paineite deist. This stance
allowed him to defend the Almighty against the Scriptures and employ the
powerful rhetoric that the Bible itself was blasphemous because its statements about God were sometimes demeaning. One imagines that this very
concept had the capacity to lead minds with some religious furniture left in
them into an entirely new way of viewing the Bible, and it was certainly a
clever way of turning orthodox attacks against infidels on their head.

Barker's most central and probably most persuasive approach was a
moral critique of the Bible. This also was a way of hoisting orthodox critics
of skeptics with their own petard. Barker would note sanctimoniously: "it is
because my deeds are righteous, and because I wish the deeds of others to be
righteous, that I thus speak of the Scriptures."[34] This was not merely a tactic, however: moralism was the central cord that connected all of the seemingly contradictory phases of his life. Barker's infidelity was, to adapt a
phrase of T. H. Huxley's, "Victorian respectability minus Christianity." He
criticized the Bible for not adequately supporting teetotalism. Furthermore,
"it does not command cleanliness, or a regard to health [. . .] And it does not
forbid Gambling, Lotteries, or certain forms of intemperance."[35] Moreover,
this manly, scoffing, working-class lion of the platform had a streak of prud-
ery to match any current stereotype of the most pious and sheltered

Victorian Christians: "I cannot see what good it could do posterity, to be told that the first man and woman were both naked and were not ashamed. The thing might be perfectly true, and yet not necessary to be recorded, nor calculated to be of any use when recorded."[36] And this was small beer for Barker compared to the Song of Solomon, stories of fertility potions and incest, and references in the Law to genitalia. He would dramatically leave blanks in some of his Bible quotations and would often make a disclaimer such as the following: "We cannot go into the particulars of this case. Read them yourselves—when your children are not by."[37] Grant's answer to this was that many wholesome things are inappropriate in some contexts or can be made to appear unwholesome if examined in the wrong light: Barker "could in the same way make a mock of the human body, and by shrugs and innuendoes, and the tricks of mere licentiousness, make the temple of man's spirit as ridiculous and polluted as his own imagination."[38] Indeed, once one has read large portions of Barker's writings and speeches, it becomes hard to resist a temptation to employ Freudian theories and argue that he was endeavoring to suppress his own fascination with human sexual organs and activities. It certainly would not have occurred to everyone to wonder at the source of the (apparently) elderly Abraham's virility in his marriage to Keturah.[39] Nor did he always keep to the path of censorship: "several portions of the Scriptures tend to deprave man. I will read you a portion [. . .]."[40] Berg found this weak spot: "I had hoped to have the happiness of congratulating my opponent on making one speech without referring to Solomon's seven hundred wives and three hundred concubines; and in his last, I thought he would keep clear of it, and in fact, he only squinted at it. (Laughter and applause.)."[41] Nevertheless, it was surely permissible for Barker to wonder if a man who seemed to be forever expanding his harem was really the right sage for the Almighty to employ "to warn young men against harlots."[42] Barker went so far in his moral critique as to argue that the Scriptures themselves tempted people to immorality: "the Bible mentioned certain crimes which otherwise would never perhaps have entered the minds of young men, and thus exposed them to the temptation of committing those crimes, the results of which were most horrible and frightful."[43] It would be hard to find even among the most earnest of Victorian Christians a comparable impulse to bowdlerize the Bible itself.

Barker spent a great deal of time highlighting the moral failures of major characters in the Bible. He would contrast these with general statements of approbation made in the Scriptures regarding these figures and then go on to argue that therefore the Bible was condoning their immoral conduct. Abraham, David, and Solomon were the main ones to receive this treatment.

For example, he writes: "Abraham is said to have taken one of his female slaves as a wife, and had offspring by her; yet no fault is found with him for so doing; on the contrary, the Bible represents God as declaring, 'Abraham obeyed my voice, and kept my charge, my commandments, my statutes, and my laws'" (Gen 26:5).[44] The judgmental tone of these criticisms tempts one to examine Barker's own character. This, however, was exactly what he wanted: he took great pride in his personal moral purity and expected people to draw the conclusion that infidels are more upright than biblical heroes or contemporary Christians. Nevertheless, a few primary sources have survived that allow one to see a dent in his moral armor. Barker judged harshly David's feigning madness in order to save his own life, pronouncing it an example of his willingness to use "deceit and fraud."[45] Nevertheless, when Barker's personal journey into unorthodoxy was threatening the life that he knew as a celebrated Methodist New Connexion minister, his response was also deceptive. Barker had ceased to believe in the rite of baptism and acted upon this publicly several times in the presence of other ministers of the denomination by substituting a naming ceremony of his own devising. When an official of the denomination wrote a bland, nonjudgmental letter asking him to respond to these reports, Barker replied:

> I think the information which you have received on this subject is not correct; and if you will be so kind as to refer your Informant to me, I think I may be able to set him right on some particulars.
>
> P.S. Perhaps I ought not to send this without cautioning you and your colleagues to be careful how you listen to informers. You appear to me to be pursuing a very dangerous course.[46]

Nevertheless, the understandable course of action of adopting a deceitful stance under pressure formed no part of Barker's own self-perception. Instead, his moral principles were thoroughly outraged by any suspect behavior that was recorded in the Bible without being accompanied by explicit censure. It would probably not occur to many skeptics today to criticize the Bible for too often failing to adopt a moralizing tone. Barker's pride in his own moral purity reminds us that the Victorian "cult of respectability" was not confined to those who attended public worship.[47]

Barker also held less priggish moral objections to the content of the Bible, and these place him in a better explored stream of intellectual history. Like many other questioning Victorians, Barker had come to view doctrines such as substitutionary atonement and the eternal torment of the damned as morally reprehensible.[48] Moreover, Barker the moralist took the critique of the atonement one step further and argued that the end was immoral as well as the means on the grounds that justification by faith was inherently antinomian. On this basis, he branded evangelicalism itself as the enemy of self-help and respectability.[49] Again like some of his more celebrated contemporaries, Barker objected to the slaughter, cruelty, and vengeance that were recorded as having divine sanction or approval in the Bible. He had a very Victorian alternative solution to the state of wickedness that prompted the deluge: "Might [God] not have caused Noah and his family to build a few schools, and train the children? [. . .] What would have been the effect if Noah had set up a few good printing presses instead of building an Ark, and published a few good newspapers, and a multitude of interesting and useful books?"[50] Perhaps an equally effective approach was his condemnation of the notion of collective punishment. This idea is so clearly taught in some passages of Scripture that its clash with the individualism of modern Western society must have been a clear gain for Barker. Nevertheless, perhaps his approach to this theme did not fully capitalize on this advantage. Barker liked to make his points by working his way through the book of Genesis seriatim, thus his first argument against collective punishment was persistently that the Almighty "subjected every serpent, in every part of the world, and through all the ages of time, to the heaviest curses, for the sin of a single serpent."[51] Berg batted this away dryly, "My opponent spoke feelingly of the curse pronounced on the serpent. He thought the reptile had been dealt with too severely."[52] Barker's highlighting of passages which portrayed massacres and collective punishment and even his harping on issues such as the polygamy of biblical heroes probably did effectively unsettle the conviction of some of his hearers that the Bible was a paragon of moral teaching.

Barker also claimed that the Bible could not have divine authority because it made statements regarding the natural world that modern science had disproved. This line of thought also occasionally betrayed the sophomoric pedantry to which mid-Victorian, working-class autodidacts were sometimes prone. He writes on the Sabbath: "the writer of the book of Genesis appears to have supposed, that the day and night returned in every part of the earth in twenty-four hours, whereas, in truth, in some parts of the earth the day and night return only once in a year. At the poles there is but one day and one night, but one morning and one evening, the whole year round."[53] And on Christ's temptation: "we are told that the devil took Jesus into an exceeding high mountain, and showed him all the kingdoms of the world, and all the glory of them,—a proof that the writer was ignorant both of the shape of the earth, and of the power of the human eye."[54]

Nevertheless, this theme also probably had real appeal. Barker knew how to align an attractive friend on his side with eloquence and conviction: "And still, as science advances, the supernatural recedes. Science is driving supernaturalism out of the universe. All science is plainly atheistic. The greatest of all the men of science are atheists. Science is naturalism; theology is supernaturalism."[55] In an article in the *Reasoner* titled "What harm have the Scriptures ever done you?," Barker gave as his second answer: "They prevented me from reading a great many books on science, which would have given me an incalculable amount of important information."[56] On the positive side, in an article titled "What I should do if I were young again" in the *National Reformer* he tacitly advised young men, "Science should be my only theology, the laws of nature as revealed by science my only rule of life, and obedience to them my only religion."[57] The sage advice of an honored man with a powerful mind that to take the Bible as a guide was to waste one's intellectual gifts surely had some influence on his young hearers and readers.

For readers today, perhaps one of the most interesting aspects of Barker's biblical criticism is his feminism. He held this ground resolutely and persistently. After detailing sections of the Bible that seem to be unfair to women, Barker's judgment is unequivocal: "These passages show that portions of the Bible originated neither with God nor woman, but with selfish, proud, usurping man."[58] At another point he asks, "Is it a sufficient reason that a weakling simpleton of a man, should be lord and master of an intelligent and clever woman, because the first woman was deceived and led into transgression before her husband?"[59] He clearly championed the alternative, namely, gender egalitarianism, particularly within marriage.[60] His opponents usually echoed the general principle of treating women fairly, but denied that the Bible was more sexist than egalitarian. Grant, for example, argued that women were treated worse in places without the Bible such as India and ancient Greece, that prominent infidel leaders had mistreated their wives, and that the Mosaic law gave more property rights to women than did the current laws of England.[61]

Another theme that has grown in significance since the mid-nineteenth century is Barker's continual appeals to the context of religious pluralism. He insisted that the Bible should be judged by the standards of world literature. On one section of the Bible he notes: "There are many improbable stories in both accounts—stories which, if people found them in Chinese or Persian books only, would be smiled at as childish fables."[62] He insisted that every argument be weighed by this standard; and these appeals, whatever effect they had on his own generation, certainly would have force for many people today. For example, if the triumph of early Christianity against all the odds were used as a proof of its divine approval, Barker would ask: "Is it not a fact, that hundreds of sects have been formed, and that some of them have spread themselves over great portions of the world, without miraculous aid? [. . .] in spite of the fiercest opposition and cruelest persecution? Take the case of Mormonism in the present age."[63] If it were argued, "The Bible has withstood the attacks of ancient and modern infidels," he would answer, "Mohammedism and Popery have withstood the rudest attacks."[64] Contorted arguments in favor of dubious passages in the Bible rang hollow when Barker would wonder what parts of the Koran could be justified in a similar way. Grant tried to turn this attack on its head, claiming that the uniqueness of the Bible was indicated by the fact that even infidels never troubled to write or lecture against the Book of Mormon, or the Koran, or any other rival volume: "Therefore, practically, they give up all the other books, which are introduced only for an evasion. They feel the Bible is the only one they need try to destroy."[65]

One of the most fundamental differences between Barker and his opponents was that the latter treated the biblical record as self-correcting while Barker demanded that every passage of Scripture be a self-contained, complete truth. The verses of the New Testament that he most often attacked were the ones in Romans chapter 13 that call for obedience to the state. In a typical comment, he claims: "The passage commands us to 'be subject to rulers,' and adds that whosoever resisteth them shall receive to themselves damnation. It makes no exceptions."[66] For an American audience, he offered a particularly pointed application, "Is Washington damned? Are Franklin and Jefferson, Hancock and Adams, all damned?"[67] Nevertheless, one could just as easily cite the passage of the New Testament in which some of the apostles are shown righteously engaging in acts of civil disobedience. Barker's opponents assumed that the one passage confirmed the existence of exceptions to this rule which the other did not trouble to mention, but Barker himself insisted that every section of Scripture be interpreted on its own. These were two such different methods of interpretation that much of the force of the overall cases being made by the combatants depended on which one was accepted as more appropriate by any particular hearer. All of Barker's opponents argued, in the words of Berg, that "the Bible, as a whole, is a progressive revelation."[68] Therefore, it was not surprising, in their view, that the Old Testament in general and its earlier passages in particular contained ideas that are expressed more crudely than they would be if communicated now. As Bowes put it, "God in the infancy of our race gave symbols, types, pictures, as men were able to bear, all without exception, adapted to the infancy of our race."[69] Grant complained that skeptics "do not judge the

Bible fairly as a whole [. . .]. They progress backwards like a crab; and judge of endings by commencements,—of perfection by imperfections,—of the laws of Christians by the lives of Jacob, David, and Solomon."[70] This response, however, assumed that the church had correctly judged the canon of Scripture, and Barker, as a freethinker, had no such conviction. Therefore, for him, not only did each passage need to stand on its own merits, but each book had to provide its own divine credentials: "But suppose it could be proved that certain prophesies have been accomplished, would that prove that the Bible, as a whole, is of divine origin, or would it only prove that those prophecies were of divine authority? It would not show that the Song of Solomon, Ecclesiastes, the Proverbs, are of divine authority."[71] Whether many of Barker's critiques sounded reasonable or unreasonable largely depended on which way one went at such methodological forks in the road.

Barker's method of interpretation was however, in its own crude way, in keeping with some of the principles of the emerging discipline of modern biblical criticism. Although he emphasized brasher, knockdown arguments, his speeches and writings were littered with assertions in line with the main preoccupations of the young discipline. Already in 1848 Barker could write of the stories of the book of Genesis:

> It would be foolish to suppose that any single individual originated them. They were probably the production of a multitude of minds operating for ages. The person who first wrote them, only collected them perhaps, and reduced them to something like form and order. [. . .] There appear in fact, to be two or three accounts, two or three different traditions, joined together in the same book.[72]

Crucially, he went on to illustrate this by the different names for the deity that are used in different passages. In this same book he argues that various passages in the New Testament are interpolations on the grounds that the flow of the unfolding argument is disrupted, and on the question of authorship he refers tellingly to "the writer of the Epistle of Peter."[73] Some years later, he offered a more precise theory regarding the creation narratives in the early chapters of Genesis: "These two accounts have all the appearance of being fragments from two different authors, having different ideas about God and creation. With chapter 4 begins apparently a fragment from a third author, in which the Deity is called by a still other name, and at verse 25 the style of the first account appears again."[74] Barker also raised the possibility that the book of the Law, which the high priest Hilkiah claimed to have found, was actually written by Hilkiah, thus radically altering traditional theories of dating, authorship, and chronology in a way that would become widespread in English-speaking scholarly circles later in the century.[75] Barker judged other books to be compilations as well: "It is plain that we have in Samuel, as in Genesis, a jumble of contradictory stories by different authors."[76] His solution to the synoptic problem was simple: "If we suppose the authors of the gospels to have written from hearsay or tradition some fifty or a hundred years after the time to which their accounts refer; if we suppose them to have lived in different neighborhoods, or to have moved in different social circles, and each to have written an account of things as they believed in his own neighborhood and social circle [. . .]."[77] In short, Barker was introducing his hearers and readers, largely for the first time, to the kind of challenges to traditional assumptions regarding biblical authorship and dating that were central to the whole enterprise of the new, scholarly discipline of biblical criticism. However, he also was mixing these theories together with a flow of rabid anti-Christian rhetoric and arguments. Therefore, the waters were muddied for educated, believing scholars in England who wished to embrace and disseminate the findings of modern biblical criticism because a constituency of ordinary believers had already become familiar with these arguments as "infidel" ones. The existence of popular, anti-Christian, biblical criticism made the acceptance of the new discipline in Britain more difficult.

Nevertheless, as some of the quotations cited above have already indicated, there was a huge gulf between scholarly and popular biblical criticism in terms of style and content. One example of this is Barker's taste for hyperbole. Virtually every one of his writings or major series of speeches contains a statement similar to this specimen: "I will undertake now to prove that there is not a book on earth—my friend shall have the whole world to choose in—that favours to a greater extent immorality and crime, or that favours it more strongly, than the Bible does."[78] In Barker's rhetoric, the patriarch Jacob becomes "one of the greatest and vilest of sinners, one of the most cruel and unnatural of the human race."[79] Likewise King David was "one of the greatest liars and most wholesale murderers—one of the most consummate hypocrites, and vilest of profligates that ever disgraced humanity."[80] Barker was an heir of the Paineite tradition of popular biblical criticism. Anyone who has read Thomas Paine's *The Age of Reason* will recognize echoes in some of Barker's arguments and rhetoric. For example, Paine also accused the Bible of being blasphemous, claimed that "lying forgeries" were involved in its production, and drew sweeping implications from the pitfalls of textual transmission and translation.[81] Not being preoccupied with issues of sexual morality as Barker was, Paine singled out Moses as the biblical hero most ripe for character assassination: "Among the detestable villains that in any period of the world have disgraced the name of man, it is impossible to find a greater than Moses."[82] As to the wider context regarding the rate at which the findings of modern biblical criticism were widely accepted, it is interesting to note that Paine argued that the very fact that a document was anonymous or its authorship had been falsely ascribed, automatically disqualified it from having any divine authority.[83]

Barker's opponents recognized his debt to *The Age of Reason*. Grant referred to "biblical infidels, who follow, with less ability and more extravagance, the footsteps of Paine" and to "Mr. Barker and his tutor Paine."[84] He also found a double standard at work:

> But, while Mr. Barker judges of Abraham by our present standard, he actually apologies for Tom Paine's drunkenness, on the principle that Tom Paine got drunk then because everyone drank;—it was a common thing; they had not found out the laws of nature. [. . .] So that Mr. Barker makes fifty years of progress excuse Paine's drunkenness, but will not let 4000 years' progress excuse one single case of drunkenness in that grand old patriarch Noah, whom he abuses so insolently and so coarsely.[85]

But Barker admired Paine so intensely that he could not resist the temptation to defend him at every turn. Berg mocked this tendency by referring to "St. Thomas Paine." but this was, if anything, an understatement—that great, radical popularizer would grow in Barker's imagination until he became almost a substitute messiah.[86] When pointed toward the moral superiority of Jesus Christ, Barker could testify reverently: "Thomas Paine had intelligence, public spirit, liberality, philanthropy, and talents, sufficient to make a dozen or a hundred such characters as Jesus, taking him even at his best, pictured by his admirers and friends."[87] Barker, however, as we have seen, was bolder in his criticisms than Paine ever was. As an apostate evangelical preacher, Barker was more intimately familiar with the Bible and orthodox theology, and he had the kind of knowledge regarding what attacks would be most painful and damaging that only an ex-lover possesses. Armed with these added resources, Barker took his place in the Paineite tradition of popular biblical criticism and excelled therein.

Although he has been neglected, Joseph Barker was an influential Victorian in a remarkable range of arenas, including Methodism, Chartism, Anglo-American connections, popular publishing, popular freethought, and popular Christian thought. He is also an intriguing figure. He was a forceful personality, an egotist, and an insatiable controversialist. He does seem to have held all of his varied views sincerely. Nevertheless—perhaps with the aid of self-deception—he was apt occasionally to strengthen the case for his current stance by mishandling the relevant evidence. Moreover, he could not suppress a self-aggrandizing desire to seek to lead a movement as soon as he had joined it. He did have an extraordinary ability to inspire people to follow him, sometimes taking whole groups with him into a new, contradictory phase and dragging more than one spellbound disciple through several of them. He was a self-taught polemicist from humble origins who wrote populist, ephemeral works. He was not a profound thinker whose ideas and writings are of lasting, intrinsic value. This judgment, however, is also true of all the other nineteenth-century leaders of popular, organized freethought. Indeed, the most celebrated figure of them all, Charles Bradlaugh, built his reputation as a thinker and writer by articulating anti-Bible views that were similar in kind to Barker's.[88] Figures such as Bradlaugh and Holyoake are not remembered for the brilliance or enduring merit of their skeptical arguments or publications. Barker's thought does not need to be rescued for its own sake, but it is valuable nonetheless as a window into the worldview and ideas of plebeian radicals in the mid-nineteenth century. To study what he said is to study what a whole generation of plebeian freethinkers heard, thought, imbibed, and echoed, for Barker was after all—subsequent attempts to obscure it notwithstanding—their "Bible man." He was a manifestation of an entire constituency of working-class men in the era before state education and household suffrage who were thirsty for knowledge and unwilling to adopt opinions merely on the word of established authorities. The leaders of these plebeian freethinkers often read seminal works, such as those written by the eighteenth-century deists, and translations of some of the new continental thought, such as D. F. Strauss's *Leben Jesu*. They then mixed these ideas together with their own emotive, anti-Christian rhetoric and commonsense attacks on traditional beliefs, creating a heady, populist intellectual climate, which not only challenged the spread of religious orthodoxy, but also complicated the spread of biblical criticism by causing it to appear anti-Christian. Barker was one of the most celebrated and prolific figures in this world: recovering his work as a freethinker serves toward illuminating this entire milieu, and understanding the way it reacted to and influenced the flow of more well-known currents in British social, intellectual, and religious history.

Chapter 7

Biblical Criticism
and the Secularist Mentality
Charles Bradlaugh and the Case against Miracles

Charles Bradlaugh (1833–1891) was by far the most famous atheist in Victorian Britain. He also became the first openly atheistic member of Parliament. While less precise claims to being "the first" are inevitably contestable and therefore perhaps best avoided, there is nevertheless a genuine sense in which Bradlaugh was the first Briton really to find his feet as a public atheist at the popular level and to maintain that stance steadily as British society watched on. Even bitterly anti-Christian radicals often stopped short of adopting outright atheism; and those who did avow atheism for a season often pulled back from it later on. Victorian infidels looked back to Thomas Paine (1737–1809) as the patriarch of their tribe, but Paine was a deist, not an atheist. Richard Carlile (1790–1813) was the next great hero in this succession. David Berman has observed that with "the indomitable Richard Carlile there is the beginning of a cohesive, more or less continuous atheistic movement," and that Carlile was "the first public champion of atheists."[1] Nevertheless, Carlile went on to formulate his own mystical-allegorical brand of religion and to insist that he was a Christian. Carlile had endured time in prison for his services to the cause of freethought, and this example set the standard for heroes of the movement thereafter. In 1841 the *Oracle of Reason* was founded, a journal that has been described as "the first outspokenly atheistical periodical published in English, perhaps in any language."[2] Prosecutions against its rapid succession of editors (each taking up the standard as the previous one was taken off into captivity) generated three new "martyrs" of freethought: Charles Southwell, George Jacob Holyoake, and Thomas Paterson. Paterson apparently came back to the Christian fold,

Southwell emigrated to New Zealand, and Holyoake, who certainly did not believe in God, nevertheless went on to renounce the label "atheist" determinedly, choosing instead to define himself as a "Secularist" and going so far as to argue that the "Principles of Secularism do not include Atheism."[3] Thus the field was still clear for Bradlaugh to come forth as the first unabashed atheist and popular champion of atheism in Britain, and to hold his ground.

The notion of the miraculous offers a particularly promising window into people's general patterns of thought and belief, as arguments for or against miracles can be advanced in such a wide variety of ways, including philosophical, epistemological, rational, scientific, experiential, traditional, biblical, theological, and historical. This chapter will pay careful attention to Bradlaugh's critique of miracles in order to clarify the nature of his skepticism as a whole, as well as that of the world of Victorian popular unbelief to which he gave leadership. Firstly, however, it would be useful to rehearse Bradlaugh's biography. Bradlaugh grew up "in very straitened circumstances" in London.[4] His father was a confidential clerk to a firm of solicitors, and he was one of seven children, two of whom died in early childhood. His family's religious habits were typical of that milieu. His parents considered the parish church to be their church and expected their children to go to Sunday-school there, but saw no need for weekly church attendance to be a feature of their own lives. Bradlaugh's formal schooling lasted five years at the most, ending when he was eleven. By the age of fourteen he himself was a Sunday school teacher at their parish church, St. Peter's, Hackney Road. Either in that year or in Bradlaugh's fifteenth year, the bishop of London announced his intention to come to the area in order to confirm some of its young people, and Bradlaugh, as a bright young man, was set apart for this honor by the incumbent, the Reverend John Graham Packer, and prescribed a course of study by way of preparation. Confirmation was not a great value and sustaining strength of the Victorian church but, nevertheless, here is a case in which, ironically, it functioned exactly as it is intended. At the age of reason, a person, having been duly informed, is given an opportunity to embrace fully and freely the faith of their baptism: Bradlaugh faced that choice squarely and ultimately decided to reject Christianity as untenable. His preparation led him into reading the New Testament, "Whereupon, to his shocked amazement, he discovered not only a general discrepancy but even internal discord among the several Gospels."[5] Packer responded to these concerns with heavy-handed alarm, and Bradlaugh gave up going to church, finding his way instead to outdoor Sunday gatherings where popular infidels expounded their views. Meanwhile, goaded by Packer, his father was increasingly rattled by his son's open break with the church. One tangible response was to place a wall-hanging facing Bradlaugh's chair in their home that had the biblical text written on it: "The fool hath said in his heart, There is no God" (Ps 14:1; 53:1). Father and son fell out with each other, and so Bradlaugh left home at the age of sixteen.

Bradlaugh also began lecturing in the open air on freethinking themes, one Christian newspaper noting at the time hostilely, but nonetheless tellingly, that his ideas were "copied from Paine's 'Age of Reason'," the fount of almost all popular critiques of the Bible in Britain.[6] Also at the age of sixteen, he wrote his own "Examination of the four Gospels according to Matthew, Mark, Luke, and John," revising it again at the age of twenty, but it was never published.[7] At the age of seventeen he was so pressed by debt that he joined the army, serving for three unpleasant years. A civilian again, he took a lowly position as an errand boy for a solicitor. He was able to rise to the level of clerk, however, and was given more and more responsibility as his considerable talents manifested themselves. His knowledge of the law would serve him in good stead throughout his life. He was also lecturing, writing, and editing as a popular freethinker, and increasingly was giving leadership to that world. He founded the National Secular Society in 1866, an organization that became the main unifying one for English atheists (and which still exists today), serving as its first president until forced to retire due to ill health in 1890, having, as it turned out, less than a year to live. Bradlaugh first ran for Parliament in 1868 and first won a parliamentary election (Northampton) in 1880, but as Britain's most unabashed atheist he was deemed disqualified either to affirm or to take the oath of office. He was therefore barred from serving in Parliament (while still winning every subsequent election) until 1886, when he was finally admitted to the members' benches in the House of Commons on a decision of the new Speaker of the House. His modern sympathetic biographer and fellow skeptic, David Tribe, has dubbed Bradlaugh "a proselytizing atheist," and his forthright attacks on religion in general and Christianity in particular, like a kind of antidote to church bells, rang out clearly and regularly throughout the land.[8]

What kind of atheist was he, though? He developed his own definition of atheism and doggedly stuck to it, a definition that explicitly refused to equate atheism with denying that there is a god. Here is a report of an early variation on his standard definition:

> He did not deny that there was "a God," because to deny that which was unknown was as absurd as to affirm it. As an Atheist he denied the God of the Bible, of the Koran, of the Vedas, but he could not deny that of which he had no knowledge.[9]

Numerous such statements may be found littered throughout his writings and reported speech. One from a debate in 1864 arguably reveals that the scriptural text his father had set for him still rattled in his mind and perhaps even serves to expose the curious way in which he could never get away from taking the Bible literally:

> I do not stand here to prove that there is no God. If I should undertake to prove such a proposition, I should deserve the ill words of the oft-quoted psalmist applied to those who say there is no God. I do not say there is no God, but I am an Atheist without God. To me the word God conveys no idea, and it is because the word God, to me, never expressed a clear and definite conception—it is because I know not what it means—it is because I never had sufficient evidence to compel my acceptance of it [. . .].[10]

The burden of proof was on believers to explain what they meant by "God"; Bradlaugh's self-imposed task was to show them why their conceptions of the divine thus articulated were untenable.

In a lifetime in which he was perpetually churning out freethinking material for publication and continually giving lectures criticizing religion and championing atheism, it is a curious—and, as shall be shown, telling—fact that Charles Bradlaugh never seems to have chosen to make the rather obvious subject of miracles his central theme. Nevertheless, he did address the subject at length in response to the initiative of others. Walter R. Browne, a Fellow of Trinity College, Cambridge, gave an apologetics lecture, apparently as a representative of the Christian Evidence Society, in Leeds in early 1876 on "the credibility or the possibility of miracles."[11] The Leeds branch of the National Secular Society therefore challenged him to debate the subject, and Bradlaugh, the national president of their organization, agreed to represent the opposing point of view. Bradlaugh's daughter, in a rather bloated biography of her father, gave an account of all the numerous such debates in which he took part. She gave the most space to those debates in which either her father won a decisive victory or his opponent was unnecessarily offensive. The debate with Browne, however, fell into neither category, so it was given fairly short shrift.[12]

There was, of course, no hope of making progress in such a debate. In Christian terms, divine agency is essential to the very definition of a miracle, and as Bradlaugh did not believe in God, there was no common place from which even to begin such a discussion. Browne spoke first, and Bradlaugh then harried him about his unproven assumptions and undefined terms. Indeed, much of the debate degenerated into incessant attempts and demands on both sides for a whole series of words to be defined. If Browne mentioned God, Bradlaugh would simply reply, "I don't know what the word means."[13] Likewise with "creation," "supernatural," and other such words. The depths of this probing of first principles might be gathered by Bradlaugh's generous concession at one point: "Now, I will submit to you that we are both agreed apparently that there is existence, so that I need not trouble you with any kind of evidence of that."[14] For his own part, Bradlaugh defined "nature" as "all phenomena, and all possible causes for all phenomena."[15] This, of course, literally excluded the supernatural by definition, and at times Bradlaugh almost sounds like he really did believe that this linguistic slight of hand actually did disprove the possibility of miracles. Browne categorized human personality and mind as nonmaterial and thus outside of his own definition of "nature," the payoff being that this was then a category that the Almighty could also occupy, making God's status, and therefore perhaps even God's existence, more intelligible. Bradlaugh, however, saw the matter in a different light: "He says he is not nature. Well, but does he mean that he is supernatural, or extra-natural, or unnatural? (A laugh)."[16]

Browne got off to a slow start in the debate. He would go through whole rounds without seeming to realize that, if he hoped to be judged to be winning in the eyes of his audience, then he needed to score a solid punch or two before he sat back down again. He was at his worst when he tried to offer concrete examples. The nadir, for his supporters, must have been when he defended the doctrine of divine providence by pointing to the case of the American Civil War. As it led to the abolition of "that infernal institution of slavery," this, he claimed: "showed to my mind conclusively that there was a God who governs the world."[17] As with all such claims, Bradlaugh responded with questions of theodicy: if some act of goodness or justice done in the world is attributed to divine agency, then we must also blame God for having allowed the badness or injustice to exist up until that point. Therefore, the Almighty was a god "who must have thought slavery in America right as long as he let it last, because, if he had thought it wrong, he would have prevented it earlier."[18] As the Christian champion became more accustomed to the arena, however, he started to come out on the offensive. On the question of theodicy, Browne averred: "Now, I contend that Christianity is the only system which gives any account of the existence of evil at all. How does Mr. Bradlaugh account for evil according to his system?"[19] This so disconcerted Bradlaugh that he made the tactical error of immediately shouting out from his chair, "I would submit that in this debate our friend cannot ask me to account for evil. (A Voice: 'Oh.')." This undoubtedly gave the audience—who did think that turnabout was fair play however much Bradlaugh might cling to legalistic notions regarding where the *onus probandi* resided in the way the debate was structured—the impression that he was vulnerable on this point.

Browne's greatest coup, however, was latching on to free will as the underlying principle under contention. He had mentioned free will in a speech, and the president of the National Secular Society—whose relentless habit it was to challenge every term or concept that his opponent mentioned that he did not think was adequately substantiated—disputed the notion. Browne therefore transformed their conversation into a kind of latter-day clash between Luther and Erasmus. He now had a first principle that would work in the minds of the crowd before him:

> I do rest this great fundamental fact of freewill upon the testimony—the primitive testimony—of my own consciousness. It may be false; of course it may be false. Everything may be false. The whole world around us may be false. Our whole existence may be a dream. Nobody has ever answered the arguments yet by which Bishop Berkeley and others have proved conclusively that we are not certain of the existence of matter, and by which Hume proved that we are not certain of the existence of mind. We are certain of nothing, in the sense that it is impossible to conceive it otherwise. If nothing is true, then it is not worth debating about anything; but, if anything is true, then, to me, my consciousness of freewill is true [. . .].[20]

Bradlaugh baldly denied that his own consciousness informed him that there was such a thing as free will. The Cambridge Fellow retorted that there was nowhere their conversation could go since they could not find a common foundation on which to build, but he would speak to the audience members who might have a consciousness more akin to his own. He also pressed home to Bradlaugh that all of morality was built upon the assumption of free will—that without it, praising and blaming people for their actions would be irrational. Robert Owen (1771–1858), however, had brought notions of environmental determinism into the world of British popular freethought, and Bradlaugh aligned himself with this point of view.[21] For him, people were punished as a way of altering their circumstances and therefore their behavior, but Browne repeatedly pointed out that this was not equivalent to actually blaming them. This line of thought allowed him to end the last round with a series of accurate blows:

> We, in the same way, do use certain means to control, say, an idiot, and with the same object—that of exciting certain habits and correcting others; but we should not dream of blaming that idiot for acting accord-

ing to a nature which is diseased—for which he is not responsible—and I say that on Mr. Bradlaugh's theory—on the material theory—an idiot and a sane man are placed precisely on the same footing; they act as their nature bids them act, and no other way. (Applause.) [. . .] I say that all these influences which Mr. Bradlaugh has depicted are not certain in their operation; that still children reared in poverty, ignorance, and vice, do grow up good citizens—(hear, hear, and applause)—and I would be ashamed to say they did not; and that children, reared up with every possible advantage, do go hopelessly to evil—(applause)—and that that is in itself a lesson that there is somewhere the action of freewill. (Applause.)[22]

And what of Bradlaugh's side of the argument? His primary posture was purely destructive: "It is he [Browne] who has to prove miracles possible, and my duty is simply to point out the defects in the argument, as we go along."[23] He offered the classic deistic argument that miracles, as a violation of God's own laws for how the universe runs, would testify against the Almighty that he must have not been sufficiently wise and farsighted in his original arrangements. Perhaps his primary argument, already alluded to, was that in order to deem an act "supernatural," one would have to account for every possible natural force and every possible way it might work. As no one has an exhaustive knowledge of the natural world, however, one never has sufficient warrant to declare an act "supernatural," that is, a miracle. Another strong theme was that there was a direct correlation between the number of tales of miracles and the level of ignorance of a people:

> How is it that, when men were less capable of judging of them, they had them? This was well put by one of the Essayists and Reviewers, who shows the extreme difficulty there is in dealing with these things. It is not necessary to dispute the honesty of the witnesses. Go to France or to Italy today, and there among the peasants you will get pretence of miracles happening; but the whole of civilisation rejects that at once. You don't deny the truthfulness of the persons, but you say they are too ignorant and too superstitious to be capable of forming a judgment, that it is contrary to the whole of experience, and you reject them at once.[24]

He sized up shrewdly the apologetics argument that miracles were needed in order to convince people of the truth of Christianity during its infancy:

> Either, at one time of the world, they were necessary to convince men, or they were not. [. . .] Why should I have to take—with thousands of years intervening between, scores of centuries coming in between myself—the stories on the tradition of men not always trustworthy, on records not

always well kept, not always reliable, with hosts of myths and imagination around? Why should I be asked to take that as evidence from two thousand years ago, which could have come directly to me at this moment, if God had ever thought a miracle necessary for the conviction of human beings?[25]

Nevertheless, Bradlaugh's mind was not apparently that taken with a philosophical objection to miracles *qua* miracles. It is striking that it was Browne and not Bradlaugh who referred to David Hume. Indeed, Bradlaugh took immense pride in his personal library—a collection primarily focused upon works that could aid him in lecturing against Christianity and in favor of secular alternatives—yet in the over 7,000 volumes he collected there was not one that contained what is often regarded even today as the definitive critique of miraculous claims, Hume's essay on miracles.[26] Thus we come to the central argument of this chapter: Bradlaugh, and indeed the whole world of popular freethought in the Victorian era, was primarily interested in objecting to miracles only to the extent that such a line of argument served to undermine Christianity. Early on in the debate he clearly announced the payoff that he was hoping for:

> If miracles cannot be proved possible, and we are dealing now with the miracles of Christianity, then the whole foundation on which the Churches base their strength is cleared away, and the whole system tumbles at once, because you have knocked from under it its only stay.[27]

Theodicy was genuinely a looming issue in his patterns of thought. In Bradlaugh's own mind, miracles appear to be a far less absurd notion than the proposition that the world is governed by an infinitely good, all-powerful being, the suffering and injustice that we see all around us notwithstanding: "Our friend says he himself has experience that all things work together for good. Go down into your dark narrow lanes, into our police-courts, into places where there is crime and disease, and ask yourself whether all things work together for good."[28] Therefore, he could not resist having a go at Christianity whenever an opportunity arose during the debate. For example, one of his running themes was something as extraneous to the subject in hand as the assertion that the institution of slavery was "of the essence of Christianity."[29]

Browne was rattled into huffily intervening at one point in order to assert that the subject of the debate was miracles generally and not the plausibility or otherwise of Christianity in particular. Bradlaugh kept on angling for an opportunity to discuss biblical accounts of miracles. Browne was not giving it to him, however. When Browne referred casually to the miracles of Christianity, Bradlaugh tried to goad him into moving onto this ground: "He may understand what he means by the miracles of Christianity; but I do not understand, and I would ask him kindly in his next speech to state specifically the miracles of Christianity on which he relies."[30] Later on Browne did use Christ's stilling the storm as an illustration of what he meant by a miracle, but he was careful to insert the phrase "supposing that had happened as told to us" in order to underline that it was merely an illustration and not an importing of the New Testament as a (contestable) authority into the debate.[31] This left Bradlaugh merely to say that he "challenged the whole story"; having crossed the ocean himself several times, and therefore having experienced storms at sea, he would need to be offered sufficient evidence that such a thing was possible, and that evidence had not yet been presented.[32] Thus we have the contours of Bradlaugh's most concerted effort to address the question of miracles.

To stop there, however, would be to leave out the richest vein. Bradlaugh's polemics against biblical miracles were his real contribution to the debate, and this contribution lies elsewhere. David Tribe has referred to Bradlaugh's book *The Bible: What It Is* as his "*magnum opus.*"[33] The version printed in 1870, which shall be used here, was a 434-page commentary on the Pentateuch, written as an exposé. Bradlaugh lectured and wrote in an anti-Bible vein for his entire adult life, and this volume is typical of the whole of that output. He critiqued the Bible in three basic ways that he illustrated over and over again from a wide variety of texts: 1) the Bible is internally inconsistent and incoherent; 2) the morals of the Bible are inadequate, unacceptable, or positively unwholesome; 3) the Bible's portrait of the Almighty is an unworthy one. The latter point, for example, included all anthropomorphic language. Even something as seemingly innocuous as a statement that God said something would be pounced upon: "but speaking implies the possession by the speaker of the organs of speech, tongue, larynx, &c."[34] As to the middle category, there is no doubt that Bradlaugh was genuinely offended by the Old Testament's failure to be as explicit as he thought was necessary about the immorality of a whole range of behaviors. Nevertheless, even this theme appears to have been sometimes distorted by his overriding commitment to discredit the Bible in any possible way. Therefore, Bradlaugh was, on the one hand, deeply scathing about the Bible's seeming toleration of the institution of slavery. Yet, on the other, a rather fastidious morality triumphs over any sympathy for the enslaved Israelites. He found Exodus 3:22 worthy of considerable censure: "But every woman shall borrow of her neighbour, and of her that sojourneth in her house, jewels of silver, and jewels of gold, and raiment: and ye shall put them upon your sons, and upon your daughters; and ye shall spoil the Egyptians." This "borrowing" we are meant to find deeply shocking, a euphemism for ugly realities tantamount to blackmail or stealing.[35] He also censured Moses for his deceptive comment to Pharaoh that the Israelites wanted a temporary leave of absence to celebrate a religious festival when they actually wanted to escape from slavery permanently.[36] Bradlaugh's Victorian sensibilities were also offended by the mere fact that the Bible would record unvarnished accounts of heinous crimes.

His main preoccupation, however, was the game of trying to catch the Bible out on errors and inconsistencies. Bradlaugh announced at the start of *The Bible: What It Is* that his method would be to highlight "every weakness of the text, however trivial, that may serve to show that the Bible, or any portion of it, is fallible, that it is imperfect," and he must be given full credit for endeavoring to keep this promise.[37] In a debate he had with the Reverend Joseph Baylee in 1860, which was structured in an interview format so that the two men took turns interrogating each other, Bradlaugh spent the bulk of his time on such trivial questions as whether Jesus was actually in the tomb for three days or a shorter period than that according to the gospel narratives, and prima facie inconsistencies between the gospel accounts regarding how many times Peter denied Christ.[38] He thought that readers ought to find it troubling that, "The period of the sojourn in Egypt was, according to Exodus, 430 years, but was 400 according to Acts and Genesis."[39] Bradlaugh was also apt to exaggerate what was at stake in these matters. Here is a typical specimen: "upon the truth or falsity of the exception of the tree of knowledge of good and evil hangs the whole of the Christian religion."[40] Therefore, ironically, Bradlaugh was far more committed to a literal interpretation of Scripture than his Christian conversation partners.

Indeed, his repeated statements that all of theology or Christianity is destroyed if one particular point against a literal interpretation is conceded are belied by the fact that he frequently quoted liberal Christians in order to support his own position. Bishop Colenso, for example, is quoted throughout *The Bible: What It Is*, but it does not seem to occur to Bradlaugh that the bishop's ability to accept these critical points without abandoning his Christian identity testifies against his slippery-slope assumptions. Bradlaugh was aware that many Christian thinkers (he named Origen, for example) have interpreted the early portion of the book of Genesis as allegorical, but he viewed this as yet more evidence that the literal reading was untenable, while leaving his assumption that a literal reading was the only legitimate one unexamined. He also tended to elevate into Christian dogma every point (inferences even) that the Bible can be interpreted as making. For example, the notions that humanity is only 6,000 years old and that "all the animals were created at most a few days prior to man" are both declared to be biblical "doctrine."[41] At his worst, Bradlaugh could even work himself up into imagining that believers' "salvation" was at stake when endeavoring to resolve the ambiguity over "which day of the third month it was that the Israelites came into the wilderness" or that allowing uncertainty over the names of Esau's wives would overthrow all biblical authority.[42] His friend and fellow freethinker, John M. Robertson, wrote a warm memoir of Bradlaugh that was published in his daughter's biography of him. When reflecting on his many lawsuits and test cases, Robertson illuminatingly observed:

> Those who deprecated his legal way of fighting legal battles simply failed to appreciate the lawyer's method. That he was a born as well as a trained lawyer many lawyers have admitted; and he fought technically, and thwarted his enemies by technicalities, because law was to him a technique.[43]

Bradlaugh really did seem to think that he could get the Bible thrown out on a technicality.

As we move into examining Bradlaugh's handling of biblical miracles specifically, it is also worth offering a bit of a corrective to the picture thus far painted regarding the strength of his work, as these passages contain some of his most satisfying comments. At his best, Bradlaugh could give brilliantly dry commentary on biblical texts. Thus, in a way not unlike what some Christian apologists have done, he discussed aspects of natural history in the Middle East that might explain the phenomenon of manna, but only to then add, "The tendency on the part of the manna to fall in double quantities the day before the Sabbath, so as not to fall on the seventh day, is peculiar to the Bible species."[44] On the rescue of Lot from the immoral environs of Sodom, he observed, in a deftly coy allusion to one of the more unseemly narratives in Scripture: "nor does the preservation of Lot and his daughters from the destroying fire in any way result in any improvement of their moral condition."[45] Bradlaugh also had a delightful gift for high-hearted sarcasm, or even scurrility. Here he is on Melchizedek: "he had no beginning of days or end of life, and is therefore probably at the present time an extremely old gentleman, who would be an invaluable acquisition to any antiquarian association fortunate enough to cultivate his acquaintance."[46] On God's striking down Uzzah for touching the ark of the covenant in order to steady it after the oxen had stumbled: "This shows that if a man sees the Church of God tumbling down, he should never try to prop it up; if it be not strong enough to save itself, the sooner it falls the better for human kind—that is, if they keep away from it while it is falling."[47] As for the great patriarch of people of faith, he "remonstrated with the Lord, who explained the matter thoroughly to Abraham when the latter was in a deep sleep, and a dense darkness prevailed. Religious explanations come with greater force under these or similar conditions. Natural or artificial light and clear-sightedness are always detrimental to spiritual manifestations."[48] He particularly excelled, however, with the story of Balaam: "when the ass saw the angel she fell down. Balaam did not see the angel at first; and, indeed, we may take it as a fact of history that asses have always been the most ready to perceive angels."[49]

Bradlaugh's instinct to catch the Bible out on technicalities has the curious effect of almost making the more wondrous biblical narratives seem less implausible than they otherwise might. For example, the story of Adam and Eve eating from the tree of knowledge of good and evil, discovering that they were naked, and sewing fig leaves together to make themselves aprons (to use the language of the Authorized Version), is anticlimatically found to be implausible on the last point. It is unlikely that they would have had a sewing kit, he argued—this time with painful earnestness—and "admitting that there had been such things as needles, if the fig leaves were the same then as now, they were not of a nature and texture capable of holding together by such a process."[50] Likewise, to move into one of the more oft-challenged miraculous narratives of the Bible, the improbability that he most highlights when handling the book of Jonah is the unlikelihood that there would have been enough sackcloth available for the entire population of Nineveh.[51] On the other hand, Bradlaugh was on good form with the sailors' decision to cast Jonah into the sea in order to quell its unrest: "I should like to see an episcopal prophet occasionally thrown overboard during a storm. [. . .] happiness to many at the mere cost of one bishop." And Jonah's repentance: "Poor fish! [. . .] it must be disagreeable to have one's poor stomach turned into a sort of prayer meeting."[52]

So, once again, it is more the alleged absurdity of the Bible and of Christianity than that of miracles that is on display. Bradlaugh occasionally does move beyond this, however, in this material, in order to make a few epistemological observations. Like the Enlightenment figures who made doubting Thomas their patron saint, Bradlaugh read the murmurings of the Israelites against the grain:

> If the Israelites frequently doubted Moses and disbelieved in God, with the terrible series of plagues fresh in their recollection can it be wondered that we, to whom they are related in a style so incoherent, at this distance of time, should also have misgivings as to their truth?[53]

His most astute comment was, again, not one on the inherent impossibility of miracles but rather on their limited utility:

> While these wonders might have induced the Israelites to consider Moses a very extraordinary man, it is difficult to conceive how they could influence the belief of the Israelites as to the existence of God. Miracles may evidence a power out of the range of the beholder's experience, but can hardly demonstrate a theological proposition.[54]

All of this both helps to clarify an understanding of the wider world of Victorian, popular freethought and is, in turn, clarified by it. It is not at all clear that British plebeian infidelity was a coherent philosophical tradition, but it is unquestionable that it was an anti-Bible tradition. Thomas Paine might have been a deist and Charles Bradlaugh, an atheist, but what they had in common was a strong desire to debunk the Scriptures. Indeed, this was arguably the single unifying stance that brought together "freethinkers" of many different stripes and gradations throughout the nineteenth century. For example, in his debate with Browne on miracles, Bradlaugh countered his opponent's assertion that God is a person with the statement, "I cannot conceive immaterial persons."[55] Today, this might seem a rather obvious proposition for secularists to rally around, but this was not at all the case then. In fact, a considerable section of popular freethinkers were also spiritualists. Although he was not a spiritualist himself, G. J. Holyoake's popular, secularist publishing firm issued works in favor of spiritualism. As they would never have published works defending the Bible or Christian orthodoxy, one can take it that being opposed to traditional Christianity was essential to the movement, but being a materialist was not. Bradlaugh was a materialist, but given his own milieu, he had to invest many hours into researching spiritualism and to treat the topic with due respect:

> Spiritualism was a subject to which he had given considerable attention for nearly twenty years prior to this debate. He had devoted a large amount of time to the reading of spiritualistic literature and the investigation of spiritualistic phenomena. He had taken part in many *séances*, and had seen different mediums, but except in one or two cases the sittings had led to nothing.[56]

The debate referred to took place in 1872 between Bradlaugh and James Burns, the editor of *The Medium*. The president of the National Secular Society was sufficiently agitated to intervene on a point of order when Burns, who was himself opposed to Christianity, expounded on how popular radicals did not need to choose between their two movements:

> I hold before me here the "Principles, Objects, and Rules" of the National
> Secular Society, and to the whole of these I am ready to subscribe in every
> iota. And I would say further, that there is no possible collision between
> these facts of psychology and the principles of Secularism. There can be
> no possible collision. Why, the greater number of my friends, up and
> down the country, have once been Secularists. I have Mr. Shepherd, of
> Liverpool, taking the chair for me when I go to Liverpool; I have another
> gentleman, who is a Spiritualist, and is also proprietor of a Secular Hall
> in a part of Yorkshire; and I have the editor of the *Spiritual Magazine*,
> who use to stand upon the Secular platform [. . .].[57]

Numerous freethinkers, some of them prominent leaders in the movement, converted to spiritualism. They often continued to identify with the
secularist cause as well. Moreover, the movement's deceased heroes were apt
to make spectral comebacks with, for example, both Thomas Paine and
Emma Martin, a popular infidel lecturer, offering insights from beyond the
grave.[58] While very much still alive and embodied, Robert Owen himself,
the great patriarch of the popular attack on Christianity in the name of
"rationalism," converted to spiritualism. In a particular gift for the purpose
at hand, he announced his belief that communication with "departed spirits" was indeed happening by declaring that it was "an apparent miracle."[59]
As we have seen, Bradlaugh honored Owen as an elder statesman in the
movement and was influenced by his thought on the crucial subject of free
will, so his case brings the complication of the issue of popular critiques of
the miraculous closer to home.

It finds its way all the way to Bradlaugh's own domicile, however, in the
case of Annie Besant (1847–1933). By most any standard, Besant was a
remarkable woman. Accomplishments of hers as notable as becoming the
first woman president of the Indian National Congress party lie entirely outside the scope of the present discussion. For the purpose at hand, it is necessary to recall that she and her Anglican clergyman husband had
permanently separated. She then moved into infidel circles (joining the
National Secular Society in 1874) and immediately emerged as a major
leader in the movement and Bradlaugh's closest companion. Bradlaugh's own
marriage had also been an unhappy one. He had separated from his wife—
who was an alcoholic—in 1870 (she died in 1877). For about a decade,
Besant and Bradlaugh were besotted with one another. Although there is no
reason to suppose that sexual intercourse was ever a part of their relationship,
even his daughter (who did not like Besant) felt it necessary to concede in
her proper, Victorian biography of her father that "a friendship sprang up
between them of so close a nature that had both been free it would undoubt-

edly have ended in marriage."[60] Make no mistake, however, Besant was a real gift to the movement, a person of extraordinary abilities. Bradlaugh and Besant went on holidays together and speaking tours around the country. She was a regular writer for his atheistic newspaper, the *National Reformer* (and eventually coproprietor of it with him); they founded and ran together the Freethought Publishing Company; and they defiantly published a birth control manual and together as codefendants fought the obscenity charge and court case it provoked. He was president of the National Secular Society and she was vice-president. In short, she became the most prominent popular champion of atheism in Britain beside her closest friend, Bradlaugh himself.[61]

In 1889 Besant converted to theosophy. Once again, she quickly became a leader in her new movement of choice, eventually becoming president of the Theosophical Society. Theosophy meant that she was a firm believer in reincarnation and karma and, in general, that she was keen to mix components of eastern religions into her own belief system. She eventually adopted a son, Jiddu Krishnamurti, and—to the extent that a rank outsider can grasp the intricacies of theosophic thought—seems to have developed the conviction that he was the incarnation of a Hindu god who would usher the world into a new era. A few years before her death, Besant recalled (in a version of a story that had gone through several redactions) that she had been, of all places, in the offices of the *National Reformer* in the spring of 1889, when she heard a voice say, "Are you willing to give up everything for the sake of truth?" To which she—one of Britain's most famous atheists—dutifully replied, "Yes, Lord."[62]

Still, at that time, the jump from secularism to theosophy was a shorter one than one might imagine today. Bradlaugh the lawyer had always emphasized the issue of evidence. They were atheists, not because they knew there was no god, but because they lacked sufficient evidence for the existence of one. He was ready to investigate patiently the evidence for spiritualism, rather than reject it on a priori grounds. Besant simply found the emerging evidence for spiritual realities more compelling than he did. Crucially, the Theosophical Society was "aggressively anti-Christian" during these years.[63] Indeed, it appears that Helena Blavatsky (1831–1891), the cofounder of the Theosophical Society, went out of her way to recruit Besant for the movement precisely because she wanted another strong female leader who also had a pronounced antipathy toward Christianity.[64] Bradlaugh, of course, was bewildered and disappointed by this turn of events. He dismissed theosophy as "a kind of Spiritualism in Eastern phraseology," but, as has been shown, that was really to give the game away, as it had already been established, to the satisfaction of many, that spiritualism was not incompatible with secularism.[65] Indeed, although theosophy was really rather too much, what a broad tent popular freethought was at this time may be illustrated by the fact that "to the last Mrs Besant continued to write for the *National Reformer*."[66] As she could have never continued to write for this atheistic paper if she had found her way back to orthodox Christianity, the point is once again underlined that Victorian popular freethought was built more on an anti-Bible, anti-Christian orthodoxy stance than any shared, positive principles such as materialism.

Charles Bradlaugh was an atheist and a materialist, but he could not remake popular Victorian unbelief into this image. Indeed, even his own intellectual passion resided far more in criticizing the Bible and attacking Christian orthodoxy than in philosophical categories and commitments. Therefore, it was perhaps more apt than he realized that Bradlaugh adopted "Iconoclast" as his *nom de plume*. His critique of miracles was first and foremost a rejection of biblical miracles, and his followers were often even less committed than he was to the more general principles that he evoked against the miraculous. An examination of popular polemics against miracles in the Victorian era serves to underline the very large extent to which nineteenth-century popular freethought was animated and held together by a common, vehement rejection of the Bible.

Chapter 8

The Appeal of Victorian Apologetics
Thomas Cooper and the Case
for Christian Orthodoxy

In 1845, Thomas Cooper (1805–92), after having just spent two years in jail for seditious conspiracy, defiantly described himself on the title page of his poem *The Purgatory of the Suicides* as "Thomas Cooper, the Chartist." This is the Cooper upon whom historians have focused their study. The only biography of him was published in 1935, and its main focus is given in its title, *Thomas Cooper, the Chartist*.[1] Likewise, although G. D. H. Cole's sketch also covers the whole of his life, its very inclusion in a volume titled *Chartist Portraits* indicates which part of his life gained the most attention.[2] More recently, Stephen Roberts, in a master's thesis on Cooper, simply limited the scope of his study to the first half of Cooper's adult life.[3] Nevertheless, there is another Thomas Cooper. For the last three decades of his life he toured the country giving addresses on Christian apologetics, describing himself on the title page of his most popular book and four others as "Thomas Cooper, Lecturer on Christianity." Even more accurately, when his wife died in 1880, he identified her husband on the gravestone by giving himself the title "Lecturer in Defense of Christianity."[4]

Moreover, if a major portion of Cooper's life and his most popular book have largely been ignored by historians, so has the entire field of Victorian apologetics. Bernard Reardon's study of *Religious Thought in the Victorian Age*, which focused on figures such as F. D. Maurice, John Henry Newman, and Benjamin Jowett, is typical of the path generally trodden.[5] It is indicative of the general neglect of this subject that the only secondary source that integrates this area of discourse into a general view of the theology of the period is one which was itself written in the Victorian age, John Hunt's

Religious Thought in England in the Nineteenth Century.[6] Nor has a study
focusing on this particular field been produced. This is perhaps not too surprising as it is always more tempting to study past ideas that foreshadowed
what was to come in subsequent generations, and the whole point of apologetics is to take advantage of the worldview that already exists rather than to
signal the one that will emerge. It is an area of thought particularly, almost
inherently, prone to becoming dated. Nineteenth-century apologetic arguments are generally considered today to be about as convincing as those of
that other Victorian obsession, phrenology, only not nearly so entertaining.
Nevertheless, one of the chief attractions of studying the past is the insights
that can be gleaned from its very "otherness," and the neglect of this area of
theological discourse has left a regrettable gap in our understanding of religious and intellectual currents in the nineteenth century.

A study of Cooper's apologetic efforts is especially well suited to shed-
ding light on this wider field of study. Cooper was an insatiable reader.
When he once claimed, "I have read every treatise and sermon on Christ's
resurrection that I could possibly get hold of," he was not making a groundless boast.[7] Moreover, he saw the work of popularizing the best of the existing apologetic literature as a central component of his self-imposed task. A
section of one of his books is subtitled, "A Popular Treatise, designed as an
introduction to the reading of Samuel Clarke, Paley, Butler, Gillespie, etc."[8]
Cooper declared in one of his early, unpublished lectures—lectures that
revealed the apologetic style and ideas that he would maintain throughout
his final decades—that it must be remembered, "I profess to use no new
arguments for Deity—that I only produce in my own language the arguments which have been produced by different minds in different ages."[9]
Cooper's lectures are littered with recommendations and critiques of relevant
books, particularly ones that were written in the eighteenth century or after,
including recently published items from his own contemporaries. In short,
an examination of Cooper's apologetic writings cannot only help to correct
an imbalance in our understanding of the life and mind of one Victorian,
but might also serve as a starting point for surveying a much wider field of
neglected literature.

The only book of Cooper's that is still read today is his autobiography,
The Life of Thomas Cooper Written by Himself, which was reprinted in
1971.[10] In it, he recounts his impoverished childhood with his single-parent
mother, his work as a shoemaker and then a schoolmaster, his youthful religious zeal and days as a Wesleyan local preacher, his move into journalism,
his days as a militant Chartist, his trial and time in prison, his move into
freethought, his pre-reconversion lecturing activities, his literary efforts, his

return to orthodoxy, and his embarking on his final career as a Christian apologist. Two facts of his life story need to be particularly highlighted as a context for examining his apologetic efforts. Firstly, Cooper had little formal education. His thinking should be judged by the standard of the kind of self-education that it was possible for a working-class man to achieve by reading on the margins of his days the books he happened to be able to obtain, rather than by pitting it against the ideas of the most gifted intellectuals of his generation who had the freedom to do with their time as they wished and who had access to elite institutions and resources. Secondly, Cooper was a free-thinker during the 1840s and the first half of the 1850s, and as far as the debt could be laid at the door of any author, his dissatisfaction with orthodox Christianity is attributable to the intoxicating effect that reading George Eliot's translation of D. F. Strauss's *Leben Jesu* had on him. Cooper's apologetic work *The Bridge of History over the Gulf of Time* (1871) was by far his most successful publication.[11] In 1885, when he published his last book, the advertisements at the back showed this work had sold 24,000 copies, while his *Life*, which had been originally published in the same year, came in second with 14,000 copies. Therefore, not only have historians neglected the contents of his most successful book, but it is ironic that the only other of Cooper's work, which has been reprinted in recent decades, is his *Cooper's Journal*, the seemingly more ephemeral publication in which he had popularized Strauss's teaching and the very work which his *The Bridge of History* sought to undo.[12] *The Bridge of History* was the first of five volumes that his publisher called "Thomas Cooper's Christian Evidence Series." The others were: *God, the Soul and a Future State* (1873), *The Verity of Christ's Resurrection from the Dead* (1875), *The Verity and Value of the Miracles of Christ* (1876), and *Evolution, the Stone Book, and the Mosaic Record of Creation* (1878).

Two large, untabulated ledgers in which Cooper recorded his lecturing activities have been preserved. When this data is compiled, it reveals that in his Christian apologist phase alone he delivered 4,292 lectures and preached 2,568 sermons. These efforts were made in 545 different cities, towns, or other distinct localities from Inverness to Jersey.[13] Most English towns saw him repeatedly over the years. To take a typical example, he lectured in Halifax during the years 1858, 1860, 1868, 1871, 1876, 1881, and 1885. Undoubtedly, these dogged efforts at sheer physical presence were an important factor in the success of his volumes and in his general influence. Long before his reconversion, Cooper's varied career had already amply proved that he was a captivating orator. Even the Secularist journal, the *Investigator*, in an article that strove to minimize the importance of his reconversion by belittling his past achievements (including his celebrated *The Purgatory of Suicides*), was nevertheless forced to concede that he was "for several years the most popular lecturer on Free Inquiry in the metropolis, and always commanding crowded audiences."[14] In the late 1850s, when his reconversion was still a novelty, Cooper's lectures received considerable attention. The *Bradford Review* recorded in 1858:

> A good deal of interest was excited in Bradford by the announcement that Mr. Thomas Cooper, the well known author of "The Purgatory of Suicides," and other works, would deliver a series of lectures in defense of Christianity, and on Monday evening, a large concourse of people assembled in St. George's Hall, to hear the first lecture.[15]

Skeptics would come to give rebuttals, charging the atmosphere with the excitement of combat. When Cooper and the Secularist leader G. J. Holyoake agreed in 1858 to turn their separately arranged lectures in Norwich into a public discussion, "long before the time for commencement of the proceedings, the Hall was densely crowded in every corner—in fact, so inconveniently so, that the greatest disorder prevailed."[16] In the early 1870s, however, Cooper decided that these clashes were unprofitable and thereafter did not allow members of the audience to speak at the end of his lectures. This decision had a significant effect on the nature of his work:

> I found that when I sturdily refused all attempts to draw me into discussion, the Secularist working men began to fall off in their attendance on my discourses. From that time I bent all my endeavours on preventing young Christian men from falling in the Secularist snare [. . .].[17]

Efforts to find local newspaper accounts of his lectures in a range of towns in the 1870s and 1880s have all been unsuccessful, although reports have been found from these same places of his visits in the 1850s. In other words, he was increasingly preaching to the faithful—often literally so, as his venues were frequently chapels and he was often asked to deliver the Sunday sermons. For example, in 1878 Cooper wrote to a friend that he had recently been in Whitby "preaching & lecturing in the Wesleyan chapel."[18]

Not that his audience had changed completely. An atheist named Wightman who had written him a "venomous, diabolical *secret* letter" six years earlier, hounded Cooper when he came to Worcester in 1879, trying to destroy his credibility with a local minister, publishing an attack on him, and, moreover, he and other skeptics were antipathetic guests at public worship when Cooper was the preacher.[19] This took an emotional toll on the elderly apologist, who wrote to his wife, Susanna:

> I did not tell you how much I had endured, during the week, from Wightman's malignity—nor can I tell you now [. . .] The effort to throw it all off & go on with my work, as if nothing has occurred made me feel the recoil, yesterday [. . .] I cannot fully throw off the sadness yet [. . .].[20]

On the other hand, even his sermons could sometimes tempt those who normally held aloof from public worship to give him a sympathetic hearing. He reported to Susanna on Sunday evening worship in Norwich, "I had a crowded audience of young men & strangers, last night, who listened to my sermon on the Atonement, with most breathless attention."[21] Nevertheless, his main work, by default if not design, was primarily building up the resistance to skeptical thoughts of people whose faith was already fairly strong.

Throughout his life, Cooper rarely allowed maintaining a secure income to become a high priority, and therefore he frequently found himself in financially precarious circumstances. His lecturing life was not a lucrative one, and his self-imposed rules made the task of making ends meet all the harder: he always lectured for nothing and resisted the temptation to confine his itinerary to more prosperous communities. He took voluntary collections, sold his books, and hoped that these sources of revenue would be greater than the expenses involved.[22] In his daily letters to Susanna, Cooper anxiously reported the amount of money he received. A report from Tewkesbury reads: "[o]nly £1-15-0 collection & 7.6 for books last night."[23] Burton-on-Trent was one of the more remunerative places on his tour, but he nevertheless wrote: "I fear the cost of St. George's Hall & the bills will seriously lessen my receipts from the Collections—but we must remember that we depend on God—not on Man, except as God's instrument."[24] Moreover, he frequently could not resist an impulse to help those in need. In addition to supporting needy relatives, his response to a letter from a Scottish widow is typical: "[s]he has been gathering potatoes at 1/- per day [. . . and now winter is coming]. I can ill afford it—but I am sending her 10/-. 'He that giveth to the poor lendeth to the Lord.'"[25] The price Cooper paid for this attitude toward money was that he was forced to stay on the lecturing circuit despite his own advanced years and poor health.

Cooper's return to orthodox Christianity was a gradual process.[26] Its public manifestations began on 13 January 1856 when he dramatically interrupted his own lecture on "Sweden and the Swedes" to announce his belief in a Moral Governor of the universe, and culminated in his being baptized on Whit Sunday, 1859. He remained an evangelical General Baptist for the

rest of his life. Cooper's first major attempt at apologetics came in 1856 in a
series of lectures to his erstwhile fellow freethinkers at the City Road Hall of
Science in London.[27] His detailed notes for the first five of these addresses
have been preserved. They reveal many of the lines of thought that he would
expound in print in the 1870s.[28] This early foundation can also be seen in
his habit of citing in those books objections to the arguments that were made
during debates in his first years as an apologist.[29] The very first lecture was
titled, "The Being, Power, & Wisdom of God: the Design Argument re-
stated: selection of striking instances of Design," and throughout all five lectures the argument from design loomed large. Cooper believed that it was
the most useful line of apologetic reasoning available. In response to the fact
that his friend Cooper had embraced it, Holyoake made a fresh attempt to
answer the Paleyan argument. Holyoake's response, however—a logical
approach in which he attempted to show that the argument was self-defeat-
ing because its assumptions could be applied to the Almighty himself, thus
leading to "an endless rank and file of Deities"—was not obviously more
intellectually satisfying than Cooper's position.[30] A different tack taken in a
debate with Cooper by another skeptic was not irresistibly compelling either.
Joseph Barker attempted to turn the alleged evidences for design in nature
against the notion of an all-powerful deity by arguing that the need to design
was a tacit confession of weakness because necessity is the mother of inven-
tion.[31]

The argument from design was undoubtedly attractive to Cooper per-
sonally. A major outlet for his enormous intellectual curiosity was the natural world. As a boy Cooper "often longed to know the names of flowers,
which none could tell."[32] Susanna shared this passion. Some correspondence
between the Coopers and their horticultural friend, Mr. Whitwell, has survived. It reveals the avid and systematic way in which the couple collected
plants. Cooper begins yet another request for a coveted cutting with the
words, "[m]y dear blue-stocking will not be content."[33] The natural world
never failed to delight him, and Cooper, as a Christian, instinctively felt that
this wonder should provoke praise for the Creator. This personal sense of the
fitting nature of the argument from design dovetailed with Cooper's not
unrealistic assessment that it was a mode of thinking that it was not easy for
freethinkers to dismiss. This latter perspective even tempted Cooper in his
1856 lectures to taunt his opponents with the challenge that they could not
explain what power had caused the evidences of design in the natural
world:

> Is this Power—"Nature"? Then what is Nature? Is Nature material—or is
> it composed partially of the immaterial or spiritual? "Oh, no; we are

materialists," it will be replied; "we acknowledge no spiritual existence whatever.["] Well then shew us how matter can adapt itself—how it can form man & beasts & birds and fishes, and insects and plants & so on. You cannot shew us how Matter or Nature can do all this.[34]

Despite the widespread assumption today that the Darwinian theory of evolution stripped Paley's argument of its force, this impression was not quickly made. When Cooper debated the atheist Charles Bradlaugh in 1864 (five years after Darwin's *On the Origin of Species* had been published) not only was he still using the argument from design (as he would do for the remainder of his life), but Bradlaugh himself made no reference to theories of evolution in his attempt to refute it. Instead, like Holyoake and Barker, he expounded a philosophical response, which was not obviously more compelling than Paley's logic.[35] In this case, Bradlaugh claimed that the argument was based on a false analogy because it is "impossible to reason from design of that which is already existing, and thus to prove the creation of that which before did not exist."[36]

Because the so-called "battle between science and religion" in general and the evolution debate in particular has already generated a great deal of scholarship, it would not be particularly profitable to center a study of Cooper's views on revisiting this territory.[37] Nevertheless, as it was one of the themes of his lectures and writings, it is necessary to give this subject some attention before moving on to discuss less explored regions of Victorian thought. The first thing that needs to be said is that not only did Cooper formulate his apologetics in a pre-Darwinian intellectual environment, but he also (like many others) evaluated and rejected theories of evolution during those earlier years. In one of his 1856 lectures he criticized "the school of Lamarcks [sic], the French Naturalist," which has "striven to restore the old exploded Greek doctrine of appetencies or desires."[38] He also had already made a careful reading of *Vestiges of the Natural History of Creation* (1844).[39] Nevertheless, although Cooper was already set on an apologetic tack from which he would not be deflected and he approached the debate somewhat with the air of a man who thinks he has heard it all before and already answered it, he still made a serious effort to tackle this new intellectual challenge. In 1878, when he was seventy-three years old, Cooper wrote playfully to Whitwell:

> *So: you* are reading periodicals,—while I am toiling through big books—Haeckel—& other monsters! I am determined to know what they *all* say, & to know it *thoroughly*. I have just gone through Lyell's "Principles of Geology" for the 2nd time. Many parts of it are delightful reading.[40]

Cooper's volume on evolution and geology, published in 1878, endeavored to offer a historical summary of the books that were considered landmarks in these fields, and his more argumentative sections are filled with references to an array of thinkers. In addition to mentioning the ideas of the major British contributors to the current debate—Darwin, Lyell, Wallace, Huxley, Tyndall, and Spencer—he alludes to the American, Asa Gray; the Germans, Haeckel, Virchow, Nageli, and Carl Vogt (as well as Goethe); and the Frenchmen, Lamarck, De Maillet, Geoffroy St. Hilaire, and Doucher de Perthes. Beside praising the older science of Cuvier, Linnaeus, Buckland, Sedgwick, and their heirs, Sir Roderick Murchison and Dr. Whewell, Cooper cites a wide range of figures to add weight to specific scientific points he is making. One of his main lines of attack is to argue that Darwin has unreasonably demanded "unlimited time" for his evolutionary process.[41] Cooper, while accepting a much older earth than some conservative readings of the Bible would allow (citing the theologians Drs. Chalmers, Vaughan, and Hamilton in order to reassure members of the faithful who might be uneasy with this) and giving his approval to "the Nebular or Cosmical theory of Laplace," nevertheless argues that the existing geological evidence clearly indicated that the earth was not as old as Darwin needed for his theory to be viable, citing the work of Helmholtz, Sir William Thomson, and Professors Croll and Tait in support of this judgment. Moreover, this summary is by no means an exhaustive list of the scientists and other thinkers referred to by Cooper. As to specifically apologetic works, Cooper recommended Dean Buckland's Bridgewater treatise and Sir John William Dawson's *The Origin of the World, according to Revelation and Science* (1877).

In short, Cooper primarily criticized Darwinism by appealing to the authority of other scientific opinions rather than that of revelation. The need for such an attempt to be made, however, and its inclusion in a series of apologetic writings, of course, indicated his belief that this theory could undermine orthodox Christianity. One reason for this conviction was that it was becoming clearer that Darwin's theory was a threat to his cherished argument from design. One almost gains the impression that he found it hard to imagine an orthodox Christian denying this argument, thereby virtually turning it into a doctrine and creating an ironic situation in which an apologetic has to be developed in order to defend an apologetic.[42]

His central objection was the extent to which Darwin's theory denied the uniqueness of the human race and the destructive implications this was felt to have in the field of moral philosophy. In Cooper's last book, a collection of essays on everything from industrial strikes to Handel's *Messiah* titled *Thoughts at Fourscore and Earlier,* he included an essay on "Charles Darwin, and the fallacies of evolution" and another one on "The Origin of Man." His comments on Darwin himself are gracious, claiming that he was "undoubtedly, a benefactor to his race" and taking several paragraphs to describe his personal virtues before going on to critique his theory with such now familiar points as that it was not based in "*real* proof: *Fact*-proof." His main argument, though, was that there is a huge gulf between humans and apes. The differences he perceived between the two species he catalogued in detail, ending with what in his view was the most crucial one, humanity's possession of a moral and spiritual nature.[43] In the other essay, he admitted that some Christian young men and even ministers had told him that "a man may be a good Christian, and yet hold the whole of Darwin's doctrines to be true," but he nevertheless warned that if this theory spread, so would skepticism. He then went on to promote the more noble views of humanity articulated by Max Müller.[44] Moreover, Cooper had read Strauss's last book, *The Old Faith and the New,* which was published in London in 1874, and the connection between evolution and unbelief was surely reinforced in his mind by seeing his rejected master abandoning orthodoxy yet more thoroughly and replacing it with Darwinian thought.[45] Even the nonreligious phase of Cooper's life might have helped to reinforce these intellectual instincts: he was deeply rooted in the culture of self-help, which was in turn grounded in an emphasis on human dignity. When he was still a freethinker, he wrote a popular pamphlet titled *Eight Letters to the Young Men of the Working-Classes.* In one of these letters he encouraged them to learn classical languages, answering those who questioned the utility of this with the explanation: "[I]t will give you the key to unlock a grand treasury of thought— the most valuable riches to every man who does not pride himself on being merely an animal."[46] Cooper could not reconcile some of his core beliefs with an evolutionary view of "the descent of man," and his solution to this tension was to reject Darwin's theory.

Some scholars have wrongly (and anachronistically) deduced from this stance and other emphases of his that Cooper was a fundamentalist. John Saville, in his introduction to the reprinted *Life,* refers in the very first paragraph to Cooper's "fundamentalist Christianity" and condemns the volumes that this chapter explores with the words: "[h]e wrote and published a great deal of fundamentalist theology, now all unreadable."[47] An annotated, critical bibliography edited by John Burnett, David Vincent, and David Mayall claims that Cooper published "fundamentalist theology."[48] At the time of the 1856 lectures, Cooper was by no means a conservative Christian. In one of them he denied the traditional teaching on hell, confessing "if I admitted the doctrine of eternal punishment & endless misery for men's errors, I must give up my conviction of God's perfect goodness."[49] Nevertheless, he did eventually settle into being an evangelical and perhaps it would be fair to say one of the old school. He was not, however, a forerunner of the new school that was to come, fundamentalism. While fundamentalism is not a monolith, the comments listed below, most of them gleaned from the apologetic writings themselves, could, taken together, hardly be found a place in any variety of it. On the issue just covered, Cooper denied a literal six-day creation, admitted that the earth was millions of years old, and occasionally even seemed to concede the possibility that the theory of evolution might be valid for forms of life below the human.[50] He censured Christians who stirred up interest in the possibility of Christ's second coming being imminent.[51] Cooper candidly admitted that his studies had convinced him that the ending of Mark's gospel given in the Authorized Version did not belong to the original document.[52] He confessed that he thought the biblical accounts of Christ's temptation in the wilderness might be merely "a parabolic description of His own mental conflict."[53] Finally, he wrote on what would become the shibboleth of fundamentalists:

> Whatever may be pronounced, at some future period of the Church's history, to be the *true* theory of inspiration (for, although eighteen centuries have passed away, the Christian Church, as yet, has *not* pronounced what is the *true* theory), it will be a theory which admits the fact that *verbal* inspiration does not characterize every part of the Scriptures [. . .].[54]

The label "fundamentalist" is therefore misleading unless it is used in such a sloppy way that it is synonymous with orthodox Christianity or evangelicalism.

Although he did not feel the force of theories of evolution, his beloved Paleyan approach to apologetics was not free from assault, even in the privacy of his own thoughts. For Cooper, "the most formidable objection to the design argument" was "the existence of pain and suffering."[55] Indeed, in his freethinking days he had found this critique decisive. Holyoake took delight in reprinting various reports from the *Reasoner* on Cooper's skeptical lectures, including one in 1848 in which he confessed "the very fact of there being *adaptions in [the universe] for pain and misery* make me *doubt that it had any Designer at all.*"[56] As an apologist, Cooper's lame response to this objection was to try to minimize the problem: "I find there is not so much Pain and Suffering in the world, as I formerly thought there was." He went on to illustrate this in various ways, including quoting a passage from a book by the missionary-explorer, David Livingstone, the point of which was to argue that being eaten by a lion was not nearly so unpleasant as some might suppose.[57] Repeatedly, Cooper resolved intellectual tensions in his own mind in this unsatisfying way. In their debate, Barker used the problem of pain as his main line of attack, and in the course of his response Cooper made the questionable decision to try to deny that infant mortality was an evil.[58] These arguments were a perverse tribute to how forcibly Cooper continued to feel the objection that if there were an all-good, all-powerful deity, there would not be suffering and evil.

A recurring theme in Cooper's apologetic work is his determined effort to refute Strauss, whose ideas challenged the historical reliability of the Gospels, including Christ's miracles and bodily resurrection. A large portion of *The Bridge of History* is devoted to marshalling evidence against Strauss, whom he summarizes as teaching:

> that the reason why upwards of 300 millions of human beings are now numbered among the professors of Christianity, the reason why the highest and wisest nations of the earth now profess this religion, and why millions upon millions have professed it in past centuries, is solely because a weak fanatical woman first imagined she saw Jesus in the garden where his sepulchre was [. . .].[59]

The bulk of his response to Strauss is an ingenious presentation of conservative biblical criticism in the generic sense—what might be called anti-biblical criticism in the sense that he was, in defiance of the currents of the modern discipline, endeavoring to demonstrate the truthfulness of traditional beliefs concerning the gospel narratives. Cooper was convinced, not least from his own experience, that Strauss's ideas were potent: "[t]hese blows have knocked many a man down, to my certain knowledge: many a man who has never got up again."[60] *The Bridge of History* was his most original contribution to apologetic thought. In contrast to the rest of his Christian evidence writings, Cooper does not cite many authors in the anti-Strauss section of this book, and he seems largely to have developed his own response to what he called "the mythical theory." In 1850, the clergyman and author Charles Kingsley had confided to a correspondent:

> But there is something which weighs awfully on my mind,—the first number of Cooper's Journal, which he sent me the other day. Here is a man of immense influence, openly preaching Straussism to the workmen, and in a fair, honest, manly way, which must tell. Who will answer him? Who will answer Strauss?[61]

Ironically, Cooper seems to have answered this call himself. He carefully examines the biblical texts, finding what he believes are internal clues regarding their time and place of composition and, most of all, marks of authorship corresponding to what is said to be known of Matthew, Mark, Luke, and John. He particularly excels with the second gospel, which he claims Mark based on the preaching of the apostle Peter. Taking the account of Christ calming the storm, he shows how Mark alone mentions that the Lord was asleep on "a pillow," which, moreover, Cooper says should have been translated from the Greek as "the pillow," a detail that only Peter would mention because he fondly remembered that "he had always provided a pillow for his dear Master's head, in his own boat, and most likely, had not one himself."[62] He goes on to show that Mark provides the most precise statement about the cock crowing as a sign of Peter's denying Christ, and that while other gospels merely say that Peter wept, Mark says, "[w]hen he thought thereon, he wept," thus indicating that this gospel writer had heard him speak of his thoughts. Mark's habit of using the word "immediately" betrays the "phrase and manner of an energetic speaker."[63] Peter was preaching in Rome, and this explains why Mark's gospel includes explanations of Jewish customs, which, if written in Jerusalem, would have been "like carrying coals to Newcastle." A case is made for the traditional authors of the other gospels as well. For example, Luke, who is said to have been a doctor, does not deny that the woman with the issue of blood could not be healed by her physicians, but, in contrast to Mark, he does not admit that her condition grew worse under their care: "he will not let his profession down."[64]

Cooper made another major effort to refute the mythical theory in his volume on Christ's resurrection. Much of the book is dedicated to answering criticisms arising from alleged difficulties in the biblical narrative. Although he addresses many specific points in detail, his general reaction to the synoptic problem is to note: "[I]f half the effort were made to unravel the difficulties in the Gospel narrative, which is often made by a company of clerks to correct the week's accounts in a bank ledger, the 'divarications' in the last chapters of the Four Gospels would soon vanish."[65] He then goes on to provide some ingenious attempts to solve some of these problems, such as identifying the three days Christ was said to have been in the tomb, on the grounds that "experience has taught me that it is better to remove the smallest causes of cavil from the minds of workingmen, than to let them go unanswered."[66] Cooper confesses that he feels it is his duty to provide a little entertainment in order to keep an audience of laborers awake for a night lecture, and he contemptuously dismisses, but plays for laughs, the solution "a real Cockney" gave at one of his lectures to the question of how Christ obtained his postresurrection clothes: he found them in a nearby garden shed; hence Mary Magdalene thought he was the gardener.[67] Demonstrating that the narrative is internally coherent, however, falls considerably short of proving that someone has been raised from the dead. His response to this wider issue is merely to pay double or nothing with what is at stake by arguing that most people would like to believe in an afterlife and Christ's resurrection is the only sure ground for such a belief. Anticlimactically, he also notes, in a delightful bow to respectable Victorian sensibilities, that if Christ did not rise from the dead then there are no grounds for keeping the Christian Sabbath.

All of this, however, was merely negative—an attempt to refute the mythical theory. In his *The Verity and Value of the Miracles of Christ*, however, although Cooper explicitly answers his own *Cooper's Journal* and the Straussian ideas it contained, he also moves beyond this into a personal apologetic regarding his own abandonment of freethought and a more positive line of argument. Cooper tellingly reveals that whatever else he had doubted, he had always continued to admire Christ's "moral beauty." This proved to be a wedge that opened a way out of Strauss's castle: "[g]radually, the strong conviction grew within me that the perfectly holy and spotless character of Christ itself was a miracle, and the greatest of all miracles."[68] This account of his intellectual and spiritual journey is confirmed in his private correspondence. Cooper had confided to Kingsley in 1856: "[c]an you tell me what to do—anything that will help me to Christ? Him I want. If the Four Gospels be half legends I still want him."[69] In the end, for Cooper, the figure of Christ revealed in a traditional reading of the Gospels was more compelling than the theories of Strauss.

Although Cooper viewed the argument from design as the most effective one he had to offer, the one that most satisfied his own mind was the moral argument. This line of thought was central to Cooper's own intellectual history and took a prominent place in the worldview that he developed. He had answered Strauss by using Christ's perfect moral nature as a door leading into the whole realm of orthodox Christology, and he believed that the existence of a moral nature in human beings functioned in a similar way on the more general issue of theism. Cooper challenged his audience to think about their own moral nature:

> How come you to have it? There is but one possible answer:—Because it has been given to you by the Moral Governor to Whom you are responsible. Your very possession of the Moral Nature proves His existence. And it was the conviction of the great thinker, Immanuel Kant, that it is the strongest and most undeniable of all the proofs of God's existence.[70]

Cooper was sincerely and deeply impressed by the moral argument. He was still teaching it in his last book, recalling as an octogenarian that it was this argument that had conquered his unbelief all those years ago.[71]

Cooper's apologetic efforts largely consisted of popularizing the various lines of argument that had already been well established by others. Although he appealed to Kant's authority to bolster the moral argument, he was not deterred by the fact (assuming he recognized it) that "the great thinker" believed that more traditional apologetic arguments lacked force. Cooper placed the moral argument side by side with the classic a priori argument and the argument from design as a trilogy of proofs of God's existence. Holyoake ridiculed this the-more-the-merrier approach in a pamphlet he wrote on Cooper's lectures as "a companion to his missionary wanderings" in 1861. Holyoake claimed that his old friend had "opened a theological Curiosity Shop," noting, "[a] priori, à posteriori arguments, abandoned even by the Evangelical Alliance, Mr. Cooper galvanizes and sets in motion again."[72] Undeterred, Cooper persisted in this approach in his book God, the Soul and A Future State.

The a priori argument was, in Cooper's hands, a mixture of philosophy, logic, common sense assertions, and the occasional suspiciously sharp turn in the argument. The section of his book that outlines it is indebted, as he freely acknowledges, to a contemporary work, W. H. Gillespie's The Argument, a Priori, for the Being and Attributes of the Lord God (1833).[73] On the question of the existence of the soul, Cooper attempts to refute a materialist view of human nature by marshalling various bits of scientific theory and medical case studies. This material is used to develop a pseudoscientific argument, which claims that all the cells of our bodies are repeatedly replaced over the course of our lives and therefore the merely physical cannot give us the continuity of identity that is demonstrated by our memories. On the existence of an afterlife, he uses various approaches, including another look at what having a moral nature implies, but his favorite and perhaps most original argument is an endearing reflection of the man. Cooper, the self-educated shoemaker whose obsessive study habits led to a physical break-down, suggested that the desire within a human being to know ever more was a clue to a nature designed for immortality:

> And do we not all know that the more we learn to know, the more we thirst to know? It is only sheer ignorance that has no desire for knowledge. [. . .] Is the wisdom of God so abortive as to make a being of boundless desires for knowledge, only at the end of a few years to put him out of existence? [. . .] The Progressive Nature of Man—if I use the most cir-

cumspect language—is a strong *presumptive* argument for a Future Life for Man.[74]

Cooper's Christian evidence writings are littered with references to a wide range of authors, from apologists to skeptics, from scientists to poets. This is well illustrated by his volume on miracles. Originality is not the aim, but rather exposing working-class men to the ideas of the cogent books and great minds that have taken the orthodox view. He freely remarks after popularizing one argument: "I would not have you suppose that this is any discovery of mine."[75] Although he also refers to items published recently, one of his main approaches is to claim that the current skeptical objections had all been raised and answered in the eighteenth century. He identifies the works of "the Old English Freethinkers": notably, Shaftesbury's *Characteristics*, Blount's *The Oracle of Reason*, Tindal's *Christianity as Old as the Creation*, Woolston's *Discourses*, and Hume's *Essay on Miracles*.[76] He also lists those who endeavored to answer them, authors who together comprise a "library of 'Apologetics'": Bentley, Samuel Clarke, Boyle, Stillingfleet, Locke, Leslie, Chandler, Hugh Farmer, Campbell, Gilbert West, Lord Lyttelton, Lardner, Leland, Ray, Derham, Smallbrook, Sherlock, Bishop Watson, and, of course, Paley and Butler.[77] Cooper then makes this appeal: "[l]et me earnestly recommend young working men to read their books, which take up all the objections to Miracles current in their times, and which fully answer those objections."[78] For good measure, Cooper notes that a contemporary freethinker, John Stuart Mill, had also criticized Hume's argument.[79] He also praises Prebendary Row's *The Supernatural in the New Testament*, Ralph Wardlaw's *On Miracles* (1852), and James Mozley's 1865 Bampton lectures. The various arguments of these works are popularized, strung together into an unfolding argument, and leavened with Cooper's own ideas, opinions, and illustrations.

Cooper's own intellectual curiosity rings out in his *God, the Soul and A Future State* in his references to various works of secular learning from Aristotle's *History of Animals* to Sir Astley Cooper's *Lectures on the Principles of Surgery*. Abandoning all apologetic purposes, he even printed as an appendix an extract from a work by the medical pioneer, William Harvey, just in case his illustration had aroused interest in a particular theme of anatomy.[80] Cooper does cite Huxley's *Lay Sermons* (1870) and criticize such thinkers as Hume, Spinoza, and Darwin, but many of his targets are from his own milieu of popular radicalism: Holyoake, Robert Owen, a Sheffield Socialist named Richard Otley, and various unnamed people whom he had heard make contributions to discussions and debates.

In addition to the mythical theory, *The Bridge of History* makes a lengthy response to "the sun theory," the argument that what is called Christianity is only a new form of the old fable of the sun personified as a god, found in ancient Egyptian, Persian, Greek, and Indian thought.[81] Cooper identifies Drummond's *Oedipus Judaicus*, Higgin's *The Anacalypsis*, and Volney's *The Ruins of Empires* as in this tradition. He also notes that in his own lifetime these ideas had been promoted among English freethinkers by Robert Taylor, who taught them in London and included them in his book, *The Diegesis* (1829). In response to this theory, Cooper seeks to demonstrate the historicity of Jesus Christ. He works backwards from the present, identifying the nineteen "arches" on "the bridge of time," which represent the nineteen centuries from Christ. Sometimes he does little more than recount secular history. "The arch of King Alfred" prompts him to talk of the English love of liberty and even to praise some words of Gladstone on extending the franchise that had warmed "the heart of the old Chartist prisoner." The apologetic purpose he rescues from this arch illustrates a wider theme that Christian Englishmen are part of a noble tradition: "our religion is the religion of Alfred, it is the religion of Wyckliffe, and Latimer, and Lord Bacon, and John Milton, and Oliver Cromwell, and Sir Isaac Newton."[82] And so it goes on, back to the "arch of the Apostles," ostensibly demonstrating that there was no plausible point in time when a god such as the sun theory requires could have been invented but, on the contrary, there is good historical evidence for believing that Jesus actually did exist.

Thus we have the main arguments of a leading popular Christian apologist of the 1870s. It might be useful, however, to examine, in addition to what he was saying, what Cooper thought he was doing—to look at his views on the role of apologetics and his expectations regarding what he might achieve. He had no illusions that his task was an easy one, but one of his goals, especially initially, was nothing less than to set people on an intellectual journey that might lead them back to Christ. He once gave a glimpse of his own view of his mission:

> I do not imagine, or expect, that I can win over, at once, to Christianity, the minds of sceptical workingmen, who may be listening to me. I know too well, by personal experience, how hard it is to part with sceptical convictions—how difficult it is to bring a mind, which has become strongly warped in the direction of unbelief, to enter upon a determined, steady, and persevering consideration of the Christian Evidences. And without this—without an earnest and devoted study of Christian Evidence—no thinking sceptic (for I am not addressing vulgar scoffers) can ever become a real Christian.

> I seek no flighty converts from your ranks—no sudden passing over to our side from yours, of some hot, excited partisan, who is incapable of thinking. I seek to lead you to accept what I believe to be Truth, by inducing you to practice the daily reflection, the steady conning over and over again of each item of the Christian Evidences, which effectually cured my doubts, and rendered me a settle and grateful believer.[83]

But even that, he confessed elsewhere with remarkable candor, was not enough without some predisposition toward faith:

> Common as it is for writers on the Evidences to assert, that it needs but the employment of their ordinary powers of understanding for men to become convinced of the Truth of Christianity, I believe that that is not true [. . .] I find that I must receive many things for solid truth which I cannot reason out, logically [. . .] I cannot live in a world of cold negations. It is a wonder to me that other men can live in such a world. But I do not condemn them for it. I only wish that they felt the satisfaction, the happiness, the thankfulness that I feel in receiving Christianity.[84]

In conclusion, a few more general comments need to be made regarding the nature, content, and, most of all, context of Cooper's apologetic work. Cooper was not a particularly original thinker, but his lack of originality is beneficial when it comes to exploring the wider scene of Victorian apologetics: his approach being to review all the arguments in defense of orthodox Christianity being utilized at that time and the best of the literature expounding them, both from the previous century and his own day. Cooper's task was not to be a seminal thinker but to be an effective popularizer. Moreover, he was a veteran Chartist who was explicitly seeking to influence the working classes, particularly young, working-class males. Britain had a fair number of respectable, professional theologians and ecclesiastics engaging in the work of articulating an erudite defense of Christian doctrine, and the country had numerous humble ministers faithfully proclaiming the traditional gospel; but a working-class layman who had imbibed a significant portion of the learned literature for and against orthodox beliefs and who endeavored to distill it in an apologetic form for mass consumption was a rarer breed. This is where Cooper's true significance lies. In 1856, when he had still not quite found his way back to orthodoxy, Cooper remarked prophetically to Kingsley: "I preached Christ as the living Saviour, during 7 years of my life, while a Wesleyan Local preacher. It is not *that* I want to do again: I think I have a much more important work to do than that."[85] His *The Bridge of History* was published in July 1871 and during that very same month his publisher, Hodder and Stoughton, also brought out *Modern Scepticism*, the first volume sponsored by the newly founded Christian Evidence Society. This society, however, represented very different worlds from those of the former shoemaker from Gainsborough in terms of class, learning, and ecclesiastical distinction. The contributions to that first volume included essays by two Oxford professors, three bishops, the archbishop of York, and a preface by a peer of the realm. C. J. Ellicott, the bishop of Gloucester and Bristol, commented in an "explanatory paper" on the nature and purpose of this new organization that these lectures "were specially designed to meet some of the current forms of unbelief among the educated classes."[86] Apparently the Society was willing to leave the rest of the work to men such as Thomas Cooper.

PART THREE

The Politics of Free Church Polity

Chapter 9

Free Church Ecclesiology
Lay Representation
and the Methodist New Connexion

Unless they happen to have exhibited particularly exotic or quixotic traits, historians usually do not have much time for small, defunct, religious denominations. The Methodist New Connexion, founded in 1797, made the mistake of championing fairly innocuous and sensible ideas that later became ubiquitous throughout Methodism, and has paid the penalty of having its history neglected. For example, even a volume with such a promising title as *Conflict and Reconciliation: Studies in Methodism and Ecumenism in England, 1740–1982* manages to ignore the Methodist New Connexion altogether.[1] The few modern discussions of this denomination that have been produced are all around thirteen pages or less in length.[2] Nevertheless, an examination of this largely forgotten movement has the potential to provide a uniquely illuminating case study of the relationship between evangelicalism and the rise of the laity.

No one was more likely to raise the question of the Methodist New Connexion's denominational *raison d'être* than its own champions and leaders. William Cooke, a prominent New Connexion minister, noted in a sermon in 1847:

> We are members of the Methodist New Connexion. We exist apart from the Parent Body; there must be a cause for this [. . .] the most fastidious need not murmur if we give a reason for our Denominational existence, and our distinctive principles.[3]

The *Methodist New Connexion Magazine* argued in 1850 that, "Every member ought, especially in the present day, to understand our system, and be able to give to every man a reason why he prefers it to other systems of Methodism."[4] Some ministers would even adopt a catechetical style on this point: "But if we are so much like the Wesleyans, why are we not one body? I will tell you."[5] This was a denomination with a sense of its own mission and fidelity to truth.

The notion of "emancipation" was central to this self-perception. The words "freedom," "liberty," and "rights" are littered throughout New Connexion writings. A review in the denominational magazine of a memoir of Alexander Kilham, the most prominent founder of the denomination, claimed that the book would be treasured by "every lover of religious liberty" and that its subject labored "in the cause of Christian freedom."[6] The marble monument at Kilham's grave declared that he was "a zealous defender of the rights of the people."[7] The preface to the denomination's jubilee volume looked forward to the day when "the church [would] be emancipated from priestly assumption," the point being that the Methodist New Connexion was in the vanguard of this movement and from its happy position could not resist extolling the joys of liberation.[8] In 1854 there was a widespread movement to change the denomination's name on the grounds that their connexion could no longer be considered "new" with accuracy. One of the most popular alternatives proposed was "The Methodist Free Church." Some people felt that this might be invidious, but William Cooke argued that they need not be ashamed to proclaim their emancipated condition: "The truth is we believe ourselves to be '*Free*.' We are '*Free*,' not only in doctrine but '*Free*' in every branch of our polity."[9]

The Dissenting community as a whole placed a high value on taking a stand on principle, and the New Connexion prided itself on existing solely in order to assert and exemplify great principles.[10] It is a matter of public record that at the denomination's jubilee tea party in 1846 the faithful consumed 1,000 pounds of currant bread, 1,000 pounds of plain bread, 130 pounds of butter, 50 pounds of tea, 300 pounds of coffee, 47 gallons of cream, and 300 pounds of lump sugar.[11] Nevertheless, they did not live by currant bread alone, and we are assured that at this same event "the benignant and scriptural principles of the New Connexion were fully appreciated; and it is only proper to say that there never was a time when they were so ardently admired, or so warmly espoused, as at the present day."[12] The *Methodist New Connexion Magazine* could wax eloquent on this subject: "Yet God has been graciously with us. He has given us to see that our principles are immortal, and become fresher with age."[13] It even went so far as to note solemnly that "those who know, and understand, and prize our pure, scriptural principles, should hold by them to the death."[14] The core members of the New Connexion held to their principles sincerely and tenaciously and were determined to exist as a denomination for as long as it was left to them to maintain this witness.

So what was it that they thought they had been emancipated from and what were the principles they espoused? The jubilee volume defined the principle that was the denomination's *raison d'être* as: "That the Church itself is entitled, either collectively, in the persons of its members, or representatively, by persons chosen out of and by itself, to a voice and influence in all the acts of legislation and government."[15] Fifty years later, in the centenary volume, the relevant passage included more details of the denomination's constitution:

> The office of the ruling elder in the Methodist New Connexion is the distinguishing feature between it and the Parent Body. The admission of an officer so called to the exercise of power alongside the teaching elder, so as to give ministers and laymen equality of authority in all deliberative and legislative assemblies, is the sole point remaining out of the many causes of dissension and final rupture in the struggle for Methodist reform one hundred years ago. This indeed was the main cause of difference then [. . .].[16]

This principle was often referred to more succinctly as "lay representation." The denomination's magazine spoke of "their distinctive principle—lay representation."[17] The specific formula used to enact this principle was an equal number of ministers and lay representatives at all levels of collective decision making including most particularly the highest one, Conference itself. Those governed by it were reminded that, "The Conference was formed on the principle of admitting an equal number of preachers and lay representatives, freely chosen by the people from amongst themselves."[18]

This principle was grounded in various arguments, with the biblical one not necessarily being preeminent. The jubilee volume could happily slip it into the middle of a list: "truth, reason, scripture, and justice, required this concession to the people."[19] An article published in 1847 listed four major reasons for embracing it:

1. We think it *reasonable* and *just* [. . .].
2. We find the principle is recognized in the New Testament [. . .].
3. The principle of Lay-representation was maintained in the ancient Church *after* the times of the Apostles [. . .].
4. The principle of Lay-representation enters into the economy of all Protestant denominations [. . .].[20]

Indeed, its "reasonableness" was often the first apologetic offered, and denominational writers seemed to take a particular delight in finding this practice reflected in the church government of other denominations and in the writings of the early church fathers. Notably, the jubilee volume (mainly by inserting sizeable extracts from other books) felt a need to ground the polity of liberal Methodism in references to Clement, Ignatius, Polycarp, Tertullian, Cyprian, Origen, Ambrose, Augustine, and "the Rev. Dr. Buchanan's account of the Syrian Christians."[21] Nevertheless, such material was invariably coupled with a careful sifting of the relevant biblical clues. The New Connexion used as a kind of motto to encapsulate the rightness of lay emancipation a quotation from Matthew's gospel: "one is your Master, even Christ; and all ye are brethren" (Matt 23:8). Moreover, to set these arguments in competition with each other is to defy how the members of the denomination themselves actually perceived their interrelationship: "On this subject, as on every other of practical importance, Reason and Revelation are seen—not in hostile attitude, employed in the demolition of each other's work, but harmoniously uniting." In terms of theological reflection, the principle of lay representation was said to be an expression of the Protestant notion of the priesthood of all believers. The *Methodist New Connexion Magazine* claimed in 1872, "When the royal priesthood of believers—of *all* believers—is understood, this question will be happily settled."[22] It was routinely argued that Methodism as a whole had emancipated laymen to works of service such as local preaching and that then to thwart them with the other hand by excluding them from rule was unjust, vexatious, and untenable. The Wesleyan body, however, as several modern scholars have ably shown, was by the early Victorian period articulating a rival principle that asserted the rights and dignity of the pastoral office.[23]

Notwithstanding its championship of lay rights, the New Connexion was not crudely anticlerical. The assessments in the centenary volume perhaps owed something to the respectability to which the denomination aspired in the late Victorian era rather than faithful historical perspective, especially when they claimed that the New Connexion "was established not more to vindicate the proper standing of the laity in the Church, than to obtain for the ministry its proper functions and prerogatives," and that the Connexion sought "to emancipate the preachers."[24] Nevertheless, such claims were grounded in incontrovertible historical facts. Kilham began his career as a reformer by publishing a pamphlet in which he argued that Methodist preachers should be allowed to administer the Lord's Supper. The Wesleyan Conference disapproved of his actions and sent him to Aberdeen as a punishment.[25] Nevertheless, he continued to campaign for the preachers to be granted full ministerial rights. Moreover, a tone of respect for the ministry can be found throughout the history of the New Connexion. In 1854, for example, the *Methodist New Connexion Magazine* published a long discourse titled "Loving Esteem for Ministers."[26] The Connexion saw the maintenance of a perfect balance between the rights of ministers and laymen as part of the genius of its system. In 1839 the magazine included an article titled "The Wesleyan, Congregational, and Methodist New Connexion Systems Compared." With the term "compared" acting as a euphemism for "contrasted," the article set out to demonstrate that its own polity achieved the golden mean:

> Our Conference, the governing assembly of the connexion in all general matters, being constituted of an equal number of Preachers and Lay-representatives, must necessarily lend its aid, to prevent the ministry being trampled upon, as complained of under the congregational system; and, as necessarily, [unlike Wesleyanism] it must act for the general benefit of the people, in accordance with their properly expressed wishes.[27]

Whatever views it might hold of Congregationalism, the New Connexion's witness against the Wesleyan system was much more germane to its *raison d'être*. Simply put, it justified its existence on the grounds that while Methodism was a good and necessary thing, the principle of lay representation was sufficiently important to make continuance within a denomination that did not recognize it as an unacceptable compromise. The jubilee volume justified the denomination's existence with a rather sharp analogy:

> Popery necessitated Protestantism, and so long as the Church of Rome cleaves to its errors and corruptions, so long must Protestantism be perpetuated, both as a witness against it, and as a means of reforming it. And so long as the Wesleyan constitution and government remain unaltered, so long must the New Connexion remain a system of antagonism.[28]

When someone suggested in 1854 that the denomination's name be changed to the "Wesleyan Free Church," a correspondent spoke for many when he claimed, "to call us 'Free Wesleyans,' would be about as incongruous as to speak of [. . .] free bondmen."[29] Even as late as 1875, abusive language was still in order:

> The Wesleyan Conference [. . .] has a spice of the arrogance of ecclesiasticism. It prides itself in its pastoral prerogatives and its clerical separateness. It has a pharisaic consciousness (not to say boastfulness) of these

things, and it robes itself with hauteur respecting the validity of its ecclesiastical superiority which contrasts rather strongly with its professed spiritual humility.[30]

One hundred years after the bitter fights that occasioned the first secession
from Wesleyanism, the wounds were only just healing.[31]

The Wesleyans, equally, were not above hurling abuse at the opposite
camp. A favorite technique was to attack Kilham. Repeatedly, articles
appeared in the *Methodist New Connexion Magazine* that were prompted by
Wesleyan aspersions on the most eminent of the denomination's founders:
for example, "The Wesleyan Magazine and Mr. Kilham" (1843); "The character of the Rev. A. Kilham and of our Connexion Defended" (1848); and
"The Rev. Alexander Kilham defended against the malignant slanders of the
'Watchman'" (1854).[32] On the positive side, the magazine deemed it necessary in 1851 to reprint a sympathetic obituary of Kilham from the supplement to the *Gentleman's Magazine* for 1798.[33] Notwithstanding their habit
of vindicating their ancestor, New Connexion apologists were sensitive
about their denomination being too strongly identified with Kilham and did
not wish to defend him in such a way that might be construed as denominational devotion to an individual. The following is a typical disclaimer: "It
has been a prevalent impression that our body originated in *personal sympathy* with Mr. Kilham [. . .]. But the impression is not correct. The Connexion
did not originate in personal sympathy, but in *principle*."[34] The article even
goes on to argue that Kilham was not the founder of the New Connexion;
he was only one of the founders and not the one who became its first president. The habit of referring to members of the New Connexion as
"Kilhamites," which is indulged in by some modern Methodist historians
(most of whom sympathize with the Wesleyan view of the ministry championed by Jabez Bunting), would have appeared to those concerned as inaccurate, insensitive, and unfairly partisan.[35] The New Connexion was ready and
willing to engage in a vigorous debate about principles and resented being
confronted instead with *ad hominem* attacks.

Members of the New Connexion always hoped that disgruntled
Wesleyans would not establish a new denomination, but would consider the
New Connexion their natural haven. Although they missed the big catches,
this expectation was reasonable enough to cause a great deal of flirtation.
One of the hazards of becoming a self-declared home of freedom is that it
constitutes an open invitation for rivals to emerge who claim to offer even
greater liberty. Following abortive negotiations for a union between the New
Connexion and the Wesleyan Methodist Association in 1837, Robert

Eckett, the dominant figure in the Association, began to champion a new principle, "circuit independency," boasting of the superior freedom it secured. When the next crop of reformers emerged in the late 1840s and the first half of the 1850s, the New Connexion again tried to direct the traffic toward itself. In a notice in the *Methodist New Connexion Magazine* concerning a pamphlet by a Wesleyan Reformer, which advocated union with the New Connexion, the reviewer suggested that "our lay friends should purchase copies by hundreds and thousands for gratuitous circulation."[36] Robert Currie has observed that during "times of agitation in Wesleyanism, the New Connexion Book Room's output increased by 25–50 per cent."[37] Eckett, who was busily fishing in the same pool, responded by repeatedly attacking the New Connexion without worrying too much about whether his actions gave the impression of being animated by malice. The *Methodist New Connexion Magazine* probably devoted more space in 1850 to refuting and counterattacking Eckett than to any other subject.[38] By the time the jubilee volume was in circulation, Eckett's judgment was viewed in New Connexion circles as so perverse as to be the exception that proved the rule: "It will, however, gratify our friends to learn that every review or notice given by editors of other publications has been of a decidedly favourable character, except that written by Mr. Eckett."[39] Nevertheless, his actions appeared to bear fruit: the Reformers ultimately decided to join forces with the Association, thereby creating the United Methodist Free Churches. The New Connexion was repeatedly hampered in such negotiations by its tendency to view the proceedings as a takeover rather than a merger. No longer the vanguard in the cause of Methodist freedom, the New Connexion was left to emphasize that there were evils on the left as well as the right. The magazine quoted approvingly the disillusioned Reformer who claimed that his body was "degenerating into the wildest notions of ultra-democracy."[40] Even the irenic Primitive Methodists were attacked for alleged imperfections in their polity, which was said to lean to the opposite extreme from that of the Wesleyans. As late as 1897, by which time ecumenism was very much in the air, Primitive Methodist church government was summarized in this combative manner: "Its features are ministerial disability in relation to the Conference, legal predominance to lay officialism, and the absence of provision for the direct representation of the Church."[41]

The propaganda of certain Wesleyans notwithstanding, Kilham and the early members of the New Connexion cannot justly be accused of having been Jacobin revolutionaries.[42] A more plausible charge might be that the New Connexion sought to import the secular values of a liberal democracy into the church. This accusation presumes that these two forces ought to be incompatible. Many people, however, would shrink for the extreme expression of this opinion made famous in Jabez Bunting's dictum that, "METHODISM [was] as much opposed to DEMOCRACY as to SIN."[43] For better or worse, New Connexion apologists unashamedly argued that the spirit of the age was correct in its liberal tendency and that they were proud to be in step with it in this regard. They did not even blush to tell the church that it ought to catch up with the British constitution: "The representative system of government, which, as Britons, we hold so dear, and on which alone, as we have been made to feel, our civil liberties can securely rest, is equally adapted to religious society [. . .]."[44] Such comments are ubiquitous in New Connexion literature. If the charge of Jacobinism had to be endured, the countercharge was also hurled that the Wesleyan powers were "ecclesiastical tories."[45] The New Connexion was dimly aware that some would argue that it was undignified and corrupting for the church to borrow its beliefs from the body politic: "Civil government, we are told, is earthly [. . .] but the Christian church is a purely Divine institution." It answered this objection with the claim that "great principles and modes of procedure may exist which are equally applicable to both."[46] For those who were still uncomfortable, the eye of faith might just be able to see the process as happening in reverse: "The method of government practised in the Apostolic Churches in many respects resembles that embodied in the civil constitution of England."[47]

The suspicion that the New Connexion was flowing with broad currents of British social and political thought rather than simply being propelled by the abstract logic of great principles is reinforced by its failure to emancipate laywomen. Even though the laity was represented in all the decision-making bodies of the denomination, only laymen were eligible to be representatives. Even classes comprised entirely of women were required to find a man to represent them.[48] In 1869, when a plan to unite with the Bible Christians had reached the stage at which all potential obstacles needed to be addressed, the New Connexion was reassured on the issue of women preaching: "It was stated to the Committee that this usage was gradually passing away, there being now only one female preacher among the Bible Christians."[49] The jubilee volume included a section on "The usefulness of Females," but the problematic nature of the role of women was amply illustrated by the wistful reflection that it was unfortunate that Methodist women were unable to become nuns.[50] The charge that unreformed Methodism emancipated the laity when it came to works of service but then thwarted it when it came to the exercise of power would have been even more apt if it had been applied to the situation of laywomen.[51]

The New Connexion was always a small body in comparison to both Wesleyan and Primitive Methodism: it began in 1797 with around 5,000 members, had around 10,000 in 1822, 30,000 by the end of the century, and ended its separate existence as a denomination in 1907 with approximately 40,000 members.[52] Currie has noted Methodism's general "sensitivity to statistics," and in demonstration of this, the New Connexion was clearly embarrassed by its failure to mushroom into a great force. A recurring feature of its literature is interminable, statistical articles attempting to prove that, although significantly smaller than many other denominations in absolute terms, its rate of growth was equal to or greater than that of those larger bodies.[53] One such article, titled "They say we don't get on: is it true?," having browbeaten would-be critics with an impressive mathematical barrage, proceeded to an anticlimax with the words: "all we want now is cordiality, prayerful exertion, and strong faith in the promises, and soon the little one shall become a thousand, and the small one a strong nation."[54] This sensitivity, together with a predictable interest in the wider cause of its *raison d'être*, encouraged the New Connexion to take a great deal of vicarious pleasure in witnessing the spread of the principle of lay representation among other Methodist bodies. It would patiently rehearse the intricacies of the constitutions of every body from the Bible Christians to the Primitive [i.e. Church] Methodists of Ireland, noting how each embraced the principle of lay representation, and it never tired of noting: "that the Methodist New Connexion is the Leader of Liberal Methodism. All the other Bodies of Methodists, apart from the Old Connexion, *have adopted its distinctive principle* [. . .] they have not adopted a *new principle*."[55] Moves toward increased lay participation in Methodist bodies were tracked with the keenest interest. The following comments on events in the Methodist Episcopal Church of America in 1859 typify the New Connexion's triumphalist attitude on this matter:

> The above resolution shows that the principles for which our forefathers in the New Connexion struggled and suffered are rising to the ascendant; for if the above resolution be adopted by the General Conference of America, as recommended, the great principle which fifty years ago had no advocates in Methodism, except among our own people, will be incorporated by four out of every five of the whole Methodist people: and, in fact, our friends of the British Conference, and those under its care, will be the only residue, forming a small minority, who refuse its adoption; and even of these we see no reason for despondency. *The Truth is mighty, and must prevail.*[56]

Concomitant with such optimism was the question of Methodist union: if the denomination's distinctive principle was no longer distinctive, then the question of its continuing separateness needed to be reopened. From the 1830s onwards, the New Connexion sporadically flirted with the idea of union with various other Methodist bodies. Nevertheless, as the original standard-bearer for Methodist reform, it could smugly argue that it was the task of the newer denominations to explain what distinctive principle they espoused that kept them from throwing in their lot with the New Connexion. A more fundamental question concerned the implications of favorable moves that were evident in the parent body. Already in 1847, Cooke, commenting on changes that had allowed Wesleyan laymen onto various committees that served Conference, observed that:

> Since Lay-men are taken to the very doors of Conference, it can scarcely be expected they will not, ere long, be taken a little further. We hail these advances, and should rejoice to see the day when such further advances will be made in the economy of Wesleyanism, as will annihilate all remaining distinctions, and prepare the way for all the branches of the Methodist family [. . .] to become identically one [. . .].[57]

From 1878 onwards Wesleyan laymen were represented in Conference itself. Members of the New Connexion claimed that the structure of this concession (notably a ministerial "upper house") and the restrictions that hedged it round precluded any assumption that the Old Connexion now embodied their distinctive principle. This alteration, however, undoubtedly indicated that for any subsequent generation sufficiently inspired to pursue union, the barriers would not be found to be insurmountable.

The movement toward union became complete when the Methodist Church was formed in 1932, a body that embraced the principle of lay representation and that merged the Wesleyans and the Primitive Methodists with the United Methodist Church. The United Methodists were themselves the product in 1907 of a merger between the United Methodist Free Churches, the Bible Christians, and the Methodist New Connexion.[58] Thus the triumph of the New Connexion's distinctive principle had deprived it of its *raison d'être*, thereby signaling its extinction as a separate body, and its relegation to historical obscurity. If it could never boast that it had enlisted vast numbers of people into its ranks, it could justly take pride in having fought and won the battle for the emancipation of Methodist laymen. Moreover, it also appears to have possessed the gift of prophecy. The centenary volume of 1897 had predicted:

Our witness to the rights of the laity in the government of the Church will not be forgotten. But there is less need of that testimony to-day than at any period in the past, and as other Churches continue to travel on the same lines as ourselves the need will diminish still more and more as time advances. Bearing such testimony is therefore likely to be a matter whose importance will recede until it reaches the vanishing point, and whose principal interest will be for the student and the historian.[59]

Chapter 10

Free Church Politics
and the Gathered Church
The Evangelical Case for Religious Pluralism

As the decades of the first half of the nineteenth century progressed, English evangelical Dissenters increasingly aspired to reform society in line with the ideal of religious equality before the law.[1] The disestablishment of the Church of England was the central, specific objective at the heart of this developing project. At a cursory glance, it might appear sufficiently natural that those excluded would harbor a desire to destroy the offending institution that one could easily overlook the fact that this stance was far from inevitable, and that it needed to be, and was, grounded in a precise, coherent worldview articulated in cogent language. This point is underlined if contrasting examples are brought into view: both the Unitarians and the Wesleyans endured their exclusion from the church establishment in the first half of the nineteenth century without embracing the cause of disestablishment. Moreover, an objection to church establishments in principle was not even the historic stance of the two denominations at the center of this chapter: the Congregationalists (or Independents) and the Baptists. Most of their forebears in the Cromwellian era took the idea of a state church for granted, and some of their coreligionists who emigrated to New England even went so far as to establish Congregationalism.[2] It is perhaps least satisfying of all to imagine that evangelical Dissenters had imbibed a secular program of reform, as there was no English secular current in favor of disestablishment strong enough to pull them along, and Dissenters had been as horrified as anyone by the antireligious spirit manifest in the French Revolution. A more persuasive grounding for this reform movement needs to be uncovered.

The most important internal change in the life of these denominations in the late eighteenth and early nineteenth centuries was their embracing of evangelicalism.[3] The dynamism of the evangelical movement is the principal reason for the remarkable numerical growth that the Congregationalists and Baptists enjoyed during this period.[4] The result of both this new wind of the Spirit and the growth it produced was a fresh sense of self-confidence. A reforming ethos was nurtured by a rising belief in their own importance and power: they now saw themselves as a force in the land that had the potential to provoke change. Several occasions when Dissent felt a need to flex its social and political muscles and duly made an impression gave momentum to this view: the defeat of Lord Sidmouth's bill (which was aimed at restricting Dissenting preachers) in 1811, the repeal of the Test and Corporation Acts (which officially, though not usually in practice, excluded Dissenters from public offices) in 1828, and the defeat of Sir James Graham's factory bill in 1843, clauses of which would have placed control of the education of the young firmly in Anglican hands.

The theological exactitude and earnestness of evangelicalism precipitated a deepening rift with the Unitarians which became a formal breach in 1836.[5] As the Unitarians had generally nurtured a desire for a comprehensive church establishment, and as they had often taken the lead in representing the political and social interests of Dissent as a whole, removing their influence fostered the further development and articulation by evangelical Dissenters of their own distinctive vision for reform.

Even before the so-called "age of reform," the notion that church establishments were wrong in principle was widespread in English Dissenting circles. The continuity of this tradition throughout the period 1780–1850 is neatly illustrated by a volume that unequivocally expressed an objection to all religious establishments, *The Protestant Dissenters' Catechism*, which was first published by the Independent minister Samuel Palmer in 1772 and which reached its twentieth edition in a version revised by the Baptist minister William Newman in 1831.[6] A prominent Congregational layman, Josiah Conder, published *On Protestant Nonconformity* in two volumes in 1818 and an abridged version in one volume in 1822. This work also offered a careful investigation of the establishment principle with the aim of demonstrating that it was erroneous.[7] On the other hand, Conder began his discussion of this issue apologetically by addressing the charge that Dissenters were unpatriotic criminals and walked gingerly thereafter. It was only after the repeal of the Test and Corporation Acts in 1828 that Dissenters felt sufficiently secure and confident in organizing to propagate their reforming views.

The first such effort, founded in 1830, was the Society for Promoting Ecclesiastical Knowledge, which, its vague title notwithstanding, was a vehicle for presenting the case for the separation of church and state.[8] Perhaps the very coyness of its name indicates that Dissenters were still uneasy about making a firm stand in public. From 1835 this society published relevant articles in its own organ, the *Ecclesiastical Journal.* A bolder public step was made in Manchester in 1834, when George Hadfield, a leading Congregational layman, who in addition to being a champion of the Dissenting vision for reform was also leading the attack on the Unitarians, recorded the event in his unpublished journal-*cum*-autobiography. Hadfield wrote that on 5 March 1834:

> The Manchester Dissenters held a public meeting at the Exchange Rooms, Mr. Harbottle in the chair two nights, and resolved on a petition to the House of Commons for the separation of the Church & State which received 34,000 signatures [. . .].[9]

Moreover, various local voluntary church associations were created in the mid-1830s with the aim of championing the alternative to the establishment principle. For example, the Birmingham Voluntary Church Society was founded in 1835. A lecture it published introducing itself to the public, however, was also extraordinarily apologetic in tone, consisting mainly of assertions of what its goals were not: it did not intend to excite unfriendly feelings between Christians, to destroy or injure the Episcopal Church, to appropriate the Church's wealth, to deprive the poor of the means of grace and salvation, to subvert the constitution of the country, to undermine the Protestant faith, or to retard the progress of evangelical piety.[10] At the end of 1839, the Evangelical Voluntary Church Association was founded and, in the following year, another organization, the Religious Freedom Society, held its first annual meeting. All of these associations were created in order to oppose state establishments of religion and were supported by an impressive array of leading Dissenting ministers and laymen.

This flurry of activity reflected the mainstream of English Dissenting thought. This fact is well illustrated by a pastoral address that the venerable Congregational minister, John Angell James, gave to his congregation in 1834, in which he expounded at length the reasons why religious establishments were inherently wrong.[11] This groundswell of reforming opinion was finally channeled into a militant organization energetically engaged in pressure-group politics when the Congregationalist Edward Miall, editor of the *Nonconformist*, founded the British Anti-State Church Association in 1844 (later known as the Liberation Society), but it is essential to realize that the convictions that animated this association were very widespread, even if more moderate Dissenters were initially uneasy with its forthright tone and aggressive tactics.

One principal reason why it might be tempting for some scholars to assume that the disestablishment campaign was merely an application by Dissenters to their own peculiar situation of the general currents of reforming thought that had leavened social and political discussions in Britain, France, and America is that the slogans were virtually interchangeable. Dissenters encapsulated their demands in the words "liberty," "equality," and "freedom" and bolstered them with the notion of "rights," even "inalienable rights." All of these words, for example, can be found in the full title and fundamental principles and objectives of the Religious Freedom Society.[12] Arguably, given the larger context, it should hardly seem remarkable that a reform movement might arise during this period among a reasonably large and self-confident group experiencing discrimination in which the members of that group would demand "liberty" and "equality" for themselves.

Once one probes beneath this surface, however, there is a whole, unique and largely neglected world of thought and argument that repays careful exploration. It is not coincidental that eminent historians who largely have been dismissive of the reforming project of Nonconformists—one thinks of Elie Halévy, Norman Gash, and Owen Chadwick—have also demonstrated scant awareness of the spiritual and theological underpinnings of this movement.[13] The judgments of these scholars seem far less measured and sound once the reforming project of Nonconformists is rethought from a perspective of theological literacy in Dissenting terms. It is not enough merely to discuss their reforming efforts in terms of political tactics, because the mentality and rhetoric of evangelical Dissenters was profoundly religious. The reform movement that came clearly to the surface in the 1830s in Nonconformist circles was a public manifestation of biblical, theological, and religious lines of thought that were deeply ingrained in the Dissenting community. In this subculture, one was more apt to discuss the nature of the church than the role of the state; more apt to be moved by what was perceived to be righteous than what was perceived to be expedient; just as apt to discuss the rights of Christ as the rights of man.

It is time to explore the religious foundations of the public actions of Dissenters. The *raison d'être* of the Congregationalists was their distinctive convictions regarding the nature of the church of Christ, and the Baptists shared this ecclesiology fully. These Dissenters thought a great deal about what the church is, or ought to be, and generated a prodigious amount of discussion and literature on this subject. According to the theological tradition they inhabited, a local church ought to be gathered, voluntary, and independent. "Gathered" meant that it was comprised only of true believers who had been separated from the world. This view was in direct contrast to the territorial idea of the state church and its parochial system, which presumed that every individual in a given locality, in some sense, belonged to the established church. "Voluntary" meant that those so gathered had freely chosen to do so. They voluntarily took upon themselves the obligations and disciplines of this corporate life of faith. This view contrasted with the element of compulsion in the establishment system where duties such as church rates were enforced by the strong arm of the state. "Independent" meant that a local congregation was answerable only to the Almighty for its actions, a principle that stood in direct contrast to any desire the government might have to control the religious life of the people. *The Protestant Dissenters' Catechism* answered the question, "What do the Dissenters think to be the scripture idea of a Church of Christ?" as follows:

> A congregation, or voluntary society of Christians, who meet together to attend gospel ordinances in the same place. And they think every such society has a right to transact its own affairs according to the judgment and conscience of the members thereof, independently of any other society whatsoever, or without being accountable to any but Jesus Christ, or restrained by any laws but his.[14]

These beliefs were the historic convictions of Congregationalists and Baptists. One clear manifestation of this pattern of thought and behavior, which has not received the scholarly attention it deserves, was the practice of creating church covenants. A group of Dissenters, when they wished to found a local church, would sign a covenant which asserted that they had freely entered into the responsibilities of this new community, and delineated what those responsibilities were. A congregation might also reaffirm this covenant at various points in its subsequent life. This tradition, which was very much alive in the first half of the nineteenth century and beyond, can be traced back to the mid-seventeenth century. To take an example from the early part of the period under discussion, the following is the preamble of the covenant that was signed by the members of the Particular Baptist Church meeting in the Horse Fair, Stony Stratford, Buckinghamshire, in 1790:

> We whose names are underwritten do now declare, that we embrace the word of God as our only guide in matters of religion, and acknowledge

no other authority whatever as binding upon the conscience. Having, we hope, found mercy at the hands of God, in delivering us from the power of darkness, and translating us into the Kingdom of his dear Son, we think and feel ourselves bound to walk in obedience to his divine commands. On looking into the sacred scriptures, we find it was common in the first ages of Christianity for such as professed repentance towards God and faith in our Lord Jesus Christ, voluntarily to unite together in Christian societies, called in the New Testament, Churches. Their ends in so doing were, to honour God and promote their own spiritual edification. Having searched the written word, we trust, with a degree of diligence, in order that we may know how to act, so well as what to believe, and sought unto God by prayer for divine direction, we heartily approve of, and mean to follow their example. With a view to this, we now solemnly, in the presence of the all-seeing and heart-searching God, do mutually covenant and agree, in manner and form the following.[15]

It is not difficult to see how a people schooled in such an intense, intentional, and independent form of spirituality would find it a monstrous impertinence for the government to presume that it ought to organize their religious lives for them, imposing whatever rites and doctrines on them that it deemed fit.

Dissenters believed firmly that they knew what the church was, and from that ecclesiological starting point they identified any interference in matters of religion by the state as a tainting influence on the pure, legitimate, voluntary, spiritual societies that the Almighty desired. J. A. James reminded his people that religious establishments:

> are injurious to the *Church* which they take into alliance with the secular government, by destroying her independence and making her a vassal of the state. Instead of maintaining her purity, dignity, and liberty, she becomes a slave of the kings of the earth [. . .].[16]

The Evangelical Voluntary Church Association published a tract with the revealing title, *Worldliness Engrafted Upon the Episcopal Church, Through Her Connexion with the State*.[17] Thus they objected, for religious reasons, not merely to doctrines and practices in the Church of England that they believed to be unscriptural but to the very notion of state involvement in matters of religion. A tract published in 1812 titled *An Answer to the Inquiry, Why Are You a Dissenter from the Church of England?* made this point clear from the outset: "The FIRST GENERAL PRINCIPLE on which we found our dissent is this,— *That no civil magistrate can have any right, authority, or power over the consciences and religion of men.*"[18] Moreover, to place questions of religion in the hands of kings, politicians, and magistrates—men who might lead unrighteous lives that offered scant evidence of having been transformed by a divine work of grace—could not but be viewed as an enormous declension from the perspective of a covenant community in which the doctrine, spirituality, and behavior of every member has been carefully tested and approved. The Independent James Bennett observed:

> Should I hear that a Yorkshire ploughman, who understands, no language but his county brogue, was appointed professor of Arabic in the university of Cambridge, or that a blind man was chosen by the manufacturers of Leeds to judge of the colour of their cloths, it would appear to me unspeakably less absurd, than for mere worldly men, destitute of the knowledge or of the spirit of the Gospel, to bear any office in the church of Christ, or possess any authority in the management of its concerns.[19]

In other words, the confidence these Dissenters possessed was first and foremost a religious confidence, a belief in their own right to act as spiritual beings and to answer only to the Almighty for such actions, and this confidence produced a concomitant indignation that the state should not acknowledge this right but rather presume to preside over the cure of souls. Ernst Troeltsch has taught those who analyze religious groups to think in terms of the church-type and the sect-type. The former sees itself as belonging to the whole population and aligns itself with the social and political powers of the society as a whole:

> The sects, on the other hand, are comparatively small groups; they aspire after personal inward perfection, and they aim at a direct personal fellowship between the members of each group. From the very beginning, therefore, they are forced to organize themselves in small groups, and to renounce the idea of dominating the world.[20]

Much has been written about the process whereby a sect evolves over time into a church. Those who narrate this trajectory often take great delight in chronicling the increasing worldliness and respectability of such groups. There is a much more complicated and interesting process than this one, however, in which a sect, finding that it has become considerably larger and more influential, then seeks to use its new position to apply sect-type values and insights to the structures of the wider society.

In what has been presented thus far, an effort has been made to uncover the sect-type religious culture that is a neglected aspect of the true nature of Dissent in this period. Dissenters were people banded together for fellowship in congregations that sought to maintain their own purity. Moreover, this culture, mentality, and theological vision occasioned a particular attitude toward the role of the state, namely, that the government should not establish a religion, but rather it should leave every person free to follow his or her own conscience without interference. If these denominations would have remained numerically small and socially insignificant, these ideas would have remained internal matters for the faithful. As Dissent became larger and more self-confident, however, rather than abandoning these convictions for the church-type model of religious establishments and territorial churches, it sought to champion in the wider society the values it had already developed, and thereby fostered a very particular kind of reform movement.

Moreover, this new assertiveness and social and political engagement also prompted Dissenters to begin to think more boldly, systematically, and creatively about the possible implications of their convictions when applied to society as a whole. In the eighteenth century, Nonconformity had no hope of reconstructing civil society and therefore no incentive to develop its own distinctive political worldview. By the 1830s, however, Dissent was increasingly convinced that it could instigate reform, and so Nonconformists began to ask new questions and develop new answers concerning the role of government. The split with the Unitarians allowed disestablishment to enter the deliberations of their pressure-group organizations, and this in turn also gave an impetus to a greater exploration of a whole web of ideas that might develop regarding the true role of the state. Some of the possible implications of Nonconformity's own, traditional lines of thought—as they were then applied to the public sphere for the first time—might initially appear counterintuitive. There are two central examples of this. Firstly, Dissenters—far in advance of most other Englishmen and women—were increasingly willing to accept the notion that British society should accommodate itself to religious pluralism. This may seem surprising because the theological views of evangelical Dissenters were so precise. After all, evangelical Dissenters were convinced that whether one had embraced religious truth or error on quite a wide range of doctrinal points was literally a matter of life and death, as their obsession with evangelistic and missionary efforts amply demonstrated. This point is also made by their newly found interest in engaging in a private war with the Unitarians. Nevertheless, all this notwithstanding, such views usually did not translate into a desire to see the theologically incorrect discriminated against.

Quite to the contrary, many Dissenters went out of their way to help those whose religious opinions and practices they considered anathema to find a securer, more equitable place in English society. The principal body, that campaigned for Dissenting rights in the first half of the nineteenth century, was the London-based Protestant Dissenting Deputies. The "Protestant" in its name notwithstanding, this body strongly supported Roman Catholic emancipation, even petitioning Parliament in favor of this cause during the heat of the debate over this issue in 1829.[21] In the north, Edward Baines, Sr., one of the most prominent and respected Dissenting laymen, supported the cause of Roman Catholics in his influential paper, the *Leeds Mercury*.[22] Although, of course, there were also Dissenters who opposed Catholic emancipation, the majority supported it, and the trend in Nonconformist thinking—once again, well ahead of attitudes in the populace at large—was clearly moving toward systematically applying the principle of religious equality for all.[23] One could go on to discuss Dissenting attitudes to other groups as well. For example, the Protestant Dissenting Deputies also petitioned in the years 1831, 1837, and 1845 for civil discriminations against Jews to be removed.[24] Likewise, the *Ecclesiastical Journal* supported Jewish emancipation.[25] Josiah Conder, in a book he published in 1822, could reject the notion of the civil necessity for Christian tests and oaths by an argument that betrays an extraordinary openness to society's being transformed in order to make room for religious pluralism: "An oath taken upon the Koran by a Mohommedan, is as good for the purposes of society, as the oath of a Christian upon the Gospels."[26] Despite, or perhaps rather because of, the intensity of their own religious convictions, evangelical Dissenters were remarkably ready to face constructively the civic implications of religious pluralism.

Secondly, evangelical Dissenters were increasingly desirous that religion would be kept out of state-sponsored activities, that is to say, in a word, they wanted the government and those spheres of society that it administered to become more secular. This, after all, is the meaning of their slogan, "the separation of church and state." The *Ecclesiastical Journal* argued in 1835:

> The separation of the church from the state means the withdrawal of the civil magistrate *within his own proper province*, which is the care of civil society, leaving religion to be provided for by the church, to which (and not to the civil magistrate) Christ entrusted this concern.[27]

When the notion of state education began to gain currency, a considerable number of Dissenters became convinced that no religious instruction should be offered at all in state schools. For example, the prominent and well-respected Congregational minister John Pye Smith noted in 1839: "My own opinion is decidedly in favour of a national measure of purely secular education, which millions would cry down as *infidel and atheistic*."[28]

Nonconformists also had a long history of protesting against royal procla-
mations of fast days and days of thanksgiving, arguing that it was not appropriate for the sovereign or the government to call the people to prayer. For
example, a statement against this practice was decided upon by the Yearly
Meeting of the Society of Friends (the Quakers) in 1833. Evangelical
Dissenters—once again, well ahead of English opinion at large—wished to
see the state purged of its religiosity.

It might complete the process of rethinking Dissent in this period at the
expense of some ingrained perceptions to note that their commitment to
religious equality and state noninterference in matters of religion, along with
some other influences, made many Nonconformists wary of projects for
moral reform that involved government action. For example, on the issue of
temperance, Dissenters were not convinced of the need for prohibition until
the 1870s, which was arguably fairly late in the day. By way of contrast, the
infidel newspaper, the *Yorkshire Tribune*, supported prohibition at its founding in 1855.[29] No Dissenting denominational journals or newspapers supported this cause at that time, and the *Nonconformist* was still actively
opposing it for many years to come. The *Baptist Magazine* did not even lend
its support to teetotalism, let alone prohibition, during the 1840s, 1850s,
and 1860s. When the bill for lowering the hurdles for obtaining a divorce
came before Parliament in 1857, the *Nonconformist* wished that it would
become law "as speedily as possible"; its only suggestion for improving the
measure being that it ought to make the standards as low for wives as they
were to be for husbands, thereby removing the offence of gender inequality
from the law.[30] Too many scholars have assumed that because Dissenters, as
voluntary members of sects, embraced and preached rigid standards for personal behavior, they inevitably must have wished to impose these same standards on their neighbors through legislation.

In fact, the quest for religious equality for all was the reform movement
that epitomized Nonconformity in the early and mid-Victorian period.
Dissenters were often sympathetic to movements for political reform. Many
prominent Dissenting laymen were publicly and passionately committed to
the Reform Bill of 1832, and a significant number of Dissenters expressed
their sympathy for a wide range of radical political movements at home and
abroad. Nevertheless, it was difficult for Dissenters to ground these instincts
firmly in their religious habits of thought and collective action, and so the
bodies, which officially spoke on behalf of Nonconformists such as the
Baptist and Congregational Unions and the Dissenting Deputies, did not
make pronouncements on such issues. The same is true of the issue of prohibition during the 1850s and 1860s. Moreover, both political reform and

prohibition were issues upon which prominent Dissenters expressed differ-
ing opinions publicly. On the other hand, the Dissenting community was
unanimously and publicly in favor of Jewish emancipation. All the organs of
Dissenting opinion championed this cause when it entered the world of
practical politics in the 1840s, and, to take a random example of an official
body, the Yorkshire Baptist Association passed a resolution in its favor.[31]
Religious equality, not moral reform or franchise reform, was at the heart of
the Dissenting political agenda.

The pattern of Dissenting beliefs and behavior outlined thus far
arguably offers an interesting sidelight on the theory of secularization. Two
scholars in this field, Roy Wallis and Steve Bruce, have noted, following a
standard definition of secularization devised by Bryan Wilson:

> We have no brief for a definition of "true religion" and little worthwhile
> evidence of the "depth" amongst the faithful. Hence with Wilson we set
> a more restricted test of secularization, namely that of the diminishing
> social significance of religion.[32]

What is interesting about this definition in light of the reforming project of
evangelical Dissenters is that, however much it might upset a scholarly desire
for quantification, Dissenters were nevertheless profoundly preoccupied
with the issues of "true religion" and the "depth" of religious experience, and
these sincerely religious people were also actively campaigning to diminish
the social significance of religion and were thus, according to the standard
definition then currently in use, prime agents of secularization.

This juxtaposition brings us back to the religious worldview of English
Dissenters. To underline the point once again, their starting point was the
church, not the state. They saw the separation of church and state, not as the
creating of a godless government, but rather as the creating of a purified
church. At the founding meeting of the Anti-State Church Association the
delegates were clearly preoccupied with the purity of the church; they spoke,
following an entirely different logic from that of those interested in the theory of secularization, of "the disenthralment of religion from the securaliz-
ing influence of state control."[33] The sect-type mentality cares little for the
veneer of religion that society might wear; it is not impressed by a nominal,
diffused religiosity, which might make up for in breadth what it lacks in
depth. The Test Act that required public officials to take the Anglican sacra-
ment annually, might appear as a safeguard against secularization from the
church-type mentality, but from the perspective of earnest religious
Dissenters it was abhorrent that something as sacred as communing with the
Almighty could be degraded into a civic show: according to this perspective,

public society was not being imbued with religion, but rather religion was being tainted with secular concerns. What some might see as the church's retreating from its strongholds in society, evangelical Dissenters viewed as the state's being forced to retreat from its squatter holdings in the land of Zion.

In a sect-type mentality everything that is not "true religion," as defined by the exacting standards of the lights of one's own spiritual community, is "the world." A truly small and insignificant sect is forced to withdraw into itself, its members being well aware that it would be futile to endeavor to change the structures of the surrounding society. English evangelical Dissenters, however, during the first half of the nineteenth century, had grown large enough and influential enough for a ghetto mentality no longer to be their only option. By the end of this period, a generation of rapid growth was made official: Nonconformists read the Religious Census of 1851 as heralding the fact that the sects were on the verge of overtaking the Church in terms of numerical strength. Rather than abandoning their principles, however, they sought to apply them to the wider society, developing new political ideas in the process. Their theological traditions had taught them to value religion that was gathered, voluntary, independent, sincere, pure, and satisfying to one's own searching heart, mind, and conscience. When applied to English society, such a tradition could be seen to recommend that the Church of England should be disestablished, government officials should refrain from endeavoring to promote religion by coercion, and men and women should have the liberty to follow their own consciences without discrimination, even if they chose to pursue Roman Catholicism, Judaism, or any other system of belief. In other words, this process of translating their own, internal values into a public reforming project had the seemingly paradoxical effect of inspiring disciplined, earnest, and theologically dogmatic covenant communities into becoming some of the foremost champions of a more pluralistic society and a more secular state.

Chapter 11

Free Church Politics
and Contested Memories
The Historical Case for Disestablishment

In the providence of God, St. Bartholomew's Day, 1862, fell on a Sunday, just as it had two hundred years before. On that earlier Sabbath some 2,000 ministers were ejected from their livings because they could not conscientiously swear their "unfeigned assent and consent to all and everything contained and prescribed" in the new Prayer Book or meet some of the other requirements of the new Act of Uniformity. Rejected by the Established Church, many of these men continued to fulfill their callings outside her pale and thereby gave a major, new impetus to Dissent. As the bicentenary of "Black Bartholomew's Day" approached, Victorian Nonconformists resolved to make the most of "the opportunity which God's providence has brought round to them."[1] In this retrospective year, historical claims became powerful weapons in the struggle between Church and Dissent; and the past became contested territory, which both sides sought to appropriate in order to add legitimacy to their present positions.

During the years just prior to the bicentenary, some Churchmen had begun to make concerted efforts to thwart the plans of militant Nonconformists and their political organization, the Liberation Society, which had as an objective the disestablishment of the Church of England. Although it had existed since 1844 (originally as the "Anti-State Church Association"), Churchmen had begun only recently to pay it serious attention.[2] In 1859, the Church Institution, a national organization for Church defense, was founded.[3] In 1861, a bill to abolish church rates, a major legislative goal of Dissenters, was defeated in the Commons for the first time since 1854.[4] The days when Churchmen would disdainfully ignore the activities of militant Dissenters had come to an end.

157

Throughout the early decades of Victoria's reign, there was an underlying divide in Dissent between militants, who wanted defiantly to advance a radical political agenda, and moderates, who were uneasy with such extremism. Moderates wanted to maintain cordial relations with their fellow Christians in the Established Church. The Church defense movement initially succeeded in tempting some moderates to distance themselves from the actions of their more extreme coreligionists. For example, the wealthy Baptist railway contractor, Sir Morton Peto, MP, quietly severed his connection with the Liberation Society in April 1860.[5] A year later he went out of his way to assert his moderate credentials, telling the Commons "he had never been an enemy to the Church of England, and had never taken part in any agitation against her" and that "no one deplored more than he did the existence of such societies as the Liberation Society."[6] At the start of the 1860s, the activities of militant Nonconformists were under intense scrutiny, and moderate Dissenters did not wish to be held responsible for their excesses.

The Liberation Society was stung by the sudden change of climate. Its minutes for September 1861 include an introspective special report, which acknowledged that the Society had lost much ground because of this counterattack by Churchmen. It recommended that the Society should revitalize itself from the grass roots through a campaign to spread its principles among its natural constituencies. Included in the report's list of specific proposals was the observation that the bicentenary "will afford an opportunity for the inculcation of the Society's principles." Because it was officially nonsectarian, the Society could not take the lead in this, but nevertheless, the report recommended that members of its committee should take an active part in the commemorations that, it hoped, explicitly Dissenting bodies would initiate.[7]

Dissenters did not require any prompting to feel a need to commemorate this great event. The Congregationalists were already making preparations. The eminent layman Joshua Wilson prepared a paper for the Congregational Union meeting in October 1861 in which he suggested various ways the denomination could mark the forthcoming occasion. These included an energetic program of chapel building, the promotion of publications and lectures related to the themes of the bicentenary, and the establishment of a denominational hall in London.[8] These suggestions were accepted and to them was added memorial fundraising for every conceivable good work done in the name of the denomination. Congregationalism, at least, planned to fare well out of the memory of the ejected ministers.

Some Baptists and other Dissenters had hoped for a unified committee, but the Congregationalists would not abandon their independent scheme. Nevertheless, the "Central United St. Bartholomew Committee of Evangelical Nonconformists" was formed as well. It was not exactly a rival: there were four men on it who also served on one of the two Congregational Union committees in 1862. No fewer than seven members of the Bartholomew Committee were also on the Liberation Society committee, including its most prominent personality, Edward Miall, and the two employees who kept it running, J. C. Williams and H. S. Skeats. These various committees were all physically connected through the presence of the ubiquitous Samuel Morley, a wealthy textile manufacturer. The Bartholomew Committee included some prominent Baptists, notably William Brock, J. H. Hinton, and Sir Morton Peto. The word "united" in the committee's full title was given added credibility by the presence of a few men from other denominations, such as William Cooke from the Methodist New Connexion and Robert Eckett from the United Methodist Free Churches; and the qualifying word "evangelical" reminded Unitarians that unity had its limits.[9] Although Edward Miall was himself a Congregationalist, he realized that the Bartholomew Committee was the one that was more likely to enlist the memory of the ejected ministers in the cause of militant Dissent.[10]

Almost as soon as Nonconformists had expressed their intention to commemorate, some Churchmen began to protest. Central to their criticism was the allegation that Dissenters were misusing history. On one level, they offered a straightforward tit-for-tat of historical facts, concentrating on the persecutions that the puritans themselves had inflicted. A fine example of this response was the much circulated tract by George Venables, *How Did They Get There? or, the Non-Conforming Ministers of 1662. A Question for Those Who Would Celebrate the Bi-Centenary of St. Bartholomew's Day, 1662.* This strident piece brought a blitzkrieg of counterhistory to bear; its blanket coverage of all possible target areas extended even to the treatment of Native Americans by the Pilgrim Fathers.[11] A variation on this theme was attempts to restore or refute specific historical details, such as whether or not 2,000 was an accurate estimate of the number of ejected ministers and whether their number was larger or smaller than the victims of the puritans.[12] Such points were a continuation (and sometimes a mere repetition) of the work done by the Nonconformist historian Edmund Calamy, and the response made to it by the Churchman John Walker in the early part of the eighteenth century.[13]

Many Church defenders saw the whole commemoration as a ploy for advancing the political agenda of militant Dissent. One of their number, J. B. Clifford, published an address titled *The Bicentenary, The Liberation Society; And To What Do Its Principles Tend?* The crux of his argument was that "the Bicentenary is being observed for Liberation purposes," but Nonconformists should have "read history a little more closely" before they attempted this stunt.[14] The *Quarterly Review* likewise asserted that the bicentenary was "not to be simply a Dissenting Saints' Day," but rather "a great political agitation."[15] Generally, the point was made that the ejected ministers were not militant Dissenters; they had no objection to church establishments *per se*. For example, Canon John Miller, a prominent evangelical clergyman, helpfully reminded his audience that the word "ejectment" implied "the removing of a person who does not want to go."[16] Moreover, the Two Thousand were mainly Presbyterians, so they could not be justly coopted into the cause of Congregationalism; and what possible historical claim on these men could be made by such groups as the United Methodist Free Churches? In short, Church defenders argued that Victorian Nonconformists were so different from the ejected ministers that it was almost dishonest of them to evoke their memory. The Congregational minister R. W. Dale summed it up well when he said, "We are charged with a kind of historical felony."[17]

Because the battle had been initially joined through these preemptive strikes, by the time Dissenters actually started publishing and lecturing, they were well aware of the case that they needed to answer. A few Nonconformists opted for direct defiance. The Congregational minister J. G. Rogers, in his bicentenary lecture, cited many of the charges before he reiterated his conviction that "the principle I think best worth teaching in connection with this celebration is that of the Liberation Society."[18] Some sought to show that the ejectment "strikingly illustrates the evils of the State-Church principle," whether or not the ejected recognized it.[19] Others appealed to the idea of historical development. The Dissenting journal, the *British Quarterly Review*, argued by analogy that Englishmen could look back with gratitude to "those sturdy barons who wrung the provisions of the Great Charter from the hands of King John," even though these men may not have approved of the House of Commons.[20] A Dissenting minister in Macclesfield appealed to biblical imagery in order to show that Victorian Nonconformists were the "valid successors" of the ejected men. He argued that "[t]he spiritual sons of spiritual fathers are the sons who do the works of those fathers." Moreover, Nonconformists would never join the Church of England because they would not "put their necks beneath a yoke which neither they nor their fathers would be able to bear."[21]

Generally, however, Dissenters took note of the arguments against them and tailored their remarks accordingly. The Congregational committee published a volume of addresses and stated that it desired its "aims and objects in the Bicentenary Commemoration may be judged of by what is found in these pages, and not by the mistakes or misrepresentations of others." In the volume, one of the writers explained on their behalf that they wished to honor the ejected ministers because of their "manliness," "love of truth," "fortitude," and "faith." He admitted that some might say that he had "proved too much" by listing characteristics common to "all good men," but expounding on "faith," he claimed that the desire to "obey God rather than men" was "the root principle of all Dissent."[22] Even that qualification, however, hardly explained why they did not just commemorate St. Bartholomew himself. Even the Bartholomew Committee followed suit:

> No identity of ecclesiastical or theological faith between the willing Nonconformists of 1862 and the forced Nonconformists of 1662, is required to give a meaning to such a commemoration. It is not to the opinions, but to the conduct of the ejected that the present is a fitting occasion to do honour. Their heroic spirit, not their convictions—their fidelity to conscience, not their articles of belief—their unswerving loyalty to their spiritual King, not their ideas on questions of Church relations and Church government, commend them to attention, to sympathy, to imitation, in these times.[23]

If the desirability of disestablishment was a lesson too tenuously connected to the text at hand, these sweeping generalities were too common to innumerable texts—whether Protestant or Catholic, Christian or pagan. A lesson between these extremes needed to be identified; one which was historically sensitive, but nevertheless useful to the cause of Dissent. The evils surrounding clerical subscription, as laid down in the Act of Uniformity, matched this requirement well. The *Baptist Magazine* confidently announced: "*This* is the great lesson which Bartholomew's-day should recal [sic] to mind—that HONEST MEN CANNOT USE FORMULARIES WHICH THEY THINK TO BE UNTRUE, OR CONTRARY TO THE WORD OF GOD."[24] The Bartholomew Committee dedicated an entire tract to this point.[25]

This piece of ground was chosen; and a bitter battle ensued. In January 1862 Canon Miller had moved the principal resolution at a meeting that was called for the purpose of founding a Church defense association in

Birmingham. In support of it, he drew attention to the Dissenters' bicentenary plans, and warned that their behavior was becoming so hostile that,
despite a tradition of working together in nondenominational societies, "it
became a serious question as to how far that co-operation was possible in the
future."[26] In the following month he delivered a lecture for the newly
formed "Birmingham Church of England Defence Association" titled
*Churchmen and Dissenters: Their Relations as Affected by the Proposed
Bicentenary Commemoration of St. Bartholomew's Day, 1662.* In it he proph-
esied correctly that this "Commemoration seems likely to affect the relation
in which Churchmen and Dissenters will stand in this country, for some
time to come."[27] In response, R. W. Dale gave a lecture under the same title
in the Birmingham Town Hall. He aimed squarely at the Church of England
in his own day, claiming that almost every party in it was uncomfortable
with some part of the Prayer Book. He targeted the evangelical clergy in particular, citing passages that seemed to teach baptismal regeneration as incompatible with their true convictions. Dale concluded:

> The truest, fittest, sublimest celebration of the Bicentenary, would be for
> eight or ten thousand of the Evangelical Clergy who object to these ser-
> vices in the prayer-book, but who obtained their ministerial office and
> their ministerial income by avowing their "unfeigned assent and consent"
> to all the book contains—to come out and to declare to the English peo-
> ple that they can no longer retain a position which they acquired by pro-
> fessing to approve what now at least they reject; that they can no longer
> use in the house of God and at the most touching and solemn crises of
> human history, words which their hearts condemn.[28]

Some Churchmen read this as a personal attack on their honesty and
integrity; and it was not an isolated incident. The evangelical Anglican newspaper, the *Record*, drew attention to a bicentenary tract circulating in Ipswich
that claimed "the Act of Uniformity shuts men up to this alternative—per-
jury or secession." The *Record* warned: "If moderate Dissenters do not wish
to have a complete and final rupture with Churchmen, they must speak
out."[29] Dissenters often implied that Churchmen were resorting to the
Jesuitical ploy of accepting the wording in its "non-natural" sense or with
"mental reservations."

Dale's appeal did not inspire Canon Miller to resign his living. Instead,
he resigned his presidency of the Central Association of the Birmingham
Auxiliary of the British and Foreign Bible Society.[30] Sir Culling Eardley, the
animating spirit of the Evangelical Alliance, tried to mediate between the
two Birmingham men, but without success. Even more tellingly, he was

unsuccessful in his attempt to dissuade Sir Morton Peto from taking the chair at a bicentenary meeting where Dale was scheduled to speak, despite Peto's desire during the two preceding years to distance himself from the activities of militant Nonconformists. The best he could do was obtain a letter in which Peto said that if clergymen claimed to be satisfied that their convictions were reconcilable with their subscription, then he would not "sit in judgment upon them," even though he did not fail to add, "I cannot see myself how they can be." This was enough to please the irenic Eardley, but others were less impressed.[31] The appeals of Churchmen to moderate Dissenters had gone unheeded. The bicentenary commemorations and their attacks on subscription, far from driving a wedge between militants and moderates, were unifying influences within Dissent. The wedge was being driven between Nonconformists and Churchmen.

The truth was that some Churchmen were themselves uneasy about subscription. A High Church clergyman published a letter to Dale in which he praised his lecture and agreed with him that the evangelical clergy did not hold to the teachings of the Church. He smugly claimed that what he and Dale had in common was "English honesty."[32] Lord Ebury introduced into the Lords his "Act of Uniformity Amendment Bill."[33] The clergymen who supported the Liturgical Revision Society were *ipso facto* admitting that change was desirable. One of their number wrote his own bicentenary tract in which he declared, "Never had the Church of England such an opportunity as that which this year presents of expressing regret for the past, by repealing or *amending the objectionable clauses in the Act of Uniformity.*"[34] Even the protest of Churchmen that Dissenters could not judge their consciences had its own internal taunt, for just a year earlier virtually every bishop in the land had signed a letter concerning the controversial *Essays and Reviews* in which they remarked, "We cannot understand how these opinions can be held consistently with an honest subscription to the formularies of the Church."[35] One clergyman, Christopher Nevile, actually did resign his livings, citing as his reason the need for a revision of the Prayer Book.[36] He took his place as a hero of Dissent, coming forward to speak at the Liberation Society conference "amid loud cheers."[37] Nevile and Miller, however, were both mavericks in their own ways; 1862 produced no mass exodus to match the Two Thousand, either from the Establishment or the Bible Society.

The irony of this story is that Church defenders, by labeling the bicentenary a political plot, actually achieved the worst of both worlds. Dissenters who took this accusation to heart stumbled into an attack on the Church itself, rather than just its Established position. The Liberation Society had

always avoided criticizing the Establishment as a Church; and this policy had
had some influence on the behavior of Dissenters in general. Any tendency
toward this type of quietism was now seriously undermined. On the other
hand, the perception that the Liberation Society was deeply connected with
the bicentenary, which was established chiefly through the propaganda of
militant Churchmen, if anything, increased the love Dissenters had for that
society.

Churchmen seemed unaware of the extent to which the ejected ministers had been revered by Dissenting communities for generations. It was
surely a grave tactical error for some of them to try to slur their reputations,
as George Venables did.[38] Robert Vaughan, who was known as one of the
more moderate and cultured Dissenters, wrote a reply.[39] It is interesting to
observe that Vaughan publicly recanted his opposition to the policy of militant Dissenters on state education—a position that he had fought for in
print for over fifteen years—at the very same conference at which Joshua
Wilson's paper on commemorating the bicentenary was read.[40] Vaughan was
subsequently asked to implement one of these bicentenary plans by writing
the official volume on the Ejectment.[41] The *British Quarterly Review*, which
he edited, remarked in an article attacking the Act of Uniformity:

> It seems to have been discovered by some persons that this journal has
> taken new ground on questions of this nature. But there are times when
> it may be well to say little, or even to say nothing; and there are times
> when it is a right thing to speak, and to speak unmistakeably.[42]

It was not completely disingenuous of the journal to go on to claim it had
not changed. The people behind it had always felt deeply about the ejected
ministers. If standing with them meant being lumped together with Edward
Miall, so be it. An ailing Joshua Wilson, another Dissenter who was more
moderate than extreme, painstakingly prepared for publication a defense of
the ejected ministers against the attacks of the *Quarterly Review*.[43] Even the
Record was embarrassed by the curate in Paddington who took as his text on
St. Bartholomew's Day 1 John 2:19: "They went out from us because they
were not of us."[44] All such attacks were counterproductive if quarantining
militant Dissent was the goal.

It is also worth noting that 1862 was the year in which the admirers of
Edward Miall honored him with a testimonial. A partial list of those
involved included not only a vast array of Dissenting radicals, from John
Bright on down, but also more moderate and scholarly men such as the
Reverend Drs. Angus, Halley, and Waddington.[45] Dissenters across the land

wanted to commemorate the bicentenary, and this sense of common cause served their more radical elements well.

The fuel that the bicentenary gave to political Dissent is also illustrated by the attitude of the Unitarians. Evangelical Dissenters had a habit of ostracizing them, which tempted them to think they had more in common with Broad Churchmen than with other Nonconformists.[46] The Unitarian newspaper, the *Inquirer*, had declared its disdain for militant Dissent in 1857. It attacked the name of the Liberation Society and went on to say:

> We are reminded by the Orthodox Dissenters of our common Nonconformity, and our common subservience to a dominant Church. To this we would reply that we approve the principle of a National Church, and, as English Presbyterians, have more love for the Church of England than for the Independents or Baptists.[47]

Nevertheless, Unitarians possessed a good portion of those congregations that descended from the ejected ministers, and the passions of the bicentenary were enough to push the *Inquirer* in the direction of militant Dissent:

> Our readers are well aware that on the Church and State Question we have clung hitherto, through constant opposition, to the old Presbyterian idea of comprehension. The discussions and controversies of the Bicentenary year, the strong ecclesiastical reaction in the Church itself [. . .] and the false position of Broad Churchmen themselves, have contributed materially to alter our views. [. . .] we feel bound now to give our hearty support to many of the practical propositions of the Liberation Society [. . .].[48]

Wesleyan Methodism, as a body, had always supported the Established Church and seen itself as different from the rest of Dissent. It survived the bicentenary with this balancing act intact. The *Wesleyan Methodist Magazine* explained the line that its denomination had taken:

> The Methodist people had not seen fit, as a Connexion, to rouse themselves to any special effort, or to take any prominent part in the Bicentenary commemoration. This is not because they hold the two thousand in light esteem, or think them unworthy of any wreath which Christian love can lay on their tombs. It is, rather, because they fear to depart at all from that traditional policy which has made them "friends of all, the enemies of none." It is because they fear lest they should be forced unwittingly into a position which they would regret to occupy.

This comment illustrates both the widespread desire to honor the ejected men (further remarks conceded that some Wesleyans wished to do more), and the way in which the commemorations had taken on a political hue. Moreover, the magazine was willing to join in the attack on subscription ,remarking, among other jibes, that it would like to give clergymen the benefit of the doubt, but "charity is very hard work sometimes."[49]

The practical work that the Congregationalists undertook must also take its place as part of the enduring impact of the bicentenary. Because funds were given to existing projects, which would have received some funding anyway, and people were allowed to spread their contributions over several years, not to mention the numerous purely local efforts, it is difficult to tabulate the results. In April 1863 a regional organization for erecting memorial chapels in Lancashire and Cheshire had received subscriptions amounting to £17,567 despite the economic distress caused by the Cotton Famine. At the same date the national fund had reached the sum of £195,749.[50] Memorial Hall, the proposed denominational headquarters, was eventually built as well. When it was opened in 1875, it was said to have cost £70,000, and the memorial fund had reportedly raised £250,000.[51] Welsh Nonconformists joined in the commemorations as well. They resolved to found a Memorial College at Brecon. It cost £10,000 to build and was opened in 1869.[52]

Nonconformists would perhaps have found other excuses for doing many of these good works. The more significant impact of the bicentenary was the deepening of the divide between Church and Dissent that it engendered, and the impetus that it gave to strident Dissent, both in its theological and political forms. All of the principal parties within the Church were affected. High Churchmen were leading the new work of Church defense ,and the bicentenary marked one of their first experiences of hand-to-hand combat at a unit. The Broad Churchmen suffered a weakening of their ties with their erstwhile friends, the Unitarians, as the latter rediscovered their identity as Nonconformists. Moreover, the focus on honesty in subscription caused others to glance suspiciously in their direction. The evangelicals had endured some painful personal blows, and the bicentenary left them feeling defiant and bitter.

Only one prominent Nonconformist publicly signaled his disapproval of the commemorations: the idiosyncratic C. H. Spurgeon. He complained, "I fear lest it should be made an opportunity for strife among brethren."[53] Some Churchmen made the most of this, but it proved to be cold comfort, for in two years' time he launched his own equally bitter war against the Church, beginning with his confrontational sermon on "Baptismal

Regeneration."[54] In the years that followed the commemorations, the divide, if anything, continued to deepen. Although it would be inaccurate to give the impression that R. W. Dale was confined to the narrow world of militant Dissenters, it is not insignificant that he gained his favorable national reputation among Nonconformists through the part he played in the bicentenary. His son wrote, recalling his bicentenary address, "Dale found himself suddenly lifted to a new position. The lecture—as he said, looking back on his early years—'fairly launched' him on his career of public service."[55] The vast number of publications that the bicentenary generated is one indication of the amount of passion that it unleashed. The editor of the "Congregational Literary Register" observed at the end of 1862 that his table was piled with over sixty bicentenary volumes, just counting those written by Congregational *ministers* and published during that year, and he was aware that much of the provincial literature had "not been heard of in the metropolis."[56] Indeed, one could probably find in many parts of the country tracts with titles similar in kind to *The Bicentenary Question. A Third Letter in Reply to the Second Letter of "A Churchman," Which Appeared in the "Shepton Mallet Journal," September 19, 1862.*[57] The Liberation Society could look back on the bicentenary with some satisfaction; Dissenters— moderates and militants united together—had been reminded why they were Dissenters, and they were ready to fight for it—to attempt to follow, in a way which they felt was appropriate to their own era, the heroic example of the ejected ministers.

Chapter 12

Free Church Politics
and the British Empire
The Baptist Case
against Jamaica's Colonial Governor

The bare facts of what happened in Jamaica during the last three months of 1865 are not disputed. A sufficient percentage of the black population in Morant Bay decided to defy the law to cause the authorities to lose control of that area for several days during which eighteen white people were killed and property was stolen and damaged. The colonial governor, Edward John Eyre, declared martial law to be in force over the troubled region, and although the military regained control without meeting any resistance, the officers in charge still felt the need to have 439 people killed, 600 flogged, and 1,000 homes destroyed.

The significance of these facts, however, was hotly contested in Victorian Britain. One side believed that Eyre and the military had heroically done what was necessary to suppress a great "insurrection" or "rebellion" and had thereby saved the whole white population of the island from otherwise certain death. The other side said that in response to a mere "local riot" the soldiers and their leaders had gone on a cruel, brutal, and illegal rampage, committing acts tantamount to murder. Numerous intellectual, literary, and scientific titans of the Victorian age publicly endorsed one side or the other. Eyre's defenders included Thomas Carlyle, Charles Kingsley, and John Ruskin, while John Stuart Mill, T. H. Huxley, and Herbert Spencer were among his accusers. Therefore, with such rich and tempting dishes ready to hand, it is not surprising that historians have failed to explore in depth the contributions Baptists brought to this table. Bernard Semmel, in his *The Governor Eyre Controversy*, addresses the role of Nonconformists, whom he calls collectively "Exeter Hall" (thereby conflating them with Evangelical Anglicans, who also used that venue for their meetings), by way of background in his first chapter, before launching into the heart of his story in chapters that include in their very titles the names of Mill, Kingsley, Carlyle, Ruskin, and Darwin.[1] Likewise, Eric Williams divides the two camps in numerous different ways—conservatives vs. radicals, aristocrats vs. workers, literary vs. scientific men, imperialists vs. Home Rulers, defenders of the South vs. supporters of the North in the American Civil War—but the equally relevant issue of religious affiliation is not touched upon in his analysis.[2] The most notable exception to this tendency is an unpublished PhD thesis by Gordon Catherall, but this source concentrates on events in Jamaica rather than the campaign against Eyre in England.[3] Nevertheless, general neglect notwithstanding, Baptists were central to this controversy. Indeed, even if one cannot resist keeping an inquisitive eye on the main pack of Victorian intellectuals, a careful study of this controversy offers vignettes such as the Baptist journal of missions, the *Missionary Herald*, reporting on a meeting in support of Baptist missions held in a Baptist chapel at which the case against Eyre was given in speeches made by Goldwin Smith and Thorold Rogers, both of whom were Churchmen and Oxford professors.[4] Moreover, one prominent English Baptist in particular, E. B. Underhill, a secretary of the Baptist Missionary Society (BMS), was a far more important player in this dispute than figures such as these.

On 5 January 1865, Underhill had written a letter on the current state of Jamaica to the Secretary of State for the Colonies, Edward Cardwell. The letter argued that the general populace of Jamaica was in great distress, indeed even starving, and placed part of the blame on the "unwisdom (to use the gentlest term) that has governed Jamaica since emancipation," specifically accusing the rulers of that island of depriving the people of fair tribunals and of their political rights and of unjustly taxing them.[5] Cardwell sent the letter on to Eyre, asking for his response to its statements. Eyre, in turn, circulated the letter widely to clergymen, judges, and local officials throughout the island, requesting that they send him relevant information for a reply. When the letter was published in the Jamaican press, the black population began to hold public meetings to express their grievances, which were referred to as "Underhill Meetings." The situation was not defused when Eyre demanded that a statement by Cardwell, which suggested that the poverty of the bulk of the population was largely attributable to their own laziness, be circulated under the heading "The Queen's Advice." While the fact that there was an economic depression in Jamaica was not in dispute,

Underhill's letter became a convenient occasion for the various parties concerned to articulate their explanations for its causes and their remedies for its alleviation.

The BMS occupied an important place in the hearts of Victorian English Baptists, whose denomination was one of the most missionary-minded in the kingdom. The society had been active in Jamaica since 1814 ,and its extraordinary success at gathering adherents there had made that island one of the most prominent mission fields in the eyes of English Baptists. Furthermore, the first half-century of BMS work in Jamaica had also been marked by overt tensions and conflicts of interest between the missionaries and both the planters and the authorities. The turbulent period in the early 1830s had many echoes that interested parties at this fresh moment of crisis could hardly fail to hear. At that time the authorities had sought to curb the religious freedom of Baptists, fearing that they would stir up unrest among the slave population. When a rebellion did come in 1831–1832, BMS missionaries were arrested; and, although charges were eventually dropped, suspicions were not. These events, coupled with an abolitionist platform that had grown more strident, caused English Baptists sometimes to view the planters and colonial authorities in Jamaica as actual or potential obstacles in the way of the spread of the gospel and of justice.[6] In short, both the English Baptists and the white elite in Jamaica had a history of distrust upon which to draw.

Governor Eyre himself was in no doubt that Baptists belonged at the center of this story. He wrote in an official dispatch to Cardwell during the busy days of martial law:

> Up to the present time no reasonable or intelligible cause has been assigned as the origin of this most wicked and widespread rebellion. [. . .]

> 63. I cannot myself doubt that it is in a great degree due to Dr. Underhill's letter and the meetings held in connexion with that letter, where the people were told that they were tyrannized over and ill-treated, were over-taxed, were denied political rights [. . .].

> 64. The parties who have more immediately taken part in these nefarious proceedings are:—firstly, G. W. Gordon, a member of the Assembly and a Baptist preacher; secondly, several black persons, chiefly of the Baptist persuasion [. . .] fifthly, a few Baptist missionaries, who like.........
.........endorse at public meetings or otherwise all the untruthful statements or innuendos propagated in Dr. Underhill's letter [. . .].[7]

Needless to say, the fact that the governor went on to affirm the commitment to lawful authority on the part of the majority of Baptist ministers did little to dampen the indignation of English Baptists at having their denomination in general, and a beloved figure in their missionary society in particular, slurred in this way.

Underhill dismissed the charge by noting that his letter had been a private one addressed to Cardwell, not to the people of Jamaica, and that its circulation on the island was Eyre's action, not his.[8] *The Athenæum* (of all papers) defended the secretary of the Baptist Missionary Society, declaring: "we say that Dr. Underhill would have been blameworthy had he neglected to put his special information at the service of the country."[9] Indeed, Cardwell himself, in a speech in Parliament, defended Underhill:

> The letter, which was brought to me I believe by the hon. Member for Bristol, was perfectly *bonâ fide*, and addressed to me for the purpose of obtaining practical inquiry into the subject [. . .]. If the consequences which have been said since to have resulted from that letter could have been reasonably expected by the Government of Jamaica, I think it was not necessary to give the letter publicity; and that the publishers of the letter, and not its writer, must be held responsible.[10]

Nevertheless, Eyre's defenders were not convinced. Hamilton Hume, honorary secretary of the Eyre Defence and Aid Fund, wrote a biography of Eyre in the year following these comments, in which he referred in the very first paragraph of his chapter on the background to the disturbances to "Dr. Underhill's most unwise and most improper letter to the Secretary of State for the Colonies, which materially helped to, if it did not indeed actually, fan into a flame the smouldering fires of rebellion." Hume's next chapter began with a section titled "First fruits of Dr. Underhill's letter."[11]

Moreover, Eyre's accusation against Underhill was not the only one with which the Baptists had to contend. When news of the troubles in Jamaica was just beginning to reach England, *The Times* ran a leader that began:

> There can now be no doubt that the insurrection of the negroes in Jamaica is an event of the most serious import. It has been attended with some of the most horrible outrages that have ever been perpetrated, even in that land of African lawlessness. In the old days of slavery the Jamaica negro was noted among his race for his dangerous character, and he rose against his masters, under the guidance of the Baptists, on the very eve of Emancipation.[12]

So Baptists needed to defend their role in the Jamaica of the 1830s as well as in that of 1865. Sir Morton Peto wrote a letter to *The Times* that endeavored to set the record straight, and the Baptist newspaper, *The Freeman*, offered a little history lesson of its own in which it praised the previous generation of Baptist missionaries in Jamaica: "'Under the guidance' of these Baptists the British nation rose against the savagery of the planters, and liberated the negro from liability to atrocities committed by white men."[13]

An even more important Baptist in this dispute was the second person named in Eyre's dispatch: G. W. Gordon. He did not belong to the Baptists associated with the BMS but rather, if he belonged to any Baptist grouping, it was the so-called "Native Baptists"—an indigenous group that was the fruit of the missionary labors of an African-American who came to the island in the late eighteenth century.[14] Nevertheless, Gordon had been baptized as a believer by the highly respected BMS missionary, J. M. Phillippo.[15] Gordon was a prosperous Jamaican of mixed race. He was a member of the Jamaican Assembly, a fierce political opponent of Eyre, and, by his passionate (his critics said "seditious") oratory, a focal figure for the mass of people who wanted something done about their grievances. When Eyre heard about the disturbances in Morant Bay, he immediately assumed that it was part of a widespread conspiracy being led by Gordon who, as a legislator, was the one Jamaican whose radical rhetoric was said in his hearing. Eyre put out an order for his arrest. Gordon, who was in undisturbed Kingston, promptly turned himself in. The governor, however, instead of having him tried in the functioning civilian courts, had Gordon transported to Morant Bay, where martial law was in force. There he was given the mere semblance of a trial by military officers—Gordon was not allowed to consult a lawyer or to call witnesses in his own defence—and within days he had been executed. The officers in charge had paused, however, between their judgment and the carrying out of the sentence. A report of their proceedings was sent to Eyre who in turn gave his personal endorsement of the decision to execute Gordon.[16] Gordon's case was the dramatic and legal focus of the campaign against Eyre. It seemed patently illegal and unjust. *The Freeman*, by analogy, wondered whether the Conservative Prime Minister Lord Derby could "declare martial law in Ireland, then deport [the radical, fiery orator and English MP] Mr. BRIGHT thither, and there try, and hang him by a mock court martial for speeches and letters on Ireland uttered or written half a year before."[17] To his most intractable critics, Eyre was guilty of Gordon's murder, and even many people who sympathized in general terms with the severe way in which British authority had been reestablished in Morant Bay felt that Gordon had been mishandled. The Eyre Defence and Aid Fund committee felt a need to publish every piece of information it could find that put Gordon in a bad light because: "So many persons of rank and influence in England have remarked that they 'thoroughly endorse all that Mr. Eyre did, except his allowing Gordon to be executed.'"18

As soon as the reports began to reach Britain, a section of the British public immediately began to express its outrage at what had been done in the name of martial law and to call for an inquiry that would lead to some appropriate action being taken against whoever was found responsible for these excesses. The figures associated with public meetings, resolutions, and deputations expressing these concerns in this early stage were overwhelmingly Nonconformists, with Baptists being prominent among them—although some Churchmen who were well known as abolitionists also played a part, most notably Charles Buxton, son of the great abolitionist, Sir T. F. Buxton. Dr. Underhill himself was very vocal in calling for an inquiry. Indeed, ironically, his controversial letter was itself primarily a call for an inquiry. The following report of the conclusion of a speech he gave at the Baptist chapel in Maidstone is undoubtedly typical of others he made during these weeks: "Having expressed an opinion that the Governor of Jamaica would meet with his deserts, and that a commission of English gentlemen should be sent to Jamaica, the speaker resumed his seat amidst much applause."19 This call was widely endorsed by the English Baptist community. *The Baptist Magazine* described the governor and the military officers concerned as "monsters," the trials held under court martial as "this new Bloody Assize" and judged that the "public will, beyond all question, require a strict and searching investigation into the whole subject."20 *The General Baptist Magazine* declared that in due course "Baptists in all parts of the country" should petition Parliament "demanding a full investigation of the whole affair."21 *The Freeman*, not content with talk of Eyre merely being recalled, recommended that "every Christian church in the land" consider it a sacred obligation to "memorialize Lord RUSSELL that the Governor may be put on his trial."22 The quarterly meeting of the missionary committee of the Baptist Union unanimously passed a resolution calling for an inquiry.23 By the time the deputation of the BMS met with Cardwell (Russell being ill) the government could no longer resist the pressure. The Secretary of State for the Colonies promised Sir Morton Peto, Dr. Angus, J. H. Hinton, William Brock, and the other gentlemen with them that "an inquiry should be at once instituted."24 The issue of *The Freeman* in which this development was announced contained a collection of already redundant letters calling on Baptists to throw their weight behind the campaign to obtain an inquiry. One from C. J. Middleditch, secretary of the Oxfordshire Baptist Association, endeavored to show the good example set by the Baptists he represented, and another letter argued, "If ever the denomination had a just claim to be heard, it is now."[25] Eyre's critics would have their inquiry.

The establishing of a Royal Commission created a kind of lull in the dispute. Both friends and foes of the governor needed to wait and see if the commissioners confirmed their own instincts. With all eyes on the future report, what turned out to be the severest penalty that Eyre would ever receive from the government happened without the emotional satisfaction that a sentence, which comes after a trial brings to those who wish to see someone punished: in order to remove any awkward situations for the investigating commissioners, Eyre was immediately relieved of his duties as governor and recalled to Britain. It was a victory for Eyre's critics, but it was not fully celebrated due to the onset of a season of quiet waiting. With an official report pending, most partisans in England tried to keep their opinions to themselves for the few intervening months, lest they should be accused of prejudging the findings of the commission. This was not always easy. *The General Baptist Magazine*, for example, could not resist giving an interim report of its own:

> The notes recently published of Gordon's trial more than confirm the first impression, that he was judicially murdered. We are told "to wait" before giving an opinion; but seeing that until just recently all our information was supplied by the Governor and his friends, the request was a little absurd.[26]

A speech by John Aldis, the president of the Baptist Union for that year, given at the annual meeting of the BMS in April 1866 well illustrates the difficulty of maintaining the recommended restraint. Supporting a carefully worded resolution that deplored the loss of life and property "attending the recent riot at Morant Bay," a report of this session begins with Aldis observing:

> I have learned that some have viewed with apprehension discourses on this subject in this place before the return of the commission, or before the presentation of the report which they will render. I felt myself almost disposed, therefore, to abandon the matter, and certainly I must modify the form in which the few observations I shall make to you must be presented. (A VOICE—Speak out.) I thought I was speaking out. Mr. TRESTRAIL—He means speak out your mind. (Cheers and laughter.)

He went on in his speech to praise Underhill lavishly, the first mention of the secretary's name prompting "[l]oud cheering, and waving of hats and handkerchiefs."[27]

The report of the commissioners, dated 9 April 1866, had something for everyone. Its conclusions were given in seven brief points, with the fourth one confirming the convictions of Eyre's defenders and the seventh one, those of his detractors, namely:

> IV. That praise is due to Governor Eyre for the skill, promptitude, and vigour which he manifested during the early stages of the insurrection; to the exercise of which qualities its speedy termination is in a great degree to be attributed.
>
> * * *
>
> Lastly. That the punishments were excessive
> (1.) That the punishment of death was unnecessarily frequent.
> (2.) That the floggings were reckless, and at Bath positively barbarous.
> (3.) That the burning of 1,000 houses was wanton and cruel.[28]

The commission was over, but the controversy raged on.

Two extreme, opposing camps now clearly emerged. Before the establishing of the Royal Commission, a group of Britons who had been outraged by the brutality of the days of martial law had formed themselves into the "Jamaica Committee" and this organization now resolved to see Eyre prosecuted for murder. On the other hand, upon the ex-governor's arrival in Southampton, an ostentatious banquet was held in his honor. On this occasion Lord Cardigan spoke of the good old days when a prime minister would stick by his colonial governors "no matter what might be the cruelties" committed putting down insurrections, and Charles Kingsley suggested that Eyre deserved to be elevated to the peerage.[29] *The Freeman* labelled it the "Bloody Banquet," and even moderate sympathizers with Eyre's cause generally felt there was something unseemly about it.[30] The response of this camp to the declared intentions of the Jamaica Committee was to establish an organization of their own, the Eyre Defence and Aid Fund.

An analysis of the kind of people who joined the respective committees of these two organizations reveals numerous cleavages, as the early reference to Eric Williams's work already has indicated. For example, politically, the Eyre committee had a good number of Tories while the Jamaica Committee had a large number of radicals; in terms of class, members of the aristocracy formed a conspicuous portion of the Eyre committee, while its rival was largely comprised of members of the middle classes; and in terms of professions, the Jamaica Committee had a disproportionate number of university professors, while the Eyre committee had recruited a significant number of military men.[31] Religious affiliation, however, was by no means an insignificant difference between the composition of the two committees. W. F. Finlason, in his *The History of the Jamaica Case* (1869), which he claimed was an impartial investigation of the whole affair but was actually a lengthy apologetic for Eyre, argued that the Jamaica Committee represented "religious sectarianism and extreme political Liberalism," while the Eyre Fund embraced "men of every variety of rank, profession, or pursuit, and of every variety of religious or political opinion."[32] An analysis of the two committees, however, flatly contradicts these statements in regard to religion, revealing that the Jamaica Committee was the far more ecumenical of the two. A painstaking effort has been made to identify the religious affiliation of as many of the members of both committees as possible, beginning with a trawl through such reference works as *The Dictionary of National Biography, Modern English Biography, The Complete Peerage,* and *Who's Who of British Members of Parliament.*[33] Of the sixty members of the Eyre committee, half can be identified as belonging to one of the established churches of Great Britain, and not one of them is identifiably a Nonconformist, or even a Wesleyan, or a Roman Catholic. Moreover, the Eyre committee did include two Church of England clergymen, and members of Parliament (MPs) whose views were sufficiently pronounced to merit some of the rare references to religion in *Who's Who of British Members of Parliament* such as Sir William Bagge who is described as "A Conservative; supported 'the Church of these realms as established at the Reformation'" and Colonel Henry Lowther: "a Conservative, voted against the disestablishment of the Irish Church 1869."[34]

Of the eighty-seven members of the Jamaica Committee, the religious affiliation of sixty-two (over two-thirds) has been identified. A mere eleven of these (less than one-fifth) were loyal to an established church. A third of these Churchmen were university professors who were typically kindred spirits with Mill on issues of political economy and the others included the Christian Socialists Thomas Hughes and J. M. Ludlow. Mill himself must go down as a freethinker, along with Hebert Spencer, and the committee also had three positivists or devotees of Comte's "Religion of Humanity": Professor Beesly, Godfrey Lushington, and Frederic Harrison. One Roman Catholic has been identified, Henry W. Wilberforce, and two Wesleyans, Isaac Holden and the president of the conference for that year, William Arthur. The Unitarians were well represented (seven in total) including Professor J. J. Tayler and the great veteran of the Anti-Corn Law League, J. B. Smith. The Jamaica Committee's treasurer was the Unitarian

P. A. Taylor, and its solicitor was his coreligionist, William Shaen. With ten people loyal to their denomination identified, the Quakers had the second largest representation on the committee. This undoubtedly was a reflection of their enduring interest in the campaign against slavery. John Bright, Jacob Bright, Henry Ashworth, and Charles Sturge were some of the more prominent Friends on the committee. Congregationalism, with thirteen committee members, had the largest denominational representation. These Congre-gationalists included wealthy businessmen such as Sir Francis Crossley and Titus Salt, ministers such as Dr. Alexander Raleigh and Newman Hall, and the newspaper editors, Edward Miall and Edward Baines.

The Baptists were represented by four men: Underhill, Sir Morton Peto, William Brock, and Thomas Price. Although this was a far humbler contribution than some of the less numerical significant groupings mentioned above, it was undoubtedly at least partially a reflection of a general under-representation of Baptists in the kinds of worlds where one became a household name. For example, MPs were clearly sought after as committee members, but while the tiny Unitarian community managed successfully to contribute three of them, by recruiting Peto, the committee gained the only Baptist who was an MP for the whole of 1866—the year during which the list was compiled.[35] Moreover, Peto's inclusion is particularly interesting because his political views and instincts were more moderate than many other voices in the denomination. William Brock was a highly successful London preacher. Thomas Price was well known for having edited the *Eclectic Review* for many years.

The support that Baptists gave to the Jamaica Committee is better revealed by an examination of wider lists for the two rival organizations: one is an Eyre Fund subscription list; the other, the Jamaica Committee referred to as simply the "committee" as opposed to the narrower "executive committee," but it probably amounted to much the same thing as a subscription list.[36] This Jamaica Committee list identified thirty-five people with the title "Reverend." Of these, ten can be identified as Baptist ministers, only one fewer than the eleven Congregationalists. Moreover, these two groups (which together comprised two-thirds of the total) would be ranked as offering equally large contributions if Dr. Price would have been given both of his titles like the Reverend Dr. Alexander Raleigh was. The Baptist ministers in this list included prominent figures such as Dawson Burns, J. P. Chown, George Gould, Charles Stovel, and Charles Williams. Moreover, not one of the ministers on the Jamaica "committee" is listed in the *Clergy List* for the Church of England.[37] The Eyre subscription list, by contrast, contained forty-three Reverends, a few of whom are too vaguely described for accurate identification (notably "J. Smith" without a location), but not one of the rest can be found in the list of Baptist ministers in the *Baptist Hand-book* and, extraordinarily, every single Reverend, bar one, can be positively identified on the *Clergy List* for the Church of England.[38] These clergymen included figures such as G. R. Portal, Domestic Chaplain to the Earl of Carnarvon; H. G. Liddell, Dean of Christ Church, Oxford, and Hon. Chaplain in Ordinary to the Queen; and, most interesting of all, someone claiming to be making a donation on behalf of Dr. Francis Bradshaw, a clergyman resident in Jamaica. Returning to the Jamaica Committee list, although one despairs of accurately identifying enough of the laymen (let alone their religious affiliations) to be able to make any reliable generalizations, it should also be mentioned that some Baptist names are readily apparent among them, notably that of Alfred Illingworth, the wealthy Bradford mill owner, and W. Steadman Aldis, who by achieving the position of Senior Wrangler in 1861 represented the celebrated first fruits of honors for Victorian Baptists at Cambridge University.

In short, in an analysis of these lists, every Baptist who expressed a commitment by endorsing one of these two organizations supported the Jamaica Committee, and the Eyre Defence and Aid Fund was overwhelmingly, and perhaps exclusively, supported by members of the established churches. Indeed, Eyre's father had been a Church of England clergyman, and "the Bishop, Archdeacons and the clergy of Jamaica" sent a warm address of support to Eyre in response to the news that he had been relieved of his duties and recalled from the island.[39] This address bore witness that:

> Those of us who have had the privilege of private intercourse with your Excellency are prepared to testify that never were charges of injustice and inhumanity more inappropriate than those with which your detractors have assailed you [. . .].[40]

The religious cleavage of this controversy in its Jamaican context is brought into sharper focus by recalling that no Baptist would have had this kind of social interaction with Eyre. When Charles Buxton rehearsed many of the excesses of the period of martial law in the Commons, his evidence incidentally included insights into the religious divide that was a subtext in the situation, such as Colonel Hobbs's putting into his official dispatch that what he had seen was "calculated to endear a man to the Established Church," and the case of Provost Marshal Ramsay who addressed a group of people he had just had flogged with the words, "Damned brutes: Damned Baptist brutes! Damned political brutes, lie down."[41] Hamilton Hume, in his biography of

Eyre, even cited as one of the contributing causes of the disturbances in Morant Bay the pernicious influence of "revival meetings."[42] As part of his response to the Morant Bay disturbances, Eyre tried to pass a bill restricting freedom of public worship, but the measure would have exempted Church of England, Church of Scotland, Roman Catholic, and Jewish congregations, making it clearly aimed at Wesleyans and Protestant Dissenters and probably Baptists in particular.[43] In August 1866 *The Freeman* ran an article titled "The Clergy and Mr. Eyre," which noted that the clergy of the Church of England had rallied to Eyre's side and argued that this was part of a long tradition of their supporting tyranny and opposing liberty.[44]

Some Churchmen themselves saw this dispute as primarily one with the Baptists. *The Times*'s brief outburst against the Baptist missionaries noted earlier was nothing compared to the disdain and slander indulged in by its religious contemporary, *The Church Times*. Its news summary for 25 November 1865 declared:

> It is not the first time that Baptist ministers have been identified with Negro rebels, nor is it likely to be the last, if the "Society" at home continues to employ such teachers as Dr. Underhill. Ever since these people squatted down in the island they seem to have applied themselves to two leading purposes, the demoralization of the Negroes, and the promotion of disloyal enmity against the ruling power. The utter ruin of the island in a commercial sense, the pauperization of the Negro, and two fruitless insurrections accompanied by the usual massacres of the white population, are tangible evidences of their success.[45]

Moreover, this item was itself restrained compared to another article in this same issue titled "The Baptists and the Jamaica Massacre." The author was provoked beyond what he could bear when "an unpleasant girl with a blotchy face" came to his door carrying "filthy cards embellished with smudged engravings" in support of Baptist missions in the West Indies. Her "arrival was heralded by a single knock, and who, well tutored in annoying persistence, refused to leave till she had 'an answer from the gentleman.'" This audacious attack prompted the writer to give wider exposure to his conviction that BMS funds "have been employed for two such objects as the restoration of Obeah worship among the negroes and the promotion of the massacre of the white population of one of our colonies."[46] Even the bishop of St. David's, Connop Thirlwall, a man who was often moderate and gracious and who had supported the cause of Dissenters at Cambridge University, saw this dispute as fueled by the Baptists, writing in a letter dated 19 December 1865:

But whatever may have been [Eyre's] fault, his misfortune has evidently been, not that he authorised the shooting of so many negroes, but that he provoked the hostility of a powerful denomination, which could enlist on its side the whole Dissenting interest, and could force the hand of the Government.[47]

In the opinion not just of Eyre, *The Times*, and *The Church Times* but of some prominent voices in the Church of England as well, the Baptists were central to this controversy.

The English Baptist community did lend strong support to the campaign against Eyre. *The Freeman* was loyal to the Jamaica Committee throughout the whole affair, claiming in July 1866 that it believed Eyre was guilty of "wilful murder," contending in the following month that his lack of remorse meant that "we cannot perceive that he deserves mercy from God or man" and even labeling him as late as March 1868, when the campaign to prosecute him had wearily reached its final failure: "the greatest of untried criminals; one compared with whom Fenians seem merciful."[48] *The General Baptist Magazine* was also sympathetic to the activities of the Jamaica Committee.[49]

One way in which the English Baptists demonstrated their opposition to Eyre and their solidarity with the victims of the days of martial law was by defending the memory of G. W. Gordon and embracing him as one of their own. The commissioners had hinted that Gordon had done his share to inflame passions but cleared him of being part of a conspiracy.[50] As to his trial itself, Russell Gurney, one of the commissioners and a Tory MP for Southampton (of all places), reiterated their conclusion in Parliament: "I am perfectly satisfied that the evidence on which Gordon was convicted was wholly insufficient to justify the conviction."[51] Nevertheless, Eyre's supporters continued to drag his name through the mud, with Hamilton Hume, for example, in the year following Gurney's statement, still claiming that Gordon had been "in a combination to madden the people and bring about a rebellion," and even asserting that he had attempted "to purchase a Confederate schooner, with arms and ammunition," albeit admitting in a footnote that this might have been some other black person, but he was sure the attempt was made.[52] But if the more Eyre's defenders thought about Gordon the less they liked him, the same exercise had the opposite effect for his accusers. Some English Baptists initially took the tack of noting that Gordon was not in association with the congregations connected with the BMS, and some even denied that he was a Baptist at all.[53] In November 1865, *The Freeman* was saying cautiously that it was not claiming Gordon was a saint and even that it was willing to concede the possibility that he "may have merited the death he has met with."[54] By August of the following year, however, "the Honourable G. W. GORDON" was being lauded in that newspaper as that "not only innocent, but noble and Christian man—the John Bright of Jamaica." The paper even went on to compare his trial to that of Christ, arguing that, like Caiaphas, Eyre thought, "it is expedient for us that one man should die for the people."[55] By December 1865, Baptist ministers were discussing Gordon's case in their Sunday morning sermons, with William Brock apparently not being the only one to use as his text, Luke 6:22-26, the scripture reference Gordon had added to his final letter to his wife.[56] Gordon's case became a bridge where the English Baptist community could cross over into the land of Eyre's accusers. At the autumn meeting of the Baptist Union in 1866, J. H. Hinton moved and William Brock seconded:

> That this Union thus places on record its conviction that the arrest, trial, and execution of George William Gordon, were at once illegal and unjust, and expresses its profound sympathy with Mrs. Gordon under the life-long affliction occasioned by so severe a loss.[57]

The General Baptist Magazine records that Hinton said in his speech that "he hoped the question would yet come for trial before a British jury" and that the resolution "was passed in solemn silence, the whole assembly signifying their concurrence and adoption by standing up."[58] Another resolution at the same meeting introduced a scheme to build a "Gordon Memorial Chapel" at Morant Bay. *The Freeman* took up this suggestion with enthusiasm, this time referring to Gordon as "the STEPHEN of Jamaica."[59] His beatification was complete.

One instance has been found of an English Baptist defying the campaign against Eyre: a letter to *The Freeman* by the young Arthur Mursell. Mursell was offended by what he considered the unsuitable tone of the newspaper's "Bloody Banquet" article on Eyre's arrival dinner. He went on to express sympathy for the ex-governor and to censure his accusers, calling the demonstration against Eyre in Southampton on the same night as the banquet "the counter brawl."[60] The newspaper received such a flood of letters objecting to this one that it decided to make its burden more manageable by only printing correspondents from Southampton itself, one of which pointed out that among the participants in the "counter brawl" were all of the Baptist ministers of that town.[61]

Mursell was in no way representative. The feelings of English Baptists on this issue are better captured by the way that moderate figures were willing to associate with it. As we have seen, this was the case with Sir Morton Peto. Indeed, as the bankruptcy of his firm came during this controversy, it is possible that the campaign against Eyre was the last political crusade to which he gave his public efforts. Another telling sign is the soft support that C. H. Spurgeon, a figure who often held himself aloof from political controversies, gave to this dispute. His journal, *The Sword and the Trowel*, was still in its first year of publication when he wrote on the Morant Bay disturbances:

> There does not appear to be the remotest evidence of any organized conspiracy [. . .] nor has any body of men been met in armed rebellion; but the governor has gone on shooting, hanging, and flogging, after the fashion of the Russians in Poland—making very little account of either law or justice, so long as he might but gratify the old planter thirst for cruelty and blood.[62]

At a meeting at the Metropolitan Tabernacle in December 1865, Spurgeon chose to give an address on the life of William Knibb, a Baptist missionary to Jamaica in the first half of the century who had also been accused of fuelling rebellion, and his lecture was followed by Underhill speaking about the present situation.[63] Even Baptist Noel felt an urge to join this controversy. This moderate and irenic Baptist minister from an aristocratic family went to the trouble of writing a book that set out to prove that Gordon was innocent and treated illegally: *The Case of George William Gordon, Esq.* (1866).[64] Noel, writing before the commissioners had reported, described Gordon as a "quiet, loyal and Christian man" and compared him to John the Baptist who also "had ventured to condemn the misdeeds of the great" and suffered for it, and to Christ himself who "was hated by the world, because He testified of it that its works were evil."[65] As for Eyre, Noel coyly compared him to Othello, whose groundless imaginations caused him to murder an innocent person, and he offered him this prayer of warning:

> May Mr. Gordon's enemies die with as clear a conscience and as calm a faith as he had! May Mr. Eyre [. . .] and all who took part in causing his death, have as real a knowledge of Jesus Christ, as simple a trust, and as joyful a hope as he had [. . .].[66]

As to Gordon's trial itself, Noel pronounced:

> He had no more chance of fair play than Faithful had in Vanity Fair. My Lord Hategood, with the gentlemen of the jury, Mr. Nogood, Mr. Malice, Mr. Lovelust, Mr. Liveloose, Mr. Liar, Mr. Cruelty, and the rest, with the

three witnesses, Pickthank, Envy, and Superstition, were no more resolved against Faithful before hearing his case than were those in power against this Christian man.[67]

The Baptist press, the proceedings of the Baptist Union, and the actions of numerous individual Baptists all reveal that the English Baptist community was decisively behind the campaign against Governor Eyre.

Eyre was never convicted of any crime. Having failed in various attempts to convince a grand jury to have him tried for murder, the Jamaica Committee doggedly attempted to have a fresh trial for a lesser charge related to the same events. The new accusation was "high crimes and misdemeanours," but this attempt, like the previous ones, came to nothing. To add another bitter blow to their defeat, in 1872 Parliament passed a measure to reimburse Eyre for the legal expenses he had incurred while successfully defying the Jamaica Committee.[68] Sir Charles Adderley, who had been Under Secretary for the Colonies when the Tory government had allegedly made a promise to pay Eyre's costs, claimed in his parliamentary speech on the expenses debate that the reason why there was a controversy in the first place was because the Jamaica Committee consisted of men who "did not think anything could justify the execution of a Baptist."[69] The Norwich mustard manufacturer, J. J. Colman, was now in Parliament, and although he was by this time a member of a Congregational church, during the years of the campaign against Eyre he had been a Baptist deacon.[70] Colman's daughter recalled in her biography of her father that he was "a sympathizer" with the "strong feeling roused against" Eyre "so ably voiced by John Stuart Mill," the chairman of the Jamaica Committee, and that Colman "expressed his views on this occasion by voting against the Motion" for paying the ex-governor's legal expenses.[71] So accusations against Baptists and the Baptist witness against Eyre were part of this controversy from beginning to end.

What conclusions can be drawn from this case study? The kind of "conscience" to which the term the "Nonconformist conscience" refers is a public one—one that inspires calls for political action. The phrase was coined in 1890 when Dissenters argued that Charles Parnell's adultery should disqualify him from holding a position of political leadership, and this term is now used by historians to refer to the politics of Dissenters in the decades before this incident as well, often with the assumption that a focus on issues of personal righteousness is its distinguishing mark. For example, Owen Chadwick writes of pressure-group campaigns in the 1850s: "The campaign for a godly Sunday was another wave in English politics of what later in the century was called the Nonconformist conscience."[72] Demanding that standards of personal morality impinge on the public sphere, however, is not the kind of political conscience that this study reveals in the English Baptist community. On the contrary, this kind of moralistic conscience was hauntingly manifest in Eyre's camp. One imagines that Charles Dickens himself could not have written a fictional episode exposing Victorian religious hypocrisy to rival the real life behavior of those who sealed Gordon's fate: he was arrested on a Friday and promptly tried and convicted on the Saturday, at which point, despite it having been argued that his immediate death was needed in order to thwart further rebellion, his execution was delayed for a day on the grounds that the powers that be did not wish to dishonor the Almighty in their proceedings by working on the Sabbath.[73] The Baptist campaign against Governor Eyre highlights a very different public conscience from this.

David Bebbington has modeled a more helpful approach than the stamping of this stereotypical view upon the whole of Dissenting politics for the whole of the Victorian age. His article, "The Baptist Conscience in the Nineteenth Century," employs the methodology of analyzing the political preoccupations of Baptists in order to discern the conscience that gave rise to these stances.[74] If this approach is followed, the campaign against Eyre would certainly qualify as a reflection of a distinctly Nonconformist political preoccupation, given the remarkable cleavage between Dissenters and Churchmen that has been demonstrated by analyzing the supporters of the two opposing organizations at the heart of this conflict. Moreover, it was a concern thoroughly adopted by Baptists, as has been demonstrated by the way the campaign enlisted the support of not just politically radical figures such as J. H. Hinton, William Brock, and Thomas Price, but even more moderate figures or individuals who sometimes chose to remain aloof from political agitations such as Sir Morton Peto, Charles Spurgeon, and Baptist Noel. Speeches and resolutions at meetings of the BMS and the Baptist Union and items throughout the Baptist press all reveal that the denomination was overwhelmingly behind this campaign.

So what was the conscience that inspired this level of concern among English Baptists? Bebbington has noted that antislavery was an "enduring component" of Baptist political convictions, and a desire to see that the former slaves of Jamaica were being treated with justice was undoubtedly a factor in this dispute. This explanation, however, fails to explain why abolitionists in the Church of England refrained from joining with their Dissenting coworkers on this occasion. Charles Buxton was a rare exception who went on to prove the rule by withdrawing from the Jamaica Committee when it went from expressing a general concern about recent events to being a vehicle for the campaign against Eyre.[75] Moreover, if Churchmen who had campaigned against slavery largely stood aloof from the efforts to prosecute the ex-governor, Eyre's defenders sometimes coupled questioning the wisdom of abolition with venting unvarnished racism.[76] *The Church Times* freely indulged in racist rants:

> Have we not unlearnt all the stupid negrophilism that was, twenty years ago, a daily lesson for us—that culminated in the homage offered to every uncouth nigger who honoured the gilded saloons of Stafford House with his odorous presence? What proportion of the English people is now prepared to swallow the statement that the Emancipation of the Negro in our West Indian Colonies was a wise measure wisely executed? And how much longer is the public to be nauseated by the presentation of "the everlastin' nigger," as the model being of creation?[77]

Thomas Carlyle famously referred to the Jamaica Committee as a "knot of rabid Nigger-Philanthropists."[78] English Baptists, however, possessed other passions that helped to curb racist attitudes toward the black population of Jamaica. Humanitarianism and abolitionism were undoubtedly motivating factors, but the fault lines between the two sides on this issue invite one to look for additional concerns that were more specifically Nonconformist and Baptist.

An issue that matches these requirements well is the desire of English Baptists to show solidarity with their coreligionists worldwide and the nature of their commitment to Christian missions. Almost all of the Baptists identified in this chapter as supporting the campaign against Eyre can also be identified as having a personal commitment to the cause of missions. For example, Sir Morton Peto's link to this controversy was undoubtedly his role as treasurer of the BMS. Likewise Thomas Price and J. H. Hinton were interested in missions as well as radical politics: the former had been a personal friend of the BMS missionary to Jamaica, William Knibb, and the latter wrote an account of Knibb's life. Dr. Joseph Angus was a former secretary of the BMS, J. P. Chown and George Gould were committee members and John Aldis, Charles Stovel, and William Brock were dedicated supporters.[79] It is not an accident that the English Baptist at the center of this controversy, E. B. Underhill, was a secretary of the BMS. A particular understanding of the then current state of missions and the worldwide fellowship that missionary endeavors produced was a motivating force behind this campaign for many Baptists.

This explanation is strengthened by noting the support for the Jamaica Committee given by someone outside the Baptist community, namely the

Wesleyan William Arthur. At first glance it would seem extraordinary that the president of the Wesleyan Conference, a body that was well known for its "no politics" rule, would be willing to take a public stand on such a divisive and political issue, particularly one that divided Tories from radicals and Nonconformists from Churchmen. Wesleyan leaders at the time of these events were not even willing to endorse the campaign against church rates, a political cause dear to Dissenters, which even many Churchmen were willing to support. Once again, factors related to missions help to resolve this puzzle: Arthur began his ministry as a missionary and, at the time of the Eyre controversy, he was a secretary of the Wesleyan Missionary Society. Moreover, the Wesleyan body was the other denomination beside the Baptists that was heavily involved in Jamaican missions. The Church of England, by contrast, although it was the established Church in Jamaica at that time, concentrated its missionary activities on other parts of the world. The Church of the plantation owners was not winning the hearts of the black population in Jamaica.[80] In short, English Baptists had an affinity with Jamaican blacks, seeing many of them as either their fellow Baptists or potentially so, while Churchmen did not have such feelings or expectations and, moreover, saw the spread of Baptist principles as one more factor demonstrating the alien nature of the Jamaican people. For example, the Tory journal, *The Quarterly Review*, argued that the situation in Jamaica had been "intensified [. . .] by the traditions of different religions, or by different conceptions of the same religion," apparently uncertain as to whether or not it could recognize Jamaican Baptists as fellow Christians.[81] As we have seen, *The Church Times* felt a need when denouncing the campaign against Eyre to attack the spiritual worth of the work of the BMS as well.[82] Indeed, this connection was also made from the opposite perspective, which brings us in conclusion back to the image with which we started: the sense of outrage that the Churchmen Goldwin Smith and Thorold Rogers felt toward the actions of Governor Eyre led them into supporting Baptist missions in Jamaica. *The Missionary Herald* ran long articles in support of E. Palmer, a black Baptist minister in association with the BMS who was awaiting trial on charges related to the recent disturbances.[83] When a resolution on events in Jamaica was discussed at the autumn meeting of the Baptist Union, S. Holt, a black Baptist minister from St. Elizabeth's, Jamaica, spoke in its support and "was received with rapturous and long-continued applause."[84] The conscience that the campaign against Governor Eyre reveals is one that caused English Baptists to look beyond differences of skin color, culture, and patriotism and to see black Jamaicans as fellow human beings and as kindred spirits in the cause of Christ (or potentially so). At the end of the day, in a

Jamaican context at least, their sympathies lay with the representatives of the BMS, more than with those of the Crown; with the black masses, more than the white elite; with radicalism in the name of justice, more than with conservatism in the name of standing by one's colonial representatives; and with the worldwide Baptist community, more than with the British diaspora. The missionary impulse and experience served to curb xenophobic instincts. It would be naive to assume that the political behavior of nineteenth-century English Baptists was always motivated by sentiments such as these, but the existence of this type of Nonconformist conscience surely warrants exploration as well.

Conclusion

Social historians, on the one hand, and intellectual historians and historical theologians, on the other, have had a tendency to assume that the field of inquiry of the other group is insignificant. Those interested in the history of ideas, like a stodgy classical musician, often stay close to a well-established repertoire of "the Greats." For the Protestant historical theologian, the path of maximum propriety leads to only half a dozen or so such figures, preeminently Augustine, Luther, Calvin, and Barth. If one must work on nineteenth-century Britain, then the equivalent subrepertoire would be John Henry Newman, S. T. Coleridge, and F. D. Maurice. This list could be expanded, of course, but only along similar lines (Thomas Arnold, Benjamin Jowett, and Charles Gore, for example). Thus, if the standard repertoire is to be trusted, it just so happens that, despite comprising perhaps half of the Christian community, no evangelicals and no Free Churchmen ever had a theological thought in the Victorian era that is worthy of a second look. Moreover, historians of ideas generally give short shrift to social history and stick rather doggedly to the perceived intrinsic worth of an idea, showing little or no interest in pursuing questions of reception, dissemination, and popular appropriation and application.

Conversely, much of social history has been shaped by a stubborn denial of the blindly obvious notion that ideas matter. Social historians have often ignored their subjects' ideas on the misguided assumption that they were irrelevant to the "real" causes of what happened and why. This habit has sometimes taken an almost tyrannical hold on various parts of the discipline of history. A scholar I know who earned a PhD in history at the University of Cambridge recalls that when he had submitted the first draft of his thesis to his supervisor, he was instructed to go through the text again and take out all the ideas! This book has endeavored to contribute to breaking down this dividing wall. It has been written upon the premise that ideas matter, that

theology matters. Nevertheless, it has also been written upon the premise
that social context matters and that popular culture matters, as does how
ideas were appropriated and applied by people at street level.

Three parts have given structure to this work. Part One, "The Social
Contexts of a Private Faith," has taken themes that are grist for the mills of
cultural and social historians—especially nineteenth-century sensibilities
regarding gender and the rise of the culture and industry of mass tourism—
and found within them the power of theological ideas at work. A genuine
commitment to think theologically about the nature of the church did push
the leaders of Dissent into a commitment to gender egalitarianism, which
had a direct, practical import for women (including in terms of property and
voting rights). Gender historians would substantially impair their ability to
comprehend what was going on in the Mill Yard case if they mistakenly
assumed that theology was not germane. Likewise, the scholarship of tourist
studies could not adequately understand Victorians' holidaying in Palestine
if it did not give due weight to their judgments regarding what forms of
Christianity were unacceptable, to the degree to which their mental lives
were shaped by the Bible, and to their covert desires for religious encounters
that would spark extraordinary spiritual growth and illumination. Every
sign indicates that cultural and social history will continue to gain a wider
and wider place within the academic study of history as a whole. This book
has sought to demonstrate that attention to theological themes pays significant dividends even in these branches of historical inquiry, the ones that
have often been the most reluctant to draw upon the history of ideas for
explanations.

Part Two, "The Social Contexts of a Contested Faith," breaks new
ground in connecting two separate bodies of scholarship: the history of the
development of biblical criticism and of theology in light of modern
thought, on the one hand, and the history of popular radicals and the
Secularist movement, on the other. Combining the two has borne fruit
repeatedly by serving to challenge, if not overturn, common assumptions
currently held by scholars. D. F. Strauss's *Leben Jesu* is a full-fledged member
of the official canon (or repertoire) of the important works in the development of theological and biblical studies in the modern period. A chapter on
Strauss is a standard feature in surveys of nineteenth-century theology. It has
long been known that *Leben Jesu* made a significant impact in England.
Nevertheless, no one has ever studied its reception in Britain or paid attention to the thoughts and views of its English critics and admirers. This study
has shown that Strauss's book was popular in Britain for exactly the opposite
reason from the one that has been universally posited—not because it

achieved a new height in aggressive iconoclasm, but rather because its critical task was pursued in a dispassionate, reverential spirit. It is only because scholars have ignored the popular tradition of radical anti-Bible rhetoric stemming from Thomas Paine's *The Age of Reason* that they have been able to assume that Strauss's work was received as a shocking (or thrilling) act of unprecedented impiety. Likewise, Bishop Colenso usually earns his fifteen minutes of fame in terms of the European context as a pioneer of biblical criticism who helped to blaze the great trail of truth and light in the English-speaking world. His critics, therefore, have been left to play the role of obscurantists, and, moreover, they have invariably been scripted in the existing scholarship with nonspeaking parts. Placing the Colenso controversy in this wider, more holistic setting, however, has served to call scholars to think afresh about the pastoral context of the debate. Matthew Arnold has a place in Victorian studies on the side of progress and modern thought rather than as an obscurantist; nevertheless, even he denounced Colenso for airing his thoughts in a way that failed to take into account the spiritual lives of the masses. To the extent that scholars of Victorian intellectual history have thought about ideas in isolation from popular, social contexts, perhaps one could say that they fall under Arnold's censure as well.

No one studying the development of biblical criticism has hitherto taken notice of the ideas of anti-Christian polemicists such as Joseph Barker. Nevertheless, the context provided by this world of plebeian unbelief was an essential element in the reception of the new discipline in England. Ideas and methods fundamental to modern biblical criticism such as questioning traditional notions of the dating, authorship, and composition of various books of the Bible, were first disseminated at a popular level in Britain as components of thoroughgoing diatribes against the Christian faith as a whole. Therefore, in this volume popular radicalism is shown to be a crucial missing key for understanding the reception of ideas in the field of theological and biblical studies in nineteenth-century Britain. Moreover, in a case study that takes as its starting point the thought of Victorian Britain's most prominent atheist, Charles Bradlaugh, on the question of miracles, a specifically anti-Christian stance is revealed to be the core of the Secularist mentality. Despite loudly employing the rhetoric of rationalism and science, the world of popular unbelief is shown to be one that was surprisingly open to alternative forms of spirituality and to discerning the existence of non-material, intelligent beings. Therefore, popular unbelief did not represent so much an alternative worldview (an echo in the intelligent lower orders of a posited march of science and ideas among the nineteenth-century intellectual elite), but rather it was Christianity's official devil's advocate, a minority, opposition party whose self-imposed task was merely to attack the party in power in every possible way on every possible occasion. Further destabilizing the conventional wisdom on modern thought, religion, and the Victorians, a study of Thomas Cooper highlights a trajectory in which an earnest wrestling with the latest ideas ultimately led to, rather than away from, an orthodox Christian faith. Cooper's mental development highlights the intellectual cogency and allure of Christian doctrine, even for someone who was greedily imbibing the latest lines of thought—ideas that scholars often declare to have been inherently corrosive to faith. Thomas Cooper was not some freak of nature with a fluke natural immunity that kept him from succumbing to the advancing plague of the loss of faith despite continued exposure to its most effective agents of contagion. To the extent that he represents (albeit in an extreme and atypical case) the intellectual resilience and vitality of Christianity in the nineteenth century, his example tells us more about faith and learning among the Victorians in general than do the loss of faith narratives regarding figures such as George Eliot and Leslie Stephen which are so prominent and considered so telling in the existing literature. This book has offered a revisionist account that sets a new agenda, calling scholars to explore the intellectual strength of the Christian faith in the Victorian period, rather than to add to the tired historiography that is built upon the old assumption of its intellectual weakness.

Part Three, "The Politics of Free Church Polity," demonstrates how much more clearly Victorian politics can be seen and how many stereotypes and confusions can be overturned when theological ideas are taken seriously. There is no doubt that the Church of England has less control over English society, and alternative religious and non-religious groups such as Roman Catholics, Jews, and atheists have much greater scope to take part in the government and life of the nation than they once did. It is also clear that changes that took place in the nineteenth century played a vital role in this transformation. The engine of these changes, however, has been almost invariably depicted by scholars as forces antithetical to Christianity such as "secularization," liberal currents in thought and society that discounted faith claims, a dechristianizing populace, and the like. This study has highlighted the fact that these changes were all championed, for theological reasons, by a large number of devout Christians—a politically powerful block of Victorians who had the ability to help to shape the future. Many Nonconformists were committed to a gathered-church theology that emphasized the voluntary, free nature of the church. A consequence in the political realm of this ecclesiology was a rejection of all use of coercion by the state in order to promote Christianity. More specifically, this meant that

Nonconformists championed the rights of Jews, Roman Catholics, and even atheists to have full equality before the law, including being eligible to serve as members of Parliament. It also meant that they opposed an established church and state funding for churches and religious education. The actual content of the political agenda of Free Churchmen, therefore, stands in marked contrast to the assumption of scholars that Dissenters were seeking to impose evangelical beliefs and mores on the population as a whole through legislation. From a Dissenting perspective, political changes that scholars have generally viewed as evidence for "secularization" or the weakening of Christianity were actually the triumph of a sound theology of the church.

The main body of this book ends with a case study of a particularly heated political controversy in Victorian Britain. English public opinion was bitterly divided over whether Governor Eyre should be praised for having (allegedly) saved the white population of Jamaica from an imminent massacre, or denounced, if not prosecuted, for authorizing a brutal and murderous military assault on the black population of that island. The Baptist community, as did many other Free Churchmen, sided resolutely and vocally with the governor's accusers. In direct contrast to their stance, Eyre's English support base was overwhelmingly, if not uniformly, Anglican. Even the Christian Socialist Charles Kingsley, an Anglican clergyman with a strong reputation for having sympathy for the oppressed masses, praised Eyre in the most extravagant of language. This case study challenges scholars to rethink the stereotype of missionaries and missions-minded denominations as agents of colonial rule and British interests. The spiritual identity of English Baptists caused them to side with black Jamaicans rather than the white elite, and with the representatives of the Baptist Missionary Society, rather than those of the Crown. Although the connection between the two is often ignored, the spiritual lives and theological beliefs of the Victorians did have direct political consequences. This book has served to demonstrate that paying attention to the former enables us to comprehend better the latter in significant and fundamental ways.

Notes

Introduction

1. Arthur Burns, *The Diocesan Revival in the Church of England, c. 1800–1870* (Oxford: Clarendon, 1999); Grayson Carter, *Anglican Evangelicals: Protestant Secessions from the Via Media, c. 1800–1850* (Oxford: Oxford, 2001); Frances Knight, *The Nineteenth-Century Church and English Society* (Cambridge: Cambridge, 1995); Peter Nockles, *The Oxford Movement in Context: Anglican High Churchmanship 1760–1857* (Cambridge: Cambridge, 1994); Mark Smith, *Religion in Industrial Society: Oldham and Saddleworth, 1740–1865* (Oxford: Clarendon, 1994); Martin Wellings, "Aspects of Late Nineteenth-Century Anglican Evangelicalism: the Response to Ritualism, Darwinism and Theological Liberalism," diss., University of Oxford, 1989 (a revised version of this research will appear shortly as a monograph published by Paternoster).
2. His most influential work in this area is his *Old Testament Criticism in the Nineteenth Century: England and Germany* (London: SPCK, 1984).
3. Edward Royle, *Victorian Infidels: The Origins of the British Secularist Movement, 1791–1866* (Manchester: Manchester, 1974). Also note its sequel, Edward Royle, *Radicals, Secularists and Republicans: Popular Freethought in Britain, 1866–1915* (Manchester: Manchester, 1980).
4. The argument in this chapter significantly expands themes that I developed in my first monograph, *Friends of Religious Equality: Nonconformist Politics in Mid-Victorian England* (Woodbridge, Suffolk: Boydell, 1999). Notably, the chronological range is much wider, the implications are broadened into new areas, and the covenantal life of Dissenting congregations is drawn upon for the first time.

Chapter 1

1. The documents related to the Trust were published by an antiquary and litigating Mill Yard minister: W. H. Black, *The Last Legacy of Joseph Davis, Senior* (London: Mill Yard Congregation, 1869). I am grateful to Mrs. S. J. Mills,

Librarian, Regent's Park College, Oxford, for drawing my attention to this source and, in general, for her helpfulness and expertise.

2. Dr. Williams's Library, General Body minutes, vol. 4 (10 April 1827–12 April 1836): 200–13. I am grateful to Mr. John Creasey, (the now former) Librarian, for permission to use this source and the other manuscripts held at this library cited below in note 20. I am also grateful to him and his staff for their valuable assistance.

3. W. T. Whitley, "Seventh Day Baptists in England," *Baptist Quarterly* XII (1946–48): 256.

4. F. H. A. Micklewright, "Some Further Notes on Mill Yard Meeting-House," *Notes and Queries,* 9 October 1946: 139; Bryan Ball, *The Seventh-Day Men: Sabbatarians and Sabbatarianism in England and Wales, 1600–1800* (Oxford: Oxford, 1994) 98.

5. E. R. Conder, *Josiah Conder: A Memoir* (London: John Snow, 1857) 261–65.

6. *Wesleyan Methodist Magazine,* 5th ser. IV (1858): 49–51.

7. See, for example, James Rigg, *Congregational Independency and Wesleyan Connexionalism Contrasted* (London: James Nichols, 1851).

8. John Stoughton, *Religion in England, 1800 to 1850,* vol. 1 (London: Hodder & Stoughton, 1884) 289–91.

9. The pre-nineteenth-century history of English Seventh Day Baptists may be found in Ball, *Seventh-Day Men.*

10. W. T. Whitley, *A History of British Baptists,* rev. ed. (London: Kingsgate, 1932) 86; F. H. A. Micklewright, "A Congregation of Sabbatarian and Unitarian Baptists," and "Some Further Notes on Mill Yard Meeting-House," *Notes and Queries,* 7 September 1946: 95–99; 2 November 1946: 185–89.

11. Dr. Williams's Library, Mill-Yard minutes, 1673–1840 (photograph copy of the original), list of members 1763–1840, nos. 10 (Joseph Slater, Jr.), 21 (Isaac Slater), 22 (John Slater, Jr.).

12. Ian Sellers, "The Old General Baptists, 1811–1915," *Baptist Quarterly* XXIV (1971–72): 30–34, 74–88.

13. Mill Yard minutes, inserted item: "Case submitted to the General Body [. . .] by the trustees of the estates of the Sabbatarian Protestant Dissenters, on the appeal and protest of the members of the Sabbatarian Church, formerly assembling at Mill Yard, Goodman's Fields," 3. (This is a briefing paper privately printed for the use of the deliberating ministers.)

14. Elizabeth Slater to the trustees, 27 August 1830: "Case," 7.

15. F. H. A. Micklewright, "W. H. Black, F.S.A.: A Manuscript Diary," *Notes and Queries,* 15 February 1947: 77.

16. This list is informed by the analysis of the prevailing notions of the roles and duties of women in Leonore Davidoff and Catherine Hall, *Family Fortunes: Men and Women of the English Middle Class, 1780–1850* (London: Hutchinson, 1987) esp. 123–26.

17. "Case," 5.

18. "Case," 5.

19. "Case," 8.
20. Smith's invariably sparse diary merely records: "Appeal cause of the Sabbat.n [sic] Baptist church in Mill Yard"; "Appeal cause"; and finally "Appeal cause; 3[r]d & last session": Dr. Williams's Library, New College and Coward Trust Collection, "Diary of John Pye Smith, 1830–42," L. 18/23, 17 [May], 26 [May], June 2 [1831].
21. See Leslie Stephen and Sidney Lee, eds., *The Dictionary of National Biography* (Oxford: Oxford, 1921–22), s.v. Halley, Robert, DD (1796–1876), 8: 993–94; Vaughan, Robert (1795–1868), 20: 175–76; Reed, Andrew (1787–1862), 16: 831–34; Binney, Thomas, DD, LLD (1798–1874), 2: 519–21; Cox, Francis Augustus (1783–1853), 4: 1336. (See also Donald M. Lewis, ed., *The Blackwell Dictionary of Evangelical Biography* (Oxford: Blackwell, 1995), s.v. Newman, William (1773–1835), 2: 822.
22. *Dictionary of National Biography*, s.v. Russell or Cloutt, Thomas (1781?–1846), 17: 475.
23. "Case," 13.
24. "Case," 12.
25. "Case," 12.
26. "Case," 12.
27. Daniel Turner, *A Compendium of Social Religion* (London, 1758) 84.
28. *The Works of John Angell James*, ed. T. S. James, vol. 11 (London, 1861) 413–15.
29. A. W. W. Dale, *The Life of R. W. Dale* (London, 1898) 89–91.
30. *Baptist Magazine* I (1809): 32, 103–05; John Briggs, "She-Preachers, Widows and Other Women: the Feminine Dimension in Baptist Life Since 1600," *Baptist Quarterly* XXXI (1986): 342.
31. Black, *Legacy of Joseph Davis*, 35–36.
32. "Case," 12–13.
33. Davidoff and Hall's generalization that Independent churches during this period had "a practice which excluded women from voting" is therefore inaccurate: *Family Fortunes,* 134.
34. "Case," 14.
35. *Works of John Angell James* 11: 414.
36. "Case," 12.
37. *Works of John Angell James,* 11: 409.
38. *The English Reports, XLVIII, Rolls Court, I* (London: W. Green, 1904) 1046.
39. "*In re* Peake's Settle Estates," *The Law Reports: Supreme Court of Judicature: Chancery Division,* ed. G. W. Hemming, vol. 3 (London: W. Clowes, 1894): 520–21.
40. Edmund H. T. Snell, *The Principles of Equity, Intended for the Use of Students— and of Practitioners,* ed. Archibald Brown, 13th ed. (London: Stevens & Haynes, 1901) 125.
41. General Body minutes, vol. 4 (2 June 1831): 213. The list of those present at the start of the day's proceedings shows forty ministers in addition to the chairman, the secretary, and five provincial guests, so either a good number of

them did not stay for the whole day or some of them were ineligible or unwilling to vote.

42. Albert Rogers, *Seventh Day Baptists in Europe and America,* vol. 1 (Plainfield, N.J.: American Sabbath Tract Society, 1910) 92.

43. Karen Smith, "Beyond Public and Private Spheres: Another Look at Women in Baptist History and Historiography," *Baptist Quarterly* XXXIV (1991): 79–87.

44. Mill Yard minutes, list of members 1763–1840, no. 31 (Elizabeth Slater, formerly Kimin).

45. Davidoff and Hall, *Family Fortunes*, ch. 2, esp. 114.

Chapter 2

1. Newman Hall, *Newman Hall: An Autobiography* (London: Cassell, 1898) 70.

2. "Hall, Christopher Newman (1816–1902)," *Dictionary of National Biography*, ed. Sir Sidney Lee, 2d suppl., 1: 186–87. Since writing this chapter, I have written my own sketch of Hall's life: Timothy Larsen, *Biographical Dictionary of Evangelicals* (Leicester/Downers Grove: InterVarsity Press, 2003) 282–84.

3. G. F. L. Bridgman, ed., *The All England Law Reports Reprinted, Revised and Annotated: 1874–1880* (London: Butterworth, 1964) 642–43.

4. *The Times,* 31 July 1879: 4.

5. *The Times,* 31 July 1879: 4.

6. *The Times,* 31 July 1879: 4.

7. *The Times,* 7 August 1879: 4.

8. *The Times,* 9 August 1879: 4.

9. *The Times,* 7 August 1879: 4.

10. *The Times,* 9 August 1879: 4.

11. Hall, *Autobiography,* 328–30.

12. *The Times,* 4 August 1879: 4.

13. *The Times,* 31 July 1879: 4.

14. *The Times,* 7 August 1879: 4.

15. *The Times,* 9 August 1879: 4.

16. *The Times,* 31 July 1879: 4.

17. *The Times,* 2 August 1879: 4.

18. *The Times,* 2 August 1879: 4.

19. *The Times,* 2 August 1879: 4.

20. *The Times,* 2 August 1879: 4.

21. *The Times,* 7 August 1879: 4.

22. *The Times,* 2 August 1879: 4.

23. *The Times,* 9 August 1879: 4.

24. *The Times,* 9 August 1879: 4.

25. Hall, *Autobiography,* 111–16.

26. Hall, *Autobiography,* 331. That was in February 1880. Newman Hall married Harriet Knipe a month later, Easter Monday, at Christ Church. For a quiet wedding there was, by Hall's own account, a large and representative congrega-

tion. His old friend, Henry Allon, of Union Chapel, Islington, officiated. A few days earlier, Hall had written to him: "I am hoping Spurgeon, if well enough, may come and close with Benediction" (Albert Peel, ed., *Letters to a Victorian Editor* [London: Independent, 1929] 320). Harriet (Knipe) Hall came from an evangelical Anglican family; her father had a house in South Kensington and another in Huntingdonshire. If Charlotte (Gordon) Hall's father was, in the context of the 1840s, almost alarmingly Radical ("His Chartism was the upholding of law in constitutional efforts to improve it [. . . but] he was maligned as a Chartist in the sense of violence": Hall, *Autobiography*, 111), her uncle, Sir William Lowthrop, was chief among Albion Chapel's founders, "a former mayor, a chief magistrate, and my senior deacon": Hall, *Autobiography*, 65. Thus each marriage was, in both church and social terms, natural and eligible. After the divorce Charlotte Hall moved to the United States.

Chapter 3

1. R. E. Prothero and G. G. Bradley, *The Life and Correspondence of Arthur Penrhyn Stanley*, 2 vols. (London: J. Murray, 1894) 2: 445–46.
2. For a recent sketch of Cook's life that pays particular attention to religion, see Larsen, ed., *Biographical Dictionary*, 155–56.
3. *General Baptist Magazine* (July 1869): 197.
4. John Stoughton, *Recollections of a Long Life*, 2d ed. (London: Hodder & Stoughton, 1894) 145.
5. Mark Twain, *The Innocents Abroad* (1869; reprint, New York: Oxford, 1996). I am grateful to my father, Kenneth W. Larsen, for drawing my attention to this source.
6. William Henry Leighton, *A Cook's Tour to the Holy Land in 1874* (London: F. James, 1947) 57.
7. Samuel Manning, *Those Holy Fields* (London: Religious Tract Society, 1874) 42.
8. *Cook's Excursionist*, 10 December 1868 (Christmas Supplement): 21.
9. Jabez Burns, *Help-Book for Travellers to the East*, 2d ed. (London: Cook's Tourist Office, 1872) 179.
10. London, Thomas Cook Archives, "Diary of George Jager," 1874 (typescript of original): 13. I owe a great debt to Jill Lomer, Archives Administrator, who patiently fulfilled numerous requests.
11. Hall, *Autobiography* ,150.
12. Prothero and Bradley, *Stanley* 2: 72.
13. *Programme of Cook's Tour to Egypt, the Nile, and Palestine, Leaving New York, January 4, 1873* (London, n.d.) 6.
14. Burns, *Help-Book*, 83.
15. H[enry] A[llon], "The Peninsula of Sinai: notes of travel therein," *British Quarterly Review* XLIII (1866): 116.
16. Edwin Hodder, *On Holy Ground* (London: William P. Nimmo, 1875) 19–20.

17. Twain, *Innocents Abroad*, 567.
18. Leighton, *Cook's Tour*, 46.
19. Manning, *Holy Fields*, 52.
20. *Cook's Excursionist*, 7 July 1870: 5.
21. Hall, *Autobiography*, 152.
22. D. P. Hughes, *The Life of Hugh Price Hughes* (London: Hodder & Stoughton, 1904) 395.
23. W. Hardy Harwood, *Henry Allon* (London: Cassell, 1894) 45.
24. Leighton, *Cook's Tour*, 62.
25. Burns, *Help-Book*, 103.
26. Allon, "Sinai," 91, 112.
27. *Cook's Excursionist*, 7 July 1870: 5.
28. Manning, *Holy Fields*, 26.
29. Stoughton, *Recollections*, 145–46.
30. *Cook's Excursionist*, 24 November 1873: 7.
31. Leighton, *Cook's Tour*, 66.
32. Hughes, *Hughes*, 395.
33. *Cook's Excursionist*, 10 December 1868 (Christmas Supplement): 37.
34. "Diary of George Jager," 18.
35. Manning, *Holy Fields*, 32, 205, 193, 140.
36. *Cook's Excursionist*, 3 May 1869: 5.
37. Burns, *Help-Book*, 66.
38. Manning, *Holy Fields*, 150.
39. Manning, *Holy Fields*, 22.
40. Stoughton, *Recollections*, 151. A useful discussion of this theme can be found in Naomi Shepherd, *The Zealous Intruders: The Western Rediscovery of Palestine* (London: Collins, 1987) ch. 3.
41. *General Baptist Magazine* (July 1869): 202.
42. Hodder, *Holy Ground*, 18–19, 330–33.
43. *Programme of Cook's Tour*, 8.
44. Stoughton, *Recollections*, 147.
45. Hall, *Autobiography*, 331.
46. Hall, *Autobiography*, 151.
47. *General Baptist Magazine* (December 1868): 362.
48. *Cook's Excursionist*, 3 May 1869: 3.
49. *Cook's Excursionist*, 24 November 1873: 7.
50. W. Fraser Rae, *The Business of Travel* (London: T. Cook, 1891) 271–72.
51. William Howard Russell, *A Diary in the East* (London: G. Routledge, 1869) 321–22.
52. See, for his denial of this charge, Thomas Cook, *Letters to His Royal Highness the Prince of Wales* (London: Cook's Tourist Office, 1870).
53. *Cook's Excursionist*, 3 May 1869: 5.
54. Russell, *Diary*, 147.
55. John Pudney, *The Thomas Cook Story* (London: M. Joseph, 1953) 188–89.

56. Rae, *Business*, 84, 215.
57. *Cook's Excursionist*, 3 May 1869: 4.
58. *General Baptist Magazine* (December 1868): 359.
59. *Cook's Excursionist*, 25 November 1868: 2.
60. London, Thomas Cook Archives, Thomas Cook to his wife, 24 March 1873; Robert Ingle, *Thomas Cook of Leicester* (Bangor: Headstart History, 1991) 48.
61. *Cook's Excursionist* (American ed.; December 1877): 11.
62. *Cook's Excursionist*, 6 December 1879: 13.
63. For a general discussion of this issue, see Boris Vukoni, *Tourism and Religion* (New York: Penguin, 1996). Also, Michael Prior, "Pilgrimage to the Holy Land, Yesterday and Today," in *Christians in the Holy Land*, eds. Michael Prior and William Taylor (London: World of Islam Festival Trust, 1995). For this and some other themes developed in this chapter, see J. G. Davies, *Pilgrimage Yesterday and Today: Why? Where? How?* (London: SCM, 1988) esp. 140–52.
64. Hall, *Autobiography*, 329.
65. For example, see "Diary of George Jager," 13, 17.
66. *Cook's Excursionist*, 5 August 1872: 2.

Chapter 4

1. The scholarship analyzing D. F. Strauss (1808–74) and his *Leben Jesu* directly is voluminous, and there is no need to rehearse it in this chapter. A short, useful introduction is Hans Frei, "David Friedrich Strauss," *Nineteenth Century Religious Thought in the West*, eds. Ninian Smart et al., vol. 1 (Cambridge: Cambridge, 1985) 215–60. For a book-length treatment see, for example, Horton Harris, *David Friedrich Strauss and His Theology* (Cambridge: Cambridge, 1973).
2. A. M. Fairbairn, "David Friedrich Strauss: a Chapter in the History of Modern Religious Thought," *Contemporary Review* XXVII (1876): 951.
3. One such classic study is James R. Moore, *The Post-Darwinian Controversies: A Study of the Protestant Struggle to Come to Terms with Darwin in Great Britain and America, 1870–1900* (Cambridge: Cambridge, 1979). The impact of Strauss's *Leben Jesu* in his native land, again by way of contrast, has generated a string of monographs. See, for example, Edwina G. Lawler, *David Friedrich Strauss and His Critics: The Life of Jesus Debate in Early Nineteenth-Century German Journals* (New York: P. Lang, 1986); William Madges, *The Core of Christian Faith: D. F. Strauss and His Catholic Critics* (New York: P. Lang, 1987); and Marilyn Chapin Massey, *Christ Unmasked: The Meaning of The Life of Jesus in German Politics* (Chapel Hill: North Carolina, 1983).
4. Royle, *Victorian Infidels*.
5. J. Guinness Rogers, *J. Guinness Rogers: An Autobiography* (London: James Clarke, 1903) 96.
6. Henry Parry Liddon, *Life of Edward Bouverie Pusey*, vol. 2 (London: Longmans, Green, 1893) 109.

7. J. R. Beard, *Voices of the Church, in Reply to Dr. D. F. Strauss* (London: Simpkin, Marshall, 1845) xiv.

8 . J. R. Beard, *The Historical Evidences of Christianity Unassailable: Proved in Four Letters Addressed to the Rev. Robt. Taylor and Mr. Richd. Carlile* (London: R. Hunter, 1826).

9. Beard, *Voices* , v.

10. Frank Turner has claimed that Strauss's *Leben Jesu* was regarded at the time "as the most advanced and destructive theological work of the day." Frank Turner, "The Victorian Crisis of Faith and the Faith that was Lost," *Victorian Faith in Crisis: Essays on Continuity and Change in Nineteenth-Century Religious Belief*, eds. Richard J. Helmstadter and Bernard Lightman, (Stanford: Stanford, 1990) 29.

11. Gordon S. Haight, ed., *The George Eliot Letters*, vol. 1 (New Haven: Yale, 1954) 13.

12. Charles C. Hennell, *An Inquiry Concerning the Origin of Christianity* (London: Smallfield, 1838) vi–vii.

13. Hennell, *Inquiry*, 370.

14. Susan Budd's research revealed that Paine's *The Age of Reason*, even in the second half of the nineteenth century, was (beside the Bible itself) the book that secularists most often mentioned as instrumental in their loss of faith. Susan Budd, *Varieties of Unbelief: Atheists and Agnostics in English Society, 1850–1960* (London: Heinemann Educational, 1977) 107–09.

15. Thomas Paine, *The Age of Reason* (London: Watts, 1938 [originally 1793/ 1795]) 128–29.

16. Gordon S. Haight, *George Eliot: A Biography* (London: Penguin, 1986) 42.

17. Haight, *George Eliot Letters*, 1: 206.

18. Daniel L. Pals, *The Victorian "Lives" of Jesus* (San Antonio: Trinity, 1982) 53.

19. Haight, *George Eliot Letters*, 1: 185 (April 1845).

20. Haight, *George Eliot Letters*, 1: 218 (May 1846).

21. *Eclectic Review*, n.s. XIX (1846): 371. Richard Whately, *Das Leben Napoleon's, kritisch geprüft* (Leipzig, 1836).

22. Henry Rogers, *Vernunft und Glaube: ihre gegenseitigen Beziehungen und Conflicte!* (Berlin, 1853).

23. Henry Rogers, *Reason and Faith: With Other Essays* (London, 1866).

24. *Edinburgh Review* XC (1849): 326, 331.

25. Rogers, *Reason and Faith*, vi, 137–66.

26. *British Quarterly Review* V (1847): 210–11.

27. *Inquirer*, 20 June 1846: 389.

28. *Inquirer*, 3 October 1846: 628–29.

29. *Eclectic Review*, n.s. XIX (1846): 364–65. Admittedly, this review had probably been commissioned before the Eliot translation had appeared.

30. Thomas Cooper, *The Life of Thomas Cooper* (London, 1882) 262–63.

31. F. E. Kingsley, *Charles Kingsley: His Letters and Memories of His Life*, vol. 1 (London: McMillan, 1901) 194.

32. *Cooper's Journal; Or Unfettered Thinker and Plain Speaker for Truth, Freedom, and Progress* (1850; reprint, New York: A. M. Kelley, 1970) 8; 1.

33. *Cooper's Journal,* 154.

34. *Cooper's Journal,* 269.

35. For a typical specimen, see *Cooper's Journal,* 108.

36. *Cooper's Journal,* 107, 272.

37. *Cooper's Journal,* 345.

38. *Cooper's Journal,* 42, 45. While Cooper was, of course, atypical, he does help to give a voice to all the popular radicals who ensured that an English translation of Strauss existed, who bought that edition and were influenced by it, who discussed Strauss and lectured on him, who attended such lectures and altered their views in light of them, and who bought the Eliot translation (which had a standing advertisement in *Cooper's Journal*) and were shaped by it.

39. Martineau's identity as the author is confirmed in his biography: James Drummond and C. B. Upton, *The Life and Letters of James Martineau,* vol. 1 (London: James Nisbet, 1902) 132.

40. *Westminster Review,* April 1847: 155.

41. *Westminster Review,* April 1847: 148.

42. *Westminster Review,* April 1847: 161.

43. *Westminster Review,* April 1847: 159.

44. *Westminster Review,* April 1847: 156–57. Instances could be multiplied of this tendency in Strauss. For example, the passage on the saying from the cross, "My God, my God, why hast thou forsaken me?" reads: "we observe that one who, as the gospels narrate of Jesus, had long included suffering and death in his idea of the Messiah, and hence had regarded them as part of the divine arrangements, could scarcely complain of them when they actually arrived as an abandonment by God." David Friedrich Strauss, *The Life of Jesus Critically Examined,* trans. George Eliot [1846], ed. Peter C. Hodgson (Ramsey, N.J.: Sigler, 1994) 688.

45. *Westminster Review,* April 1847: 161.

46. *Edinburgh Review* XC (1849): 325.

47. James Urquhart, *The Life and Teaching of William Honyman Gillespie* (Edinburgh: T. & T. Clark, 1915).

48. William Gillespie, *The Truth of the Evangelical History of our Lord Jesus Christ: Proved, in Opposition to Dr. D. F. Strauss, the Chief of Modern Disbelievers in Revelation* (Edinburgh, 1856) 16.

49. Beard, "Strauss, Hegel, and Their Opinions," in Beard, *Voices,* 10. (The pagination in this volume restarts at the beginning of each essay.)

50. Strauss, of course, viewed only a belief in miracles rather than a disbelief in them as prejudicial. For example, he argued that the instantaneous restoring of skin damaged by leprosy was "so inconceivable that every one who is free from certain prejudices (as a critic ought always to be) must involuntarily be reminded by it of the realm of fable." Strauss, *Life of Jesus,* 439.

51. *Inquirer,* 3 October 1846: 628–29.

52. Strauss frequently used the devise of naming "legend" and "tradition" as the active agents, thereby discreetly deflecting attention away from the notion that Christians were embellishing their stories in the telling. Thus, "it was tradition which converted what it met," "the primitive Christian legend might without hindrance represent," "it was not possible for the legend long to rest contented with so slight a use of them"; Strauss, *Life of Jesus*, 534, 668, 683.

53. It should be noted that Strauss's theory that what has been deemed Christ's bodily resurrection should be viewed as actually having been an internal impression experienced by some disciples was bolstered by sexist assumptions. For example, he wrote: "Lastly, how conceivable is it that in individuals, especially women, these impressions were heightened, in a purely subjective manner, into actual vision." One wonders what Eliot thought when she translated that; Strauss, *Life of Jesus*, 742.

54. Beard, "Illustrations of the Credibility of the Gospel Narratives, Drawn from Moral Considerations," in Beard, *Voices*, 73.

55. *Westminster Review*, April 1847: 154–55.

56. *British Quarterly Review* V (1847): 245.

57. *British Quarterly Review* V (1847): 223.

58. Beard, "Illustrations," 20–21.

59. *Edinburgh Review* XC (1849): 342.

60. Gillespie, *Truth*, 107–08. Strauss had written, for example, "On the mention of a blind beggar of Jericho, Mark is careful to give us his name, and the name of his father (x. 46). From these particulars we might already augur, what the examination of single narratives will prove: namely, that the copiousness of Mark and Luke is the product of the second function of the legend, which we may call the function of embellishment"; Strauss, *Life of Jesus*, 360.

61. Rogers, *Reason and Faith*, 137–66.

62. *British Quarterly Review* V (1847): 240.

63. Gillespie, *Truth*, v.

64. *British Quarterly Review* LV (1847): 260. Strauss, by way of contrast, had referred to "the inadequacy of an appeal, in a scientific inquiry, to a popular notion, such as that of the aid of the Holy Spirit"; Strauss, *Life of Jesus,* 383.

65. Beard, "Strauss," 15; Beard, *Voices*, xiii.

66. *Eclectic Review*, n.s. XIX (1846): 371.

67. Strauss, *Life of Jesus*, lii.

68. Brewin Grant and George Jacob Holyoake, *Christianity and Secularism: Report of a Public Discussion* (London, 1853), 215.

69. Although I have read a considerable amount of primary source material by Bradlaugh, I have never seen *Leben Jesu* cited or referred to in his writings and speeches.

70. *Edinburgh Review* XC (1849): 337.

71. *Contemporary Review* XXVIII (1876): 278.

Chapter 5

1. *Chronicle of Convocation,* Lower House, 11 February 1863: 1041, 1049–50.

2. *Chronicle of Convocation,* Lower House, 19 May 1863: 1180, 1184; Upper House, 20 May 1863: 1208.

3. J. W. Colenso, *The Pentateuch and the Book of Joshua Critically Examined,* part 1, 2d ed. (London: Longman, 1862) viii–ix. (The second edition replaced the first in less than a month. It contained only minor changes, all of which are listed in the front of part 2, for the benefit of those holding first editions.)

4. Letter to Theophilus Shepstone, 2 March 1863: G. W. Cox, *Life of John William Colenso,* vol. 1 (London: W. Ridgway, 1888) 236.

5. Cox, *Colenso,* 1: 235–37, 271.

6. Professor Max Müller listed Colenso with Galileo and Darwin as a defender of truth. Cox allows his subject to bask in this light in which Müller had placed him as does, in recent years, Ferdinand Deist. Cox, *Colenso,* 1: 215; Ferdinand Deist, "John William Colenso: Biblical Scholar," *Old Testament Essays,* eds. J. A. Loader and J. H. le Roux, vol. 2 (Pretoria: UNISA, 1984) 129–30.

7. Peter Hinchliff, *Benjamin Jowett and the Christian Religion* (Oxford: Clarendon, 1987) 54–56.

8. His story is told in A. J. Davidson, *The Autobiography and Diary of Samuel Davidson* (Edinburgh: T. & T. Clark, 1899).

9. A detailed examination of this work can be found in Ieuan Ellis, *Seven Against Christ* (Leiden: E. J. Brill, 1980). A magnificent, edited version has recently been published: Victor Shea and William Whitla, eds., *Essays and Reviews: The 1860 Text and Its Reading* (Charlottesville: Virginia, 2000).

10. T. K. Cheyne, *Founders of Old Testament Criticism* (London: Methuen, 1893) 196.

11. Colenso, *Pentateuch,* 1: 39–40.

12. Colenso, *Pentateuch,* 1: 57–60.

13. Colenso, *Pentateuch,* 1: xvii, xix.

14. *Record,* 13 October 1862: 2. A copy of the more unguarded version found its way into the hands of the *Record* which duly exploited the opportunity to the full. Cox, *Colenso,* 1: 195–96. Prothero and Bradley, *Stanley,* 2: 103.

15. Colenso, *Pentateuch,* 1: vii.

16. *Westminster Review,* n.s. XXII.1 (January 1863): 69. It has been tentatively suggested that Mark Pattison, one of the contributors to *Essays and Reviews,* was the author of this article. *Wellesley Index to Victorian Periodicals, 1842–1900,* ed. Walter E. Houghton, vol. 3 (Toronto: Toronto, 1966) 643.

17. The *Record* compared Colenso unfavorably with Robinson Crusoe who was not reduced to doubt by the hard theological questions posed to him by his man Friday: 19 November 1862: 2. Cheyne, *Founders,* 199–200. "Colenso, John," *Encyclopaedia Britannica,* 15th ed., 3: 445.

18. Colenso, *Pentateuch,* 1: vi–viii, xxi–xxii.

19. Colenso, *Pentateuch,* 1: 9.

20. Colenso, *Pentateuch*, 1: 149.
21. J. W. Colenso, *St Paul's Epistle to the Romans* (Cambridge: Macmillan, 1861), v.
22. *Guardian*, 9 April 1862: 353.
23. Cox, *Colenso*, 1: 135.
24. Peter Hinchliff, *John William Colenso* (London: Nelson, 1964) 41–46.
25. Cox, *Colenso*, 1: 129–30.
26. Jeff Guy, *The Heretic: A Study of the Life of John William Colenso, 1814–1883* (Johannesburg: Ravan, 1983) 26–29.
27. Letter to the Secretary, S.P.G., 31 March 1856: Wyn Rees, *Colenso Letters from Natal* (Pietermaritzburg: Shuter & Shooter, 1958) 58.
28. Colenso, *Pentateuch*, 1: 144.
29. Letter to Theophilus Shepstone, 29 December 1862: Cox, *Colenso*, 1: 234.
30. *Record*, 31 October 1862: 2.
31. Colenso, *Pentateuch*, 1: chs viii and iv.
32. *Record*, 12 November 1862: 4; *Guardian*, 10 December 1862: 1170.
33. Colenso, *Pentateuch*, 3: xii.
34. *Christian Witness* 20 (1863): 54–58.
35. *Guardian*, 3 December 1862: 1149.
36. *Guardian*, 24 December 1862: 1218; *Christian Observer* LX, CCC (December 1862): 930–31.
37. Colenso, *Pentateuch*, 1: 43–44.
38. Colenso, *Pentateuch*, 3: xvii. He expressed similar sentiments in more formal language in a letter which was printed in *The Times*, 7 February 1863: 9.
39. *Record*, 21 November 1862: 4.
40. The first was by "An Unknown Pen" [G. H. Mason] and the second by James G. Murphy. Jeff Guy, who does not cite a single item from the flood of such literature or even one of the numerous lengthy articles published in the religious press, is simply mistaken when he asserts: "There were few attempts to answer him [Colenso]." *Heretic*, 137.
41. Letter to the *Record* from "Clavis"; 10 November 1862: 4.
42. John Rogerson, whose book also manages to deal with Colenso's critics almost entirely without citing their writings, claims that "Colenso's argument did not rest upon this figure alone [the 600,000 adult males mentioned in Exodus 12], as some of his critics supposed," and then goes on to list some of the other passages in the Pentateuch in which this number is either reiterated or implied. Colenso's critics, however, whatever other deficiencies they might have had, knew their Bibles. The "harmonization hypothesis" was incorporated into this speculative explanation from the very beginning, anticipating Rogerson's objection; *Old Testament Criticism*, 221.
43. *British Quarterly Review* XXXVII, LXXIII (January 1863): 184.
44. *Christian Remembrancer* XLV, CXIX (January 1863): 245, 248–49.
45. *British Quarterly Review* XXXVII, LXXIII (January 1863): 156–58.
46. *Record*, 1 December 1862: 4.
47. Letter dated 17 December 1862: R. T. Davidson, *Life of Archibald Campbell Tait*, vol. 1 (London: Macmillan, 1891) 337.

48. *Chronicle of Convocation*, Lower House, 11 February 1863: 1036.
49. Colenso, *Pentateuch*, 1: xxxv–xxxvi.
50. *Guardian*, 19 November 1862: 1098.
51. *Record*, 12 November 1862: 1.
52. *Chronicle of Convocation*, Lower House, 19 May 1863: 1177–80.
53. Cox, *Colenso*, 1: 326. The trial, which was the work of Bishop Gray of Capetown, was not recognized as valid under English law, and therefore Colenso retained the legal rights of a bishop.
54. Colenso published a long letter he had received, which documented similar remarks made by respected figures from the church fathers to the present day: Colenso, *Pentateuch*, 3: xxxiii–xl.
55. *Chronicle of Convocation*, Lower House, 19 May 1863: 1181.
56. *Record*, 5 November 1862: 4.
57. Letter to J. Davies, 23 September 1862: Frederick Maurice, *The Life of Frederick Denison Maurice*, vol. 2 (New York: Scribner's, 1884) 423.
58. Maurice, *Life of Maurice*, 2: 424–35.
59. Letter from Sarah Colenso to Margaret Bell, 3 November 1863: Rees, *Colenso Letters*, 78.
60. *Edinburgh Review* CXVII, CCXL (April 1863): 501. *The Times* never reviewed the book and avoided expressing its own view of the controversy. The *Record* noted with disapproval the favorable review in the *Daily Telegraph*, but was delighted with the negative review, in response to it, which appeared in the Morning Post shortly thereafter, taking Colenso's decision to attempt to answer some of its points in a letter to the *Telegraph* as proof of its force. *Record*, 10 November 1862: 3; 14 November 1862: 2.
61. Letter to B. H. Hodgson, 6 December 1862; Letter to Charles Darwin, 16 February 1864: Leonard Huxley, *Life and Letters of Sir Joseph Dalton Hooker*, vol. 2 (London: Murray, 1918) 57–59.
62. For example, see *Spectator*, 25 October 1862: 1178.
63. *Spectator*, 8 November 1862: 1250–52.
64. Prothero and Bradley, *Stanley*, 2: 99–104.
65. Evelyn Abbott and Lewis Campbell, *The Life and Letters of Benjamin Jowett*, vol. 1 (London: J. Murray, 1897) 301.
66. Davidson, *Life of Tait*, 1: 341–42.
67. *Chronicle of Convocation*, Upper House, 20 May 1863: 1205–06, 1208.
68. Connop Thirlwall (1792–1875), *Dictionary of National Biography*, 19: 618–21.
69. Thirlwall gave a charge to the clergy of his diocese triennially. These comments are taken from the one that he delivered in October 1863. J. J. S. Perowne, ed., *Remains, Literary and Theological of Connop Thirlwall*, vol. 2 (London: Daldy, Isbister, 1877) 62–65, 75.
70. G. W. E. Russell, ed., *Letters of Matthew Arnold 1848–1888*, vol. 1 (London: Macmillan, 1895) 175–76.
71. *Macmillan's Magazine* VII, XXXIX (January 1863): 241–56.

72. For an example of criticism of Arnold's stance, see *Westminster Review,* n.s. XXIII.2 (April 1863): 503–16. Arnold wove his reply to his critics into his next review: *Macmillan's Magazine* VII, XL (February 1863): 327–36.

73. Owen Chadwick, *The Victorian Church,* vol. 2 (London: A&C Black, 1970) 91–92.

74. Guy, *Heretic,* 183, see also 184–88.

75. Guy, *Heretic,* 180.

76. The quotation comes from a letter to "a clergyman in South Africa," 21 March 1865: Maurice, *Life of Maurice,* 2: 490.

77. Rogerson purports to list the four main lines of approach taken by Colenso's critics, but this crucial response is not one of them. Moreover, his third point— an assumption that Colenso's alleged difficulties were overcome by special mir- acles—is hardly representative (no references are given): it would appear to have been derived from Colenso's own presumptions regarding the only way he imagined his arguments could be answered; *Old Testament Criticism,* 233–34.

78. Letter to Bishop Tait, 19 November 1862: Davidson, *Life of Tait,* 1: 338.

Chapter 6

1. Summaries of his life can be found in J. O. Baylen and N. J. Gossman, eds., *Biographical Dictionary of Modern British Radicals: Vol. 2, 1830–1870* (Brighton: Harvester, 1979) 38–41; *Dictionary of National Biography,* i, 1124–27; and Donald M. Lewis, ed., *Dictionary of Evangelical Biography, 1730–1860* (Oxford: Blackwell, 1995) 1: 60. Barker's various efforts at autobi- ography were the basis of a volume that was published after his death, J. T. Barker, ed., *The Life of Joseph Barker Written by Himself* (London: Hodder & Stoughton, 1880).

2. For this phase of his life, see Stephen Roberts, "Joseph Barker and the Radical Cause, 1848–1851," *Publications of the Thoresby Society* (The Leeds Historical Society) 2d series, I (1991): 59–73.

3. For Barker as a reconvert, see Timothy Larsen, "The Regaining of Faith: Reconversions among Popular Radicals in Mid-Victorian England," *Church History* LXX.3 (September 2001): 527–43.

4. J. M. Robertson, *A History of Freethought in the Nineteenth Century* (London: Watts, 1929) 281.

5. J. M. Wheeler, *A Biographical Dictionary of Freethinkers of All Ages and Nations* (London: Progressive, 1889).

6. *London Investigator,* January 1856: 149.

7. John Watts, "Iconoclast" [Charles Bradlaugh], and Anthony Collins, eds., *Half- hours with the Freethinkers* (London: Holyoake, 1857).

8. Hypatia Bradlaugh Bonner, *Charles Bradlaugh: His Life and Work* (London: T. Fisher Unwin, 1895) 2: 121.

9. Royle, *Victorian Infidels.*

10. J. Estlin Carpenter, *The Bible in the Nineteenth Century; Eight Lectures* (New York: Longmans, 1903).

11. Rogerson, *Old Testament Criticism*, 195.

12. *Origin and authority of the Bible. Report of a public discussion between Joseph Barker, Esq., and the Rev. Brewin Grant, B.A.* (Glasgow, [1855]) 48.

13. *Barker's Review,* 19 December 1863: 267.

14. For the challenge, see Joseph Barker, *Confessions of Joseph Barker, a Convert from Christianity* (London, 1858) 16.

15. Omaha, Nebraska, Historical Society of Douglas County, Barker Papers, Joseph Barker, Jr, to Joseph Barker, 4 April 1860.

16. *The Belief in a Personal God and a Future Life: Six Nights' Discussion Between Thomas Cooper and Joseph Barker* (London: Holyoake, [1860]) 167.

17. For the latter of these, which was the more notable one, see S. P. Putman, *400 Years of Freethought* (New York: Truth Seeker, 1894) 520–25.

18. *Origin and authority*, 4.

19. Joseph Barker, *The Popular Imperfections of the Bible. A Speech Delivered by Mr. Joseph Barker, President of the Bible Convention in Salem, U.S.* (London: Holyoake, 1854) 24.

20. *The Report of the Public Discussion at Stockport, Between Mr. John Bowes and Mr. Joseph Barker* (London, 1855) 31.

21. *Report of the Public Discussion*, 52.

22. *Origin and authority*, 37.

23. *Origin and authority*, 216.

24. Joseph Barker, *Seven Lectures on the Supernatural Origin and Divine Authority of the Bible* (Stoke-upon-Trent: George Turner, 1854) 105.

25. *Great Discussion on the Origin, Authority and Tendency of the Bible between Rev. J. F. Berg, D.D., of Philadelphia, and Joseph Barker, of Ohio* (Stoke-upon-Trent: George Turner, 1854) 159.

26. Another English plebeian freethinker, Robert Cooper, produced a vade mecum of biblical contradictions: *The Infidel's Text-book* (Hull: R. Johnson, 1846). Interestingly, for the American edition (which is the one I have been able to consult) the title was made less strident, *The Inquirer's Text-book* (Boston: J. P. Mendum, n.d.). Barker paid tribute to the usefulness of this volume: *London Investigator*, August 1854: 68.

27. *Origin and authority*, 11.

28. Barker, *Seven Lectures*, 29.

29. *Report of Public Discussion*, 26.

30. Barker, *Seven Lectures,* 15.

31. Barker, *Seven Lectures,* 40.

32. *Origin and authority*, 211.

33. *Origin and authority*, 77, 92.

34. Joseph Barker, *A Review of the Bible* (London, 1848) 5.

35. Barker, *Seven Lectures,* 111.

36. Barker, *Review*, 15.

37. *Great Discussion*, 35.

38. *Origin and authority*, 298.

39. Barker, *Seven Lectures,* 30.
40. *Report of Public Discussion,* 42.
41. *Great Discussion,* 106–07.
42. *Origin and authority,* 221.
43. Barker, *Seven Lectures,* 40. Ironically, Barker was probably subconsciously recalling biblical teaching: "Nay, I had not known sin, but by the law: for I had not known lust, except the law had said, Thou shalt not covet. But sin, taking occasion by the commandment, wrought in me all manner of concupiscence." (Rom 7:7-8 AV)
44. *Great Discussion,* 15.
45. *Origin and authority,* 137–38.
46. John Rylands University Library of Manchester, "Joseph Barker case: Barker refuses to baptize with water," *Papers, Barker to Thomas Allin,* 12 April 1841. The letter making the initial request is also here—Allin to Barker, 8 April 1841—and the controversy can be traced through the subsequent letters in this collection.
47. For the notion of respectability in this period, see Geoffrey Best, *Mid-Victorian Britain, 1850–75* (London: Fontana, 1971) 279–86.
48. For the wider context, see Michael Bartholomew, "The Moral Critique of Christian Orthodoxy," in Gerald Parsons, ed., *Religion and Victorian Britain,* vol. 2, *Controversies* (Manchester: Manchester, 1988): 166–90. For the specific issue of eternal torment, see Geoffrey Rowell, *Hell and the Victorians: A Study of the Nineteenth-Century Theological Controversies Concerning Eternal Punishment and the Future Life* (Oxford: Clarendon, 1974).
49. For example, see *Great Discussion,* 121.
50. Joseph Barker, *Noah's Flood* (London: Barker, [1863?]) 4.
51. Barker, *Popular Imperfections,* 15.
52. *Great Discussion,* 46.
53. Barker, *Review,* 8.
54. *Origin and authority,* 17.
55. *Six nights' Discussion,* 91.
56. "What harm have the Scriptures ever done you?" *Reasoner,* 17 September 1854.
57. "What I should do if I were young again." *National Reformer,* 8 September 1860.
58. *Origin and authority,* 80.
59. Barker, *Review,* 62.
60. For example, *Great Discussion,* 30.
61. *Origin and authority,* 147, 209, and 95.
62. Barker, *Popular Imperfections,* 21.
63. Barker, *Seven Lectures,* 67.
64. *Report of Public Discussion,* 79.
65. *Origin and authority,* 302.
66. Barker, *Popular Imperfections,* 23.
67. *Great Discussion,* 95.

68. *Great Discussion*, 32.
69. *Report of Public Discussion*, 46.
70. *Origin and authority*, 112.
71. *Report of Public Discussion*, 13.
72. Barker, *Review*, 12.
73. Barker, *Review*, 55–59.
74. *Origin and authority*, 6.
75. *Great Discussion*, 143, 175.
76. *Origin and authority*, 10.
77. *Origin and authority*, 16.
78. Barker, *Seven Lectures*, 38.
79. Barker, *Review*, 46.
80. *Origin and authority*, 344.
81. Paine, *Age of Reason*, 78, 128; 20–21, 58; 17, 24, 146.
82. Paine, *Age of Reason*, 77–78.
83. Paine, *Age of Reason*, 75, 81, 84, 120.
84. Paine, *Age of Reason*, 38–39.
85. Paine, *Age of Reason*, 140. For an account of Paine's life, see John Keane, *Tom Paine: A Political Life* (London: Bloomsbuury, 1995).
86. *Great Discussion*, 166.
87. *Origin and authority*, 383.
88. Bradlaugh's sympathetic, modern biographer refers to his *The Bible, What It Is!* as his "*magnum opus*": David Tribe, *President Charles Bradlaugh, M.P.* (London: Elek Books, 1971) 50. Bradlaugh's handling of the Bible is explored in chapter seven.

Chapter 7

1. David Berman, *A History of Atheism in Britain: From Hobbes to Russell* (London: Croom Helm, 1988) 201, 205.
2. Joss Marsh, *Word Crimes: Blasphemy, Culture, and Literature in Nineteenth-Century England* (Chicago: Chicago, 1998) 110.
3. Bonner, *Bradlaugh*, 1: 332.
4. Bonner, *Bradlaugh*, 1: 3.
5. Tribe, *President*, 17.
6. Bonner, *Bradlaugh*, 1: 20–21.
7. *Catalogue of the Library of the late Charles Bradlaugh* (London: Mrs. H. B. Bonner, 1891) 137.
8. Tribe, *President*, 10.
9. Bonner, *Bradlaugh*, 1: 87.
10. *Discussion between Mr. Thomas Cooper and Mr. C. Bradlaugh [1864, Hall of Science, London]* (London: Freethought, 1888) 9.
11. *Can Miracles Be Proved Possible? Verbatim Report of the Two Nights' Public Debate Between Messrs. C. Bradlaugh and W. R. Browne, M.A.* [Leeds, 1876] (London: Watts, n.d.) 1.

12. Bonner, *Bradlaugh*, 2: 44–45.

13. *Can Miracles Be Proved Possible?*, 9.

14. *Can Miracles Be Proved Possible?*, 11.

15. *Can Miracles Be Proved Possible?*, 8.

16. *Can Miracles Be Proved Possible?*, 48.

17. *Can Miracles Be Proved Possible?*, 23.

18. *Can Miracles Be Proved Possible?*, 29.

19. *Can Miracles Be Proved Possible?*, 51.

20. *Can Miracles Be Proved Possible?*, 26.

21. Bradlaugh was very gratified to have been able to play an official role at the public gathering to celebrate what turned out to be Owen's last birthday: Bonner, *Bradlaugh*, 1: 78. The literature on Owen is voluminous. For a recent, book-length study, see Edward Royle, *Robert Owen and the Commencement of the Millennium: A Study of the Harmony Community* (Manchester: Manchester, 1998).

22. *Can Miracles Be Proved Possible?*, 60, 62.

23. *Can Miracles Be Proved Possible?*, 12.

24. *Can Miracles Be Proved Possible?*, 39.

25. *Can Miracles Be Proved Possible?*, 38–39.

26. *Catalogue.*

27. *Can Miracles Be Proved Possible?*, 14–15.

28. *Can Miracles Be Proved Possible?*, 51.

29. *Can Miracles Be Proved Possible?*, 28.

30. *Can Miracles Be Proved Possible?*, 35.

31. *Can Miracles Be Proved Possible?*, 42.

32. *Can Miracles Be Proved Possible?*, 49–50.

33. Tribe, *President*, 50.

34. Charles Bradlaugh, *The Bible: What It Is* (London: Austin, 1870) 14.

35. Bradlaugh, *Bible*, 173. He made the same point elsewhere: "Iconoclast" [Charles Bradlaugh], *New Life of Moses* (London: A. Besant & C. Bradlaugh, n.d.) 4.

36. Bradlaugh, *Bible*, 176.

37. Bradlaugh, *Bible*, vi.

38. *God, Man, and the Bible. Three Nights' Discussion between Rev. Joseph Baylee, D.D., and Mr. C. Bradlaugh [then debating as "Iconoclast"], on the 27th, 28th, and 29th June, 1860, at the Teutonic Hall, Liverpool* (London: Freethought, n.d.).

39. Bradlaugh, *Bible*, 24.

40. Bradlaugh, *Bible*, 20.

41. Bradlaugh, *Bible*, 25–26.

42. Bradlaugh, *Bible*, 217, 119.

43. Bonner, *Bradlaugh*, 2: 424.

44. Bradlaugh, *Bible*, 209–10.

45. Bradlaugh, *Bible*, 106.

46. Charles Bradlaugh, *New Life of Abraham* (London: Besant & Bradlaugh, n.d.) 4.

47. "Iconoclast" [Charles Bradlaugh], *New Life of David* (London: Austin, n.d.) 4.

48. Bradlaugh, *Abraham*, 4.

49. "Iconoclast," *Moses*, 7.

50. Bradlaugh, *Bible*, 48.

51. Charles Bradlaugh, *A New Life of Jonah* (London: Freethought, n.d.) 7.

52. Bradlaugh, *Jonah*, 5–6.

53. Bradlaugh, *Bible*, 207.

54. Bradlaugh, *Bible*, 173.

55. *Can Miracles Be Proved Possible?*, 30.

56. Bonner, *Bradlaugh*, 1: 343.

57. *Human Immortality Proved By Facts. Report of a Two Nights' Debate on Modern Spiritualism, between Mr. C. Bradlaugh and Mr. J. Burns* [London, 1872] (London: Burns, n.d.) 47–48.

58. Logie Barrow, *Independent Spirits: Spiritualism and English Plebeians, 1850–1910* (London: Routledge & Kegan Paul, 1986) 12–15. This book is an excellent introduction to the cross-pollination of the two movements in general.

59. Frank Podmore, *Robert Owen: A Biography* (1906; London: George Allen & Unwin, 1923), 603.

60. Bonner, *Bradlaugh*, 2: 13.

61. There have been many studies of Besant. Perhaps the classic account of the first half of her life (including her National Secular Society work) is Arthur H. Nethercot, *The First Five Lives of Annie Besant* (Chicago: Chicago, 1960). For a recent journal article, see Mark Bevir, "Annie Besant's Quest for Truth: Christianity, Secularism and New Age Thought," *Journal of Ecclesiastical History* L.1 (January 1999): 62–93.

62. Tribe, *President*, 270.

63. Anne Taylor, *Annie Besant: A Biography* (Oxford/New York: Oxford, 1992) 233.

64. Taylor, *Besant*, 236.

65. Taylor, *Besant*, 245.

66. Bonner, *Bradlaugh*, 2: 418.

Chapter 8

1. Robert J. Conklin, *Thomas Cooper, the Chartist (1805–1892)* (Manila: Philippines, 1935). Since writing this chapter, I have written my own sketch of Cooper's life: Larsen, *Biographical Dictionary of Evangelicals*, 158–60.

2. G. D. H. Cole, *Chartist Portraits* (London: Macmillan, 1941) 187–217.

3. Stephen Roberts, "Thomas Cooper: Radical and Poet, c.1830–1860," M.Litt. thesis, University of Birmingham, 1986.

4. Lincolnshire Archives, "Canwick Old Cemetery," M.I.S., grave location: T(b)137. The original gravestone has been replaced, but the new one is faithful to the original inscription.

5. Bernard M. G. Reardon, *Religious Thought in the Victorian Age: A Survey from Colderidge to Gore* (London: Longman, 1980).
6. John Hunt, *Religious Thought in England in the Nineteenth Century* (London: Gibbings, 1896).
7. Thomas Cooper, *The Verity of Christ's Resurrection from the Dead* (London: Hodder & Stoughton, 1875) 96.
8. Title page of the first section of Thomas Cooper, *God, the Soul, and a Future State* (London: Hodder & Stoughton, 1875).
9. Lincoln, Lincolnshire Archives, Misc. Don. 2 Baptist 2, item 14, Thomas Cooper, "The Questions of Suffering in the Universe . . .," City Road [Hall of Science, London], 12 October 1856. For a similar comment, see Thomas Cooper and Robert Taylor, *A Calm Inquiry into the Nature of Deity* (London: Farrah, 1864) 22–23.
10. Thomas Cooper, *The Life of Thomas Cooper* (1872; Leicester: Leicester, 1971).
11. Conklin's work obscures this point by a copying error that turned sales of fourteen thousand copies of the *Life* into "forty" thousand: *Life*, 438. The fact that it was his best-selling volume is acknowledged in Stephen Roberts's entry on Cooper in Joyce E. Bellamy and John Saville, eds., *The Dictionary of Labour Biography* (Basingstoke, Hampshire: Macmillan, 1993) 9: 55.
12. *Cooper's Journal* (1850; New York: Kelley, 1970).
13. Lincoln Central Library, Local Studies, Thomas Cooper Mss. 5059 and 5060.
14. *Investigator*, May 1857, 22.
15. "Mr. Thomas Cooper's Lectures on Christianity," *Bradford Review*, 15 May 1858.
16. "Mr. Cooper and Mr. Holyoake," *Norfolk News*, 8 May 1858.
17. Thomas Cooper, *Thoughts at Fourscore and Earlier* (London: Hodder, 1885) 378.
18. Lincolnshire Archives, Misc. Don. 2 Baptist 3, Cooper to Whitwell, 5 August 1878.
19. Lincolnshire Archives, Misc. Don. 2 Baptist 4, Cooper to his wife, 18 and 19 October 1879.
20. Lincolnshire Archives, Misc. Don., 24 October 1879.
21. Lincolnshire Archives, Misc. Don., 8 December 1879.
22. Cooper, *Life*, 395.
23. Lincolnshire Archives, Misc. Don. 2 Baptist 4, Cooper to his wife, 28 October 1879.
24. Lincolnshire Archives, Misc. Don., 15 October 1879.
25. Lincolnshire Archives, Misc. Don., 5 November 1879.
26. Exploring Cooper's apologetic ideas also serves to illuminate the intellectual contours of a Victorian reconversion and thus provides an interesting contrast to the more explored narratives of the loss of faith. See, for example, Susan Budd, "The Loss of Faith: Reasons for Unbelief among Members of the Secular Movements in England, 1850–1950," *Past and Present* XXXVI (April 1967): 106–25. See Larsen, "Regaining of Faith," 527–43.

27. For the City Road Hall of Science and the world of plebeian freethought in this period, see Royle, *Victorian Infidels*.

28. He also toured with these lectures; for example, see "Thomas Cooper's Discourses," *Norfolk News*, 10 April 1858; "The Evidences of Christianity," *Yorkshire Gazette*, 17 April 1858.

29. Thomas Cooper, *The Verity and Value of the Miracles of Christ* (London: Hodder & Stoughton, 1876) 165.

30. G. J. Holyoake, *The Trial of Theism* (London: Holyoake, 1858) 11.

31. *Six Nights' Discussion between Thomas Cooper and Joseph Barker, held in St. George Hall, Bradford, September, 1860* (London: Ward, n.d.) 9, 14, 44.

32. Cooper, *Life*, 19.

33. Lincolnshire Archives, Misc. Don. 2 Baptist 3, Cooper to Mr. Whitwell, 21 August 1873.

34. Lincolnshire Archives, Misc. Don. 2 Baptist 2, item 10, Thomas Cooper, "The Existence, Power, Wisdom, all-pervading Presence, and Unity of God, demonstrating from a review of the teachings of Astronomy, and of the Arrangements of the Universe," City Road [Hall of Science, London], 28 September 1856.

35. John Kent also makes this point in regard to the Bradlaugh-Brewin Grant debate in 1875: *From Darwin to Blatchford: The Role of Darwinism in Christian Apologetic, 1875–1910* (London: Dr. Williams's Library, 1966).

36. *Discussion between Mr. Thomas Cooper and Mr. C. Bradlaugh* (London: Freethought, 1883 [1864 debate]) 9.

37. See, for example, John H. Brooke, *Science and Religion: Some Historical Perspectives* (New York: Cambridge, 1991); Moore, *Post-Darwinian Controversies*; and David N. Livingstone, *Darwin's Forgotten Defenders: the Encounter Between Evangelical Theology and Evolutionary Thought* (Grand Rapids: Eerdmans, 1987).

38. Cooper, "Existence, Power, and Wisdom of God," 1856.

39. Cooper relates his encounter with this work soon after its publication in his *Evolution, the Stone Book, and the Mosaic Record of Creation* (London: Hodder & Stoughton, 1878) 11. He attached to his 1856 lectures old notes from past lectures of a purely scientific nature. One has a reference to a page from *Vestiges*, see: Lincolnshire Archives, Misc. Don. 2 Baptist 2, item 14, "The Providence of God: Proofs of the continued action of God in the Universe: importance & salutariness of the doctrine of Providence," City Road [Hall of Science, London], 19 October 1856. Recently, a major scholarly study of this book has been produced: James A. Secord, *Victorian Sensation: The Extraordinary Publication, Reception, and Secret Authorship of "Vestiges of the Natural History of Creation"* (Chicago: Chicago, 2000).

40. Lincolnshire Archives, Misc. Don. 2 Baptist 3, item 7, Cooper to Mr. Whitwell, 5 August 1878.

41. Cooper, *Evolution*, 16.

42. Cooper, *Evolution*, 2–3.

43. Cooper, *Thoughts*, 132–62.

44. Cooper, *Thoughts*, 322–34.
45. Cooper, *Resurrection* 29; D. F. Strauss, *The Old Faith and the New* (London: Asher, 1874).
46. Thomas Cooper, *Eight Letters to the Young Men of the Working-Classes* (London: Watson, 1849) 13.
47. Cooper, *Life*: introduction by John Saville, 7, 24.
48. John Burnett, David Vincent, and David Mayall, eds., *The Autobiography of the Working Class: An Annotated, Critical Bibliography* (Brighton, Sussex: Harvester, 1984) 1: 80.
49. Cooper, "The Questions of Suffering," 1856.
50. Cooper, *Evolution*, 91, 109, 123, 130; Cooper, *Thoughts*, 132–62.
51. Thomas Cooper, *The Bridge of History Over the Gulf of Time* (London: Hodder & Stoughton, 1871) 157–58.
52. Cooper, *Resurrection*, 83.
53. Cooper, *Miracles*, 165.
54. Cooper, *Bridge*, 103–4.
55. Cooper, *God*, 76.
56. G. J. Holyoake, *Thomas Cooper Delineated as Convert and Controversialist: A Companion to His Missionary Wanderings* (London: Holyoake, 1861) 10.
57. Cooper, *God*, 77–79.
58. *Six Nights' Discussion*, 12.
59. Cooper, *Bridge*, 80.
60. Cooper, *Bridge*, 85.
61. Kingsley, *Charles Kingsley*, 94–95.
62. Cooper, *Bridge*, 110.
63. Cooper, *Bridge*, 114.
64. Cooper, *Bridge*, 127.
65. Cooper, *Resurrection*, 38.
66. Cooper, *Resurrection*, 54.
67. Cooper, *Resurrection*, 41–42, 127–28.
68. Cooper, *Miracles*, 167.
69. Amsterdam, Internationaal Instituut Voor Sociale Geschiedenis, Coll. Cooper, Thomas Cooper to Charles Kingsley, 22 June 1856.
70. Cooper, *God*, 99.
71. Cooper, *Thoughts*, 352–65.
72. Holyoake, *Thomas Cooper*, 5.
73. Cooper, *God*, 16. Cooper corresponded with Gillespie: Cooper and Taylor, *Calm Inquiry*, 35.
74. Cooper, *God*, 172.
75. Cooper, *Miracles*, 55.
76. Cooper, *Miracles*, 43–47.
77. For an examination of Butler's place in Victorian intellectual history, see Jane Garnett, "Bishop Butler and the Zeitgeist: Butler and the Development of Christian Moral Philosophy in Victorian Britain," in Christopher Cunliffe, ed.,

Joseph Butler's Moral and Religious Thought: Tercentenary Essays (Oxford: Clarendon, 1992) 63–96.

78. Cooper, *Miracles*, 46.
79. Cooper, *Miracles*, 47–56.
80. Cooper, *God*, 106–8.
81. Cooper, *Bridge*, 3.
82. Cooper, *Bridge*, 43–44.
83. Cooper, *Resurrection*, 131–32.
84. Cooper, *Miracles*, 160–70.
85. Internationaal Instituut Voor Sociale Geschiedenis, Coll. Cooper, Thomas Cooper to Charles Kingsley, 15 February 1856.
86. Christian Evidence Society, *Modern Scepticism*, 9th ed. (1871; London: Hodder & Stoughton, 1874) 505.

Chapter 9

1. J. M. Turner, *Conflict and Reconciliation: Studies in Methodism and Ecumenism in England, 1740–1982* (London: Epworth, 1985). Mention is made, however, of the controversies in Wesleyan Methodism that led to the secession that created the New Connexion.
2. Notably, E. A. Rose, "The Methodist New Connexion, 1797–1907. Portrait of a Church," *Proceedings of the Wesley Historical Society* XLVII (1990): 241–53; and R. E. Davies, E. G. Rupp and A. R. George, eds., *A History of the Methodist Church in Great Britain*, 4 vols. (London: Epworth, 1965–88) 2: 280–94.
3. *Methodist New Connexion Magazine* [hereafter *MNCM*] L (1847): 15–16.
4. *MNCM* LIII (1850): 72.
5. *MNCM* LIII (1850): 455.
6. *MNCM* XLI (1838): 29–31.
7. [J. Blackwell], *Life of the Rev. Alexander Kilham* (London, 1838) 394.
8. *The Jubilee of the Methodist New Connexion: Being a Grateful Memorial of the Origin, Government, and History of the Denomination* (London: W. Cooke, 1851) iv.
9. *MNCM* LVII (1854): 48.
10. For the importance of the notion of principle in this milieu, see Larsen, *Friends of Religious Equality*, 105–08.
11. *Jubilee*, 190.
12. *MNCM* XLIX (1846): 472.
13. *MNCM* L (1847): 23.
14. *MNCM* LXIII (1860): 567.
15. *Jubilee*, 73.
16. G. Packer, ed., *The Centenary of the Methodist New Connexion, 1797–1897* (London: G. Burroughs, 1897) 30.
17. *MNCM* LXXV (1872): 292.
18. *MNCM* LIII (1850): 457.

19. *Jubilee*, 56.
20. *MNCM* L (1847): 18–20.
21. *Jubilee*, 121–29.
22. *MNCM* LXXV (1872): 292.
23. The fullest treatment of this theme can be found in J. C. Bowmer, *Pastor and People: a Study of Church and Ministry in Wesleyan Methodism from the Death of John Wesley (1791) to the Death of Jabez Bunting (1858)* (London: Epworth, 1975). See also W. R. Ward, *Religion and Society in England, 1790–1850* (London: Batsford, 1972); and J. H. S. Kent, *The Age of Disunity* (London: Epworth, 1966).
24. Packer, *Centenary*, 28, 224–25.
25. [Blackwell], *Kilham*, 125–79.
26. *MNCM* LVII (1854): 417–26.
27. *MNCM* XLII (1839): 223–4.
28. *Jubilee*, 204.
29. *MNCM* LVII (1854): 52.
30. *MNCM* LXXVIII (1875): 611.
31. Packer, *Centenary*, 67.
32. *MNCM* XLVI (1843): 341; LI (1848): 427; LVII (1854): 168.
33. *MNCM* LIV (1851): 75.
34. *MNCM* L (1847): 16.
35. For example, Bowmer, *Pastor and People*, 132; Ward, *Religion and Society*, 275.
36. *MNCM* LVII (1854): 626.
37. Robert Currie, *Methodism Divided: a Study in the Sociology of Ecumenicalism* (London: Faber, 1968) 60.
38. *MNCM* LIII (1850): 215–20, 375–85, 438–39.
39. *MNCM* LIV (1851): 484.
40. *MNCM* LVIII (1855): 433.
41. Packer, *Centenary*, 207.
42. For a discussion of the origin of the New Connexion set within the wider political context, see David Hempton, *Methodism and Politics in British Society, 1750–1850* (London: Hutchinson, 1984) ch. 3. According to his biographer, Kilham's politics were "of the reforming Whig character, the same as those held by Earl Grey, Lord Erskine, Mr Fox, &c." [Blackwell], *Kilham*, 340.
43. Currie, *Methodism Divided*, 43.
44. *Jubilee*, 144.
45. *MNCM* LVII (1854): 50.
46. *Jubilee*, 146.
47. Packer, *Centenary*, 51.
48. *Jubilee*, 75.
49. *MNCM* LXXII (1869): 738.
50. *Jubilee*, 229.
51. The laywomen of some Congregational and Baptist churches, by way of contrast, enjoyed a measure of emancipation, even during the first half of the nineteenth century, as illustrated in chapter one.

52. Packer, *Centenary*, 92, 174. Rose, "Methodist New Connexion," 252.
53. Currie, *Methodism Divided*, 13. See, for example, *MNCM* XLIV (1841): 412–14.
54. *MNCM* LIII (1850): 460.
55. *Jubilee*, 200–1.
56. *MNCM* LXII (1859): 84.
57. *MNCM* L (1847): 21.
58. For Methodist union, see Currie, *Methodism Divided;* Kent, *Age of Disunity;* and H. Smith, J. E. Swallow and W. Treffry, eds., *The Story of the United Methodist Church* (London: Henry Hooks, 1932).
59. Packer, *Centenary*, 250.

Chapter 10

1. For the flowering of this trend, see Larsen, *Friends of Religious Equality*. For the politics of English Dissenters in the period prior to the one covered in this chapter (especially the 1770s), see James E. Bradley, *Religion, Revolution and English Radicalism: Nonconformity in Eighteenth-Century Politics and Society* (Cam-bridge: Cambridge, 1990). The original prompt for this chapter was an invitation to give a plenary paper at the Past and Present Society conference, "Rethinking the 'Age of Reform': Britain circa 1780–1850," July 2000, St. Anne's College, Oxford, England.
2. For New England, see E. R. Norman, *The Conscience of the State in North America* (London: Cambridge, 1968).
3. For the history of evangelicalism, see D. W. Bebbington, *Evangelicalism in Modern Britain: A History from the 1730s to the 1930s* (London: Unwin Hyman, 1989).
4. For the expansion of Dissent in the period 1791–1851, see Michael R. Watts, *The Dissenters*, vol. 2 (Oxford: Clarendon, 1995) ch. 1.
5. K. R. M. Short, "London's General Body of Protestant Ministers: Its Disruption in 1836," *Journal of Ecclesiastical History* XXIV.4 (October 1973): 377–93.
6. William Newman, *The Protestant Dissenters' Catechism* (London: Holdsworth & Ball, 1831).
7. Josiah Conder, *On Protestant Nonconformity*, 2d ed. (London: B. J. Holdsworth, 1822).
8. *The Second Annual Report of the Society for the Promoting of Ecclesiastical Knowledge* (London, 1831).
9. "The Personal Narrative of Me, George Hadfield, M.P.," Manchester: Manchester Central Library, 125–26.
10. Thomas Morgan, *A Lecture on the Views and Designs of the Birmingham Voluntary Church Society, Delivered in Cannon-Street Meeting House, April 14th, 1836* (Birmingham, [1836]).
11. John Angell James, *A Pastor's Address to His People, on the Principles of Dissent, and the Duties of Dissenters* (London: Westley & Davis, 1834).

12. Religious Freedom Society, *Report Presented to the First Annual Meeting of the Religious Freedom Society* (London, 1840).

13. For examples of this dismissiveness, see Elie Halévy, *A History of the English People in the Nineteenth Century*, trans. E. I. Watkins, vol. 4 (London: E. Benn, 1951) 184; Norman Gash, *Reaction and Reconstruction in English Politics, 1832–1852* (Oxford: Clarendon, 1965) 105; and Chadwick, *Victorian Church* 1: 409–12.

14. Newman, *Protestant Dissenters' Catechism*, 24.

15. Charles W. Deweese, *Baptist Church Covenants* (Nashville: Broadman, 1990) 127–28.

16. James, *A Pastor's Address to His People*, 14.

17. Matthew Bridges, *Worldliness Engrafted Upon the Episcopal Church, Through Her Connexion with the State* (London: J. Dinnis, n.d.).

18. Anon., *An Answer to the Inquiry, Why Are You a Dissenter from the Church of England? In a Letter to a Friend*, 5th ed. (Harlow: B. Flower, 1812).

19. James Bennett, *The History of the Dissenters, from the Revolution to the Year 1808*, 2d ed., vol. 1 (London, 1808) 101.

20. Ernst Troeltsch, *The Social Teaching of the Christian Churches*, trans. by Olive Wyon (London: Allen & Unwin, 1931) 331.

21. Bernard Lord Manning, *The Protestant Dissenting Deputies* (Cambridge: Cambridge, 1952) 204.

22. Edward Baines, Jr., *The Life of Edward Baines* (London: Longman, 1851) 141–43.

23. Stoughton, *Religion in England*, 65–66.

24. Manning, *Protestant Dissenting Deputies*, 211–12.

25. *Ecclesiastical Journal* (August 1835): 281.

26. Conder, *On Protestant Nonconformity*, 270–71.

27. *Ecclesiastical Journal* (January 1835): 2.

28. Edwin Hodder, *The Life of Samuel Morley*, 3rd ed. (London: Hodder & Stoughton, 1887) 68.

29. Royle, *Victorian Infidels*, 187.

30. *Nonconformist*, 10 June 1857: 441.

31. C. E. Shipley, ed., *The Baptists of Yorkshire* (Bradford: W. Byles, 1912) 303.

32. Roy Wallis and Steve Bruce, "Secularization: The Orthodox Model," *Religion and Modernization: Sociologists and Historians Debate the Secularization Thesis*, ed. Steve Bruce (Oxford: Clarendon, 1992): 11.

33. "Proceedings of the First Anti-State-Church Conference" (London: London Metropolitan Archives, Liberation Society Papers) A/LIB/275.

Chapter 11

1. *Objects and Plans of the Central United St. Bartholomew Committee of Evangelical Nonconformists* (London, 1862) 5.

2. For a general study of Nonconformist politics in the period 1840–1870, see Larsen, *Friends of Religious Equality*.

3. M. J. D. Roberts, "Pressure-group politics and the Church of England: The Church Defence Institution, 1859–1896," *Journal of Ecclesiastical History* XXXV (1984): 560–82.

4. J. P. Ellens, *Religious Routes to Gladstonian Liberalism* (University Park: Penn State, 1994) 167–203.

5. London, Greater London Record Office, Liberation Society, Minutes of the Executive Committee, A/LIB/2, 13 April 1860, minute 1058.

6. *Hansard*, 3rd Series, LXXII: 1024 (24 April 1861).

7. London, Greater London Record Office, Liberation Society Minutes, A/LIB/2, 27 Sept. 1861, minute 1206.

8. Joshua Wilson, *The Second Centenary of the Ejectment of the Nonconformist Ministers from the Established Church* (London, n.d.).

9. *Objects and Plans; The Congregational Yearbook* (London) for 1862, [x], and for 1863, [x]; Supplement to the *Liberator*, June 1862: 111.

10. Arthur Miall, *Life of Edward Miall* (London: Macmillan, 1884) 240–41.

11. George Venables, *How Did They Get There?* (London: Wertheim, Macintosh, & Hunt, 1862).

12. T. Lathbury, *Facts and Fictions of the Bicentenary* (Bristol: Bristol Church Defense Association, 1861).

13. *Dictionary of National Biography.* s.v. Edmund Calamy, D.D. (1671–1732), John Walker (1647–1747).

14. J. B. Clifford, *The Bicentenary* (Bristol, n.d.) 32, 15. I am grateful to the Principal and Chapter, Pusey House, Oxford, for access to this source.

15. *Quarterly Review* CXII (1862): 236–70.

16. John Miller, *Churchmen and Dissenters*, 2d ed. (Birmingham, 1862) 11.

17. Central United Bartholomew Committee, *The Willis's Rooms Lectures* (London, [1862]) 69.

18. J. G. Rogers, *Puritans, Nonconformists, and Dissenters* (Manchester, [1862]) 31.

19. *United Methodist Free Churches' Magazine* (May 1862): 276.

20. *British Quarterly Review* XXXVII (1863): 241.

21. G. B. Kidd, *Are Nonconformists of the Present Day the Valid Successors of the Ejected of 1662?* (London, 1862) 4–6.

22. Robert Vaughan, et al., *St. James's Hall Addresses* (London: Jackson, Walford, & Hodder, 1862) pref. and 35–37.

23. *Objects and Plans*, 4.

24. *Baptist Magazine*, n.s. VI (1862): 79.

25. Central United Bartholomew Committee, *On Clerical Subscription* (London, [1862]).

26. *Record*, 27 January 1862: 4.

27. Miller, *Churchmen and Dissenters*, 3.

28. R. W. Dale, *Churchmen and Dissenters* (Birmingham, 1862) 19–20.

29. Supplement to the *Record*, 26 March 1862: [1].

30. *Record*, 11 April 1862: 2.

31. *Watchman*, 14 May 1862: 157.

32. A Priest of the Church of England, *A Letter to the Rev. R. W. Dale* (Birmingham: Walter J. Sackett, 1862) 5.

33. *Hansard*, 3rd series, LXVII: 2–29 (27 May 1862).

34. Charles Girdlestone, *How Shall We Commemorate on August 24, 1862, the Bi-Centenary of the Act of Uniformity?* (London, [1862]) 7.

35. R. G. Wilberforce, *Life of Samuel Wilberforce*, 3 vols. (London: John Murray, 1882) 3: 4–5.

36. *Nonconformist*, 30 July 1862: 648–49.

37. Supplement to the *Liberator*, June 1862: 111.

38. Venables, *How Did They Get There?*, 7–8, 17–19.

39. Robert Vaughan, *I'll Tell You* (London, 1862).

40. *Nonconformist*, 16 October 1861: 827–29.

41. Robert Vaughan, *English Nonconformity* (London, 1862) iii–iv.

42. *British Quarterly Review* XXXV, LXX (April, 1862): 323.

43. Joshua Wilson, *Calumnies Confuted* (London: Jackson, Walford, & Hodder, 1863).

44. *Record*, 25 August 1862: 2.

45. Supplement to the *Nonconformist*, 14 May 1862: 437–40.

46. Dennis G. Wigmore-Beddoes, *Yesterday's Radicals: A Study of the Affinity Between Unitarians and Broad Church Anglicanism in the Nineteenth Century* (Cambridge: J. Clarke, 1971).

47. *Inquirer*, 7 February 1857: 81.

48. *Inquirer*, 29 November 1862: 834.

49. *Wesleyan Methodist Magazine* (August 1862): 732–36.

50. *Fund to Aid the Erection of Memorial Chapels in Lancashire and Cheshire: First Annual Report of the Committee* (Manchester, 1863).

51. Hodder, *Morley*, 366; Albert Peel, *These Hundred Years* (London: Congregational Union, 1931) 239–41.

52. Charles Miall, *Henry Richard, M.P.* (London: Cassell, 1889) 166.

53. Supplement to the *Record*, 26 February 1862: [2]; *Watchman*, 7 May 1862: 147.

54. Susannah Spurgeon, *C. H. Spurgeon, Autobiography*, rev. ed., 2 vols. (1897; Edinburgh: Banner of Truth, 1973) 2: 55–57.

55. Dale, *Life of R. W. Dale*, 175.

56. *Congregational Yearbook* (1863): 392.

57. James Allen, *The Bicentenary Question* (Shepton Mallet, [1862]).

Chapter 12

1. Bernard Semmel, *The Governor Eyre Controversy* (London: MacGibbon & Kee, 1962).

2. Eric Williams, *British Historians and the West Indies* (London: Andre Deutsch, 1966) ch. 8.

3. Gordon A. Catherall, "British Baptist Involvement in Jamaica, 1783–1865," diss., University of Keele, 1970.

4. *Missionary Herald*, n.s. XI (1867): 49.

5. The letter was reprinted widely in the press during the controversy and was also published as a pamphlet, Edward Bean Underhill, *A Letter Addressed to the Rt. Honourable E. Cardwell* (London: A. Miall, 1865) 11–17.

6. Brian Stanley, *The History of the Baptist Missionary Society, 1792–1992* (Edinburgh: T & T Clark, 1992) 68–105.

7. The full dispatch was printed in *The Times*, 20 November 1865: 9.

8. Underhill, *Letter*, 6–7.

9. *Athenæum*, 16 December 1865: 838.

10. *Hansard*, CLXXXIV, 1826–1827 (31 July 1866).

11. Hamilton Hume, *The Life of Edward John Eyre* (London: R. Bentley, 1867) 131, xiv.

12. *The Times*, 13 November 1865: 8.

13. Peto's letter was reprinted in the *Freeman*, 22 November 1865: 748. *Freeman*, 15 November 1865: 737.

14. For the Native Baptists, see G. A. Catherall, "The Native Baptist Church," *Baptist Quarterly* XXIV (1971): 65–73.

15. E. B. Underhill, *The Tragedy of Morant Bay* (London: Alexander & Shepheard, 1895) 89.

16. For an account of these events from a Baptist perspective, see G. A. Catherall, "George William Gordon: Saint or Sinner?" *Baptist Quarterly* XXVII (1977): 163–72.

17. *Freeman*, 19 October 1866: 391.

18. *Eyre Defence and Aid Fund* (London, [1866]).

19. *Freeman*, 22 November 1865: 748; 6 December 1865: 781.

20. *Baptist Magazine* LVII (1865): 780–85.

21. *General Baptist Magazine* (December 1865): 464.

22. *Freeman*, 6 December 1865: 784.

23. *Missionary Herald*, n.s. X (1866): 50.

24. *Freeman*, 13 December 1865: 804.

25. *Freeman*, 13 December 1865: 758.

26. *General Baptist Magazine* (February 1866): 71.

27. *Freeman*, 27 April 1866: 269.

28. *Report of the Jamaica Royal Commission*, Part I: *Report* (London: Eyre & Spottiswoode, 1866) 40–41 (Blue Book, vol. 30 [New York, 1966]: 530–31).

29. *Freeman*, 24 August 1866: 238.

30. *Freeman*, 24 August 1866: 231.

31. All analysis of the two committees, the memberships of which changed over time, is based upon the respective lists of committee members given in *Eyre Fund*. (The Jamaica Committee list was probably copied from the *Morning Star*.)

32. W. F. Finlason, *The History of the Jamaica Case* (London: Chapman & Hall, 1869) 368, 369.

33. *Dictionary of National Biography*; Frederic Boase, *Modern English Biography* (London: Frank Cass, 1965); G. E. C., *The Complete Peerage of England, Scotland, Ireland, Great Britain and the United Kingdom, Extant, Extinct or Dormant*, ed. Vicary Gibbs (London: St. Catherine, 1912); Michael Stenton, ed., *Who's Who of British Members of Parliament*, vol. 1: *1832–1885* (Hassocks, Sussex: Harvester, 1976).

34. Stenton, *Who's Who*, 15–16, 244–45.

35. D. W. Bebbington, "Baptist M.P.s in the Nineteenth Century," *Baptist Quarterly* XXIX (1981): 3–24.

36. Although lists were undoubtedly published sporadically, this analysis is based on two of them, the one in *Eyre Fund* for that committee and the other is taken from Jamaica Papers. *No. III. Statement of the Committee and other Documents* (London, [1866]) 94–97.

37. *Clergy List for 1866* (London, 1866).

38. *Baptist Hand-book for 1866* (London, 1866).

39. "Eyre, Edward John (1815–1901)," *Dictionary of National Biography*. Suppl.: January 1901–December 1911, 1: 641.

40. The address can be found in *Hansard*, CLXXXIV, 1815 (31 July 1866).

41. *Hansard*, CLXXXIV, 1777, 1780.

42. Hume, *Eyre*, 153–54.

43. *Missionary Herald*, n.s. X (1866): 54–55; 345.

44. *Freeman*, 31 August 1866: 252.

45. *Church Times*, 25 November 1865: 369.

46. *Church Times*, 25 November 1865: 372–73.

47. Connop Thirlwall, *Letters to a Friend*, ed. A. P. Stanley (London: R. Bentley, 1882) 54.

48. *Freeman*, 6 July 1866: 90; 13 July 1866: 112; 6 March 1868: 192.

49. *General Baptist Magazine* (May 1867): 154.

50. *Royal Commission*, 38 (528).

51. *Hansard*, CLXXXIV, 1834 (31 July 1866).

52. Hume, *Eyre*, 183–84, 190.

53. *Freeman*, 22 November 1865: 748; *Baptist Magazine* LVII (1865): 783.

54. *Freeman*, 22 November 1865: 747.

55. *Freeman*, 24 August 1866: 231.

56. *Freeman*, 6 December 1865: 785.

57. "Minutes of the Committee of the Baptist Union of Great Britain and Ireland" (1856—12 December 1870), 11 October 1866, minute number 16, Angus Library, Regent's Park College, Oxford.

58. *General Baptist Magazine* (November 1866): 427–30.

59. *Freeman*, 26 October 1866: 412.

60. *Freeman*, 31 August 1866: 247.

61. *Freeman*, 7 September 1866: 268.

62. *Sword and Trowel* (December 1865): 542.

63. *Freeman*, 27 December 1865: 835.

64. Baptist W. Noel, *The Case of George W. Gordon, Esq.* (London: J. Nisbet, 1866). For Noel's life, see D. W. Bebbington, "The Life of Baptist Noel: Its Setting and Significance," *Baptist Quarterly* XXIV (1972): 389–411.

65. Noel, *Gordon,* 32, 34, 53.

66. Noel, *Gordon,* 30, 57.

67. Noel, *Gordon,* 54.

68. For an account of the position and actions of the government in regards to this controversy, see B. A. Knox, "The British Government and the Governor Eyre Controversy, 1865–1875," *Historical Journal* XIX (1976): 877–900.

69. *Hansard,* CCXII, 814 (8 July 1872).

70. Bebbington, "Baptist M.P.s," 17.

71. Helen Caroline Colman, *Jeremiah James Colman: A Memoir* (London: Chiswick, 1905) 267.

72. Chadwick, *Victorian Church* 1: 464.

73. Semmel, *Eyre,* 52.

74. W. Bebbington, "The Baptist Conscience in the Nineteenth Century," *Baptist Quarterly* XXXIV (1991): 13–24. For a more general study of Nonconformist attitudes toward politics in the 1860s, see Larsen, *Friends of Religious Equality.*

75. Charles Adderley praised Buxton in the Commons for separating himself from the Jamaica Committee: *Hansard,* CLXXXIV, 1792 (31 July 1866). The *Freeman,* by contrast, attempted to refute his reasoning: 6 July 1866: 90.

76. For a discussion of this controversy within the context of British attitudes toward race, see Douglas A. Lorimer, *Colour, Class and the Victorians: English Attitudes to the Negro in the Mid-Nineteenth Century* (Leicester: Leicester, 1978) ch. 9.

77. *Church Times,* 25 November 1865: 372.

78. Thomas Carlyle, *Critical and Miscellaneous Essays* (London: Chapman & Hall, 1899) 5: 12.

79. Brief lives of all of these figures, including most of the details mentioned in this paragraph, can be found in Lewis, *Blackwell Dictionary.*

80. Brian Stanley, *The Bible and the Flag: Protestant Missions and British Imperialism in the Nineteenth and Twentieth Centuries* (Leicester: Apollos, 1990) 85–91.

81. *Quarterly Review* CXX (1866): 239, 236.

82. *Church Times,* 25 November 1865: 272–73.

83. *Missionary Herald,* n.s. 10 (1866): 189–93; 262–64.

84. *General Baptist Magazine* (November 1866): 429.

Index of Named Persons